Mary Cushing

God and Production in a Guatemalan Town

GOD AND PRODUCTION IN A GUATEMALAN TOWN

By Sheldon Annis

UNIVERSITY OF TEXAS PRESS   AUSTIN

First edition, 1987

Requests for permission to reproduce material from this work
should be sent to:
  Permissions
  University of Texas Press
  Box 7819
  Austin, Texas 78713-7819

Library of Congress Cataloging-in-Publication Data

Annis, Sheldon, date
  God and production in a Guatemalan town.

  Bibliography: p.
  Includes index.
    1. Indians of Central America—Guatemala—
Economic conditions.   2. Indians of Central
America—Guatemala—Missions.   3. Protestant
churches—Missions—Guatemala.   4. San Antonio
Aguas Calientes (Guatemala)—Economic conditions.
5. Indians of Central America—Guatemala—Textile
industry and fabrics.   6. Mayas—Economic conditions.
7. Mayas—Missions.   I. Title.   II. Series.
F1465.3.E2A56   1987   972.81'053   87-13921
ISBN 0-292-72736-4

*Dedicated to the memory of
Carmelo, Alcides, and all the others*

Contents

Figures

Tables

Acknowledgments

I OWE an immeasurable debt to the people of San Antonio for their tolerance and generosity—in particular, to my two weaving teachers, Doña Paola Santos Marín and Doña Victoria Santos Marín. To Don Bernardo López Zamora I am especially grateful. It was he who first introduced me to Protestantism in San Antonio and then prodded me to understand it. As he says, "through rectification of our ignorance we are redeemed."

Many friends helped sustain this work through completion. Elissa Miller collaborated on early rounds of fieldwork; the study would not have been done without her. Wendy Kramer, Lydia Parks, Pierre Petit, and Marines Pérez assisted in collecting data on household economy, textile production, and agriculture. From the start of this study until its finish, historian Christopher Lutz shared his enthusiasm, data, and insight into the "Quinizilapa towns." Mitchell Denburg provided the photographs that enrich this volume. Cherri Pancake collaborated on analysis of textile design and reviewed an earlier manuscript draft. Ron Weber seemed to understand my arguments better than I did as he deftly edited the manuscript. Peter Russell, of the Instituto para Nutrición para Centroamérica y Panamá (INCAP) in Guatemala City, and Alan McCutcheon, formerly of the University of Chicago Computation Center, provided indispensable assistance with data processing. David Stoll generously shared his source material on the evangelical movement in Guatemala. My former colleague at the Inter-American Foundation, Mac Chapin, badgered me mercilessly to get this work done; my former boss, Peter Hakim, helped provide a measure of space to make that possible.

Particular thanks are due to the Organization of American States for the research fellowship that allowed me to carry this work to the field, and to my wife, Barbara—who did not finance, footnote, or otherwise get involved—for taking me but not the study too seriously.

Several readers provided comments that greatly improved this manuscript: Richard Adams of the University of Texas Department of Anthropology, Robert Carmack of the State University of New

York at Albany, and Shelton Davis of the Anthropology Resource Center in Washington. Bernie Kemp, formerly of the Economics Department of Virginia Tech, provided especially useful commentary on my analysis of textile production.

I cannot properly acknowledge my debts to the University of Chicago. Certainly, the scholarly brilliance of Paul Wheatley, chairman of the Committee on Social Thought and formerly professor of geography, was the impetus that set this study in motion. Sol Tax, of the Anthropology Department, who introduced me to Mesoamerican ethnology, was a constant friend and advisor. His advice, "Write it like a letter to your mother," was especially helpful when I didn't know where to start; and so, dear Mom, let me tell you all about this town in Guatemala . . . William Pattison provided the steady encouragement that led me through the Geography Department, into the field, and through the writing of the first draft; without his support, for better or worse I would be pursuing some other career today. Norton Ginsburg made key suggestions that simplified, disciplined, and greatly strengthened this final version.

Nearly all the Catholic or Protestant fieldworkers who read this manuscript interpreted it as an attack on "their side" and an apologia for the other. In answer to the question that all of them asked me: I am neither. Actually, I am a nonpracticing, agnostic Jew; so, hopefully I have no bias other than skepticism.

Finally, with deep sadness, I dedicate this work to the thousands of Guatemalans who were assassinated during the past few years—in particular, to two whom I knew well: Carmelo Santos and Alcides López Hernández. Both died in the struggle over San Antonio's rights to its land. Carmelo was the mayor of the town, a young tailor who had no land himself but dared to become a leader. Alcides was a special friend. He was the only religious doubter I ever met in this land of believers—a warm and subtle man whose counsel and good humor I have deeply missed.

Figure 1. Mayor Carmelo Santos, at his desk, shortly before his assassination.

Figure 2. Alcides López, picking a *güicoy* from his plot in the *laguna*. (Photo by Roberto Buzzini)

God and Production in a Guatemalan Town

1

How to Get an Indian's Attention

A FEW DAYS after the earthquake of February 4, 1976, I found myself in the passenger seat of a four-wheel-drive Ford Bronco, picking my way village by village through the rubble of the central highlands of Guatemala. At the wheel of the Bronco sat Edgardo Robertson, a North American evangelical missionary.[1] For different purposes, we were each trying to assess the earthquake's damage and, along the way, help out where we could.

On the streets of his native Midwest, Edgardo Robertson would hardly attract notice: a rawboned, muscular man in his mid-thirties; short-cropped blond hair; a ruddy complexion; the look of someone who works outdoors—a carpenter, farmer, or mechanic perhaps. But in a remote, earthquake-ruined village—where the living now pause in shock to comprehend their future, where the frantic digging has just stopped—Edgardo Robertson is an imposing, even a commanding figure. The dustcloud in which he arrives in itself lends authority. Villagers look up as he steps from the gold and copper Bronco (on his feet, eight or so inches taller than any village male). They watch his hawklike appraisal of the wreckage of their material lives. A small committee falls in step for the inspection tour and answers without hesitation the questions that he poses in robust and fluent Cakchiquel. They watch, fascinated, as he jots notes, his knee propped on an overturned bed in the dust; as he stoops to toss a door jamb out of his path; as he reflectively prods a loose boulder with his boot. Here in the broken *aldea* of Paraxtuj, Guatemala, the large hands that would appear merely competent in the Midwest look as if they might be capable of mending what is so badly broken, of restoring what is destroyed. But most striking about Edgardo, surely not missed by anyone, is that when he speaks he has the intense, smoldering—almost lunatic—eyes of a biblical prophet. In a violent nightmare of earthquakes and terror, here is a man for the times.

Between towns, his fire dampened, Edgardo and I talked. He described his journey to faith and the evangelism that had engaged him for the past ten years; and I told him how, prior to the earthquake, I had expected to carry out a study on the social impact of tourism. Politely but with no great interest he listened to what I considered a most impressive array of questions—on the nature of agricultural production, land tenure, migratory labor, textile production, ritual, politics, and the like. My keenest interest was in the semiotics of handweaving, something I had called "a window on Indian culture" in my dissertation proposal. Looking for some point of contact between the hopeful scholar and the missionary, I asked, with considerable curiosity, how *he* would ask people about the meanings of the designs and colors that they wove into their clothing.

"Look around you," he said irritably, dismissing these abstractions with the rubble around us. "Do you want to understand these people? First you have to get their attention. What you're asking has nothing to do with their lives. If you want to get an Indian's attention, talk to him about God."

Here is how that is done. First, Edgardo pulls into the marketplace, smiling at acquaintances and warmly greeting his friends. He hops out of his vehicle and strides to a spot—just the right spot—directly in front of the crumbled masonry and toppled belltower of the Catholic church. As a circle gathers around him, he kneels in self-absorbed prayer. Although he is physically doing almost nothing, his presence reorganizes the marketplace. Some people begin to shift in the direction of the circle; many others hurriedly walk away. Most remain within earshot and wait.

Imperceptibly at first, then more visibly, the prophet's body starts to tremble. Clutching his worn Bible, his hand rises with a life of its own. His body seems to be struggling against itself: chin and knees pulled toward the earth, arm and Bible reaching skyward.

The arm wins, and Edgardo is on his feet, pacing lightly back and forth. As he begins to preach, his rasping voice takes on volume; his Bible slices the air.

"Look at this earthquake, your lives, your sin; look at the destruction," he cries. He rolls on and on, preaching of Christ's love and the war with Satan. Sweat rolls down his forehead. Finally, as his hoarse voice begins to calm, he leads the circle in songs and prayer. Then he goes off to discuss the reconstruction of the two toppled evangelical churches.

Certainly he had gotten their attention. But how? I looked around this town where hundreds had just died. Scarcely a house stood intact. Street patterns were barely discernible beneath the dust and crushed adobe. At the edge of the marketplace, a man struggled to lift an injured woman who sat in a chair strapped to his back. A child watched anxiously, caught between wanting to help and wanting to hold his father's hand.

I was disgusted by Robertson's theatrical manipulation of the town's tragedy. This, I felt, was not what anyone needed: to suffer disaster *and* moral responsibility for it! To those who stood near me in the crowd, I made what amounted to awkward jokes and apologies for Edgardo's performance. I wanted no association with such as he, and soon we went our separate ways. He pursued the word of God; I eventually went on to San Antonio Aguas Calientes to ask my questions about agriculture, land, migratory labor, and textile symbolism.

But in retrospect, I see that I would have done better to have listened more carefully.

What was euphemistically called "the situation" worsened dramatically in Guatemala at the end of the 1970s and during the early 1980s. Under General Romeo Lucas García, government-linked violence swept into nearly every corner of the country. Insurgency widened as the army struck out at guerrillas and the villagers who were their presumed base of support.

Compared to the north and the west of the highlands, San Antonio was relatively unscathed, but even in this tourist town the violence took its toll.[2] When I visited in late 1982, women in a makeshift refugee camp described how helicopters had landed in their isolated hamlet of Chimachoy the previous year to search for evidence of subversion and, finding nothing, burned, killed, and forced everyone out. One woman grotesquely mimicked the laughter of a soldier snipping away pieces of her son's ear, torturing good-naturedly to learn the whereabouts of guerrillas.

In March 1982, in the wake of fraudulent elections, a coup led by junior military officers ousted Lucas García. Then, on June 9, General Efraín Ríos Montt seized sole power after dissolving the ruling military junta of which he was a member.

Although he was probably intended only as a figurehead, Ríos Montt not only came out on top but, to the surprise of many, held control of the government. A graduate of both the Dale Carnegie School and counterinsurgency programs in Panama and in the United States, Ríos Montt had risen from corporal to chief of staff. In 1974, he had run for president at the head of a coalition led by the Christian Democrats. He was a populist and—by Guatemalan standards— a liberal. He campaigned for land reform and, largely on the strength of that issue, won the actual vote. Nevertheless, the electoral results were clumsily manipulated (the count had to be stopped until it could be made to come out right), and the presidency was given to General Kjell Lauguerud.[3] Ríos Montt was banished to the quiet life of a minor diplomatic post in Spain.

Ríos Montt returned to Guatemala in 1978, at the end of the Lauguerud presidency. About this time, he renounced Catholicism and joined an obscure, 1,000-member evangelical sect known as "el Verbo" (the Church of the Complete Word), which had been established after the earthquake by a southern California group, Gospel Outreach.[4] In the meantime, ironically, his brother, Mario, had risen to become a Catholic bishop, the head of the Prelature of Escuintla.

When Ríos Montt seized the government in 1982, he not only surprised everyone by securing control—he unexpectedly called upon a source of power and legitimacy far greater than the young officers who had backed him in the coup: the power of God. "Guatemalans are the chosen people of the New Testament," he cried. "We are the new Israelites of Central America."

With the same passionate, tasteless, glassy-eyed vehemence of Edgardo Robertson railing at the Indians in the marketplace, Ríos Montt railed at the nation. Commanding the national media, he excoriated businessmen, demanding that they give up their mistresses; he assailed corruption in the army and among bureaucrats; he urged everyone to quit drinking, accept Christ, and be saved. Guatemala, he said without a trace of irony, was a country ruled by the power of love.

For the most part, the intelligentsia, the foreign press, and much of the Guatemalan middle class reacted to Ríos Montt as I had reacted to Edgardo Robertson years earlier: they thought he was mad . . . or a bizarre joke . . . or an embarrassment . . . or a sham. Prophet, reformer, lunatic? *Dios* Montt was widely dubbed "the Guatemalan Ayatollah."

Yet Guatemala, like Iran to which it was compared, was a hot, in some ways mystical, and very repressed country. After so many years of killings and fear, it was repressed not only in a political sense, but in an emotional and spiritual sense as well. Many people readily responded to the certainty and moral thunderings of the holy man. The foreign press and intellectuals may have been laughing, but in the countryside and the barrios, Ríos Montt was no buffoon. At a minimum, as Edgardo Robertson might have said, he had their attention. More important, Ríos Montt had an audience of fellow officers who, though primarily Catholic, were ready to listen. Many of them were stung by their international reputation as human rights abusers and by their own knowledge of corruption. Many of them felt restored in their military pride when called upon to stand for reform, honesty, and moral cleansing.

The overriding concern of Ríos Montt's term of office was to win the guerrilla war. To do that, he mounted a program of "beans and bullets." After a short respite from the bloodshed, it soon became clear that there would be many more bullets than beans and that the Christian soldier was not going to kill his enemies any less frequently or less dead than had the non-Christian soldier who had preceded him. Yet unlike Lucas García, whose program was also beans and bullets, Ríos Montt gained ground against the guerrillas, and his army did better in the field. In fact, toward the end of his office, it was widely reported that the government, remarkably, was winning.

Why? Most critical observers would argue that the war abated only because a well-trained and brutal army killed and overkilled all possible enemies. Quite simply, after a certain point, there was no one left to shoot back. And after enough exemplary killing in the villages, there was no one to think about—or even think about thinking about—helping those who might.[5]

Although I believe that this simple explanation is the key factor, a more complicated process was also at work—for the war was always a psychological as well as a military struggle. Beyond merely wiping out guerrillas and their bases of popular support, the larger challenge faced by the army was to create a psychological identification and new social organization that would allow campesinos to *be* nonguerrillas.

During the late sixties and throughout the seventies, the guerrillas not only were fairly free to roam the countryside, but had dominated the terrain in a moral as well as a physical sense. In part, they were able to do so through their indirect identification with the Catholic Church. Though the Church historically opposed revolutions, pastoral work among the poor was nevertheless a recognizable extension of the post–Vatican II theology of liberation. As Phillip Berryman, an ex-Maryknoll priest, writes, there is a "strong grassroots connection between Christianity [*viz.* Catholicism] and revolution. Large numbers of Christians in Central America, especially peasants, have come to reinterpret their lives based on a new understanding of the Christian gospel. They have frequently then joined militant organizations."[6]

In the spirit of the era, the guerrillas were, by extension at least, liberators. Even though many of them carried heavy nontheological political baggage (along with the personal scars of war and a taste for violence), they survived in the field in part through the legitimacy they gained among campesinos as a result of both their direct and their symbolic links to the Church.

Prior to Ríos Montt, the government's claim to moral legitimacy rested largely on tired abstractions about "anticommunism" and on schoolish, nationalistic sloganeering. These themes rang hollow to the rural poor and had few authentic advocates at the village level. The emotional rallying power of jeep bumperstickers that shouted "Belize is ours" or maps with Guatemala drawn patriotically out of scale paled beside the imagery of a gun-carrying priest.

Although several thousand guerrillas could not directly defeat a fierce and well-trained army, they at least held the moral high ground. And in Guatemala, that was no small matter. It meant, for example, that whenever and wherever guerrillas were perceived to be winning militarily—as in the "Ixil Triangle" in the early 1980s—they could easily muster local support, including new recruits.[7] And in those contested areas where military control shifted back and forth— southern Quiché, Sololá, northern Chimaltenango, San Marcos— the guerrillas could rely on at least passive support or neutrality from villagers.

Because few people spoke overtly of politics in the highlands (and lived long), the secular developmentalist activities of the Church took on subtle shades of meaning. The army was right to treat suspiciously "innocent" claims such as "All we're doing here is trying to organize our marketing coop." Though a Church-organized and, say, an AID-organized coop were doing essentially the same thing, they could be doing so within very different frames of political reference. By the end of the 1970s, the Guatemalan blend of liberationist theology and developmentalism implied a social order in which the army, the government, and the wealthy were on one side of the fence, and the people on the other.

It is for this reason that, from the army's point of view, the enemy became not just the guerrillas and their civilian supporters but, eventually, social organization itself. The seemingly inexplicable onslaughts against defenseless villages made a kind of sense. There *were* endless enemies. Because the village itself was such a tangled human web—bound by blood ties, a past, its ideologies, and colored by the Church, the Christian Democrats, and even the Peace Corps— it appeared treacherous and potentially threatening. Even innocuous cooperatives, above-ground political parties, and village self-help committees looked suspect and were vaguely guilty by association.

The resulting violence has been documented extensively elsewhere.[8] What most shocked outside observers was that not only did the army kill whenever and wherever they could find an armed target, but, frustrated because generally they couldn't, they also ripped up the social fabric—and sometimes even the physical fabric, the earth itself. Scores of mayors and anyone foolish enough to be called a "leader" were shot.[9] The cooperative movement, which had been built over nearly twenty years with funding and technical assistance from AID, was decimated.[10] The previously ubiquitous local structures of *técnicos, promotores,* and village-level *comités*—the most common means used by private voluntary organizations and even government ministries to transfer resources for village-level activities—were suddenly invisible or paralyzed, unable to implement even the most mundane of development activities.

In a world where social institutions have been torn apart, there is, of course, more rather than less need for social institutions. The army helped fill the gap. The most dramatic new social institution was the model village: an entirely new community built from the ground up and populated with refugees from wrecked communities. In the larger plan, these communities were boldly envisioned as *polos de desarrollo* (poles for regional development).

In addition, virtually the entire countryside was socially reorganized by means of village civil defense patrols. At the same time that Ríos Montt decentralized military field commands and detailed city-based officers to rural posts, he also conscripted *all* males between the ages of fifteen and sixty and put them under the command of local army veterans. The local patrols watched and regulated all movement through their areas and then, as an adjunct activity, were integrated into a complex institutional network (the *coordinadora* system) for national "reconstruction."[11]

With the countryside embroiled in violence and a Protestant zealot at the helm of the government, one easy interpretation of rising membership in evangelical churches is that being reborn gave villagers a safe-conduct ticket through government-linked repression. A second "easy" interpretation is that during such times of dislocation and extreme psychological stress, villagers responded to the "hot," transcendental qualities of evangelical fundamentalism. If ever there was a time for tears, rolling on the floor, and speaking in tongues, this was it.

As far as they go, these explanations are true. However, they tend to miss the deeper cultural appeal that Protestantism offered many village Indians and the role that Protestantism may have played in tipping the war's balance in favor of the government.

Ríos Montt, I believe, not only challenged the insurgents' weak hold on the physical landscape but also loosened their firm hold on the moral landscape. Inadvertently perhaps, he helped give voice and social identity to still-inchoate forces that had been jelling for years at the grassroots. As will be discussed in later chapters, Protestantism came long before Ríos Montt and, in some senses, even before the missionaries. But Ríos Montt did bring it center stage. As counterbalance to liberationist theology, Protestant fundamentalism may not have been the deciding factor in the war, but it was certainly an important factor as the army *re*organized while it *dis*organized the countryside.

Ríos Montt built a new rural constituency upon a cultural axis that was authentically Indian. Many of the people drawn to this newly evolving moral and organizational axis were already influential in their villages because they were entrepreneurs, landholders, or the better-educated elite, and Protestantism reinforced their advantage.[12] These were generally people who were willing to participate in village civil defense patrols, villagers who saw guerrillas as Satan and for whom the theology of liberation held little subconscious appeal. In a subtle way, they shaded the civil defense committees with "secular Protestantism" in the same way that many coops had subtly been shaded as "Catholic."[13]

The fact of a new "way to be" that was physically safe, emotionally accessible, and economically rewarding created allies for the government forces. The new high ground allowed those villagers who were nominally neutral but afraid (the majority, probably, who wished only for an end to violence) to rationalize their support for the perceived winners. Thus, while the army and the paramilitary burned and scourged, evangelism helped to further alienate the guerrillas from popular sympathy, that is, "to separate the fish from the water."

Ríos Montt was ousted in August 1983 by a coup similar to the one that put him in power. He was replaced by Defense Minister Oscar Humberto Mejía Victores, who remained in power until the transition to civilian government in January 1986. Among other things, Mejía objected to the "religious fanaticism" of Ríos Montt. Despite all the changes that had occurred, Guatemala had retained its particularly strong tradition of separating church and state; and of course, the country was still predominantly Catholic.[14] At the national level, the country was not ready for a man—possibly a madman—who seemed intent on imposing a state religion (the wrong one, to boot) even if he did seem to be winning a guerrilla war.

Once overthrown, Ríos Montt quickly passed from sight and then, for a time, was jokingly reported to be seen blessing children in supermarkets in Guatemala City.[15] Yet Ríos Montt will be remembered as more than a bizarre twist in a sad epoch. Socially and politically, he left a complex legacy: what was pulled apart did not spring back to its former shape just because a junta was deposed. Both violence and the rewiring of the countryside continued. By the time the transition to nominal political democracy was made in late 1985, the loyalties, alignments, and ideologies of the rural areas were deeply and probably permanently altered.[16]

The presidential election held in November 1985 was the fairest and most honest in Guatemala's history. One interesting sidelight to the campaign was a Protestant presidential candidate, Elías Serrano, a conservative businessman who hastily formed his own *personalista* following, the Democratic Party of National Cooperation (PDCN).

Serrano had been a member of Ríos Montt's Council of State. During the election, he was closely identified with Ríos Montt and became tagged as "the Protestant candidate." A major question was whether the lackluster Serrano could inherit the still-considerable political popularity of Ríos Montt and mobilize the latent political networks that he had formed.

As it happened, he didn't. To most voters, Serrano appeared dull and technocratic. He appealed primarily to right-leaning urban voters (a group split among several candidates) and the Protestant "hard core," and placed a weak fourth.

What happened to the Protestant vote? Vinicio Cerezo, a shrewd and sometimes eloquent man who had incredibly survived twenty years in Guatemalan politics, correctly appraised the new alignments being forged. His campaign team devised messages that spoke to rural Indian voters. Making ample use of his identity as a *Christian* Democrat, he spoke of God, peace, and the need for equitable development. His right-leaning opponents, in contrast, for the most part resurrected the spectre of anticommunism and, from the rural point of view, could scarcely be distinguished from each other.

Cerezo skillfully pulled together a broad coalition of the old and new. He not only pulled the traditional (above-ground) political left and moderate right toward center but, perhaps more important, preached a kind of ecumenical message that attracted Protestant and Catholic toward a common cultural center. He recognized that Protestant/Catholic had become a major new axis in Guatemalan society. But unlike Serrano, who became identified with one edge of the axis, Cerezo aimed for and captured the middle ground. Not since the electoral victory of Juan José Arévalo in 1945 had any presidential candidate won by such a large margin over so many opponents. Cerezo easily won the vote in the capital and in twenty of Guatemala's twenty-two departments.

If, as argued above, rural Protestantism was a major force in tipping the guerrilla war and is now a significant factor in national elections and the broader power relations of Guatemalan society, what is it about village life that has caused Protestantism to flourish? In the larger historical sense, where did Ríos Montt come from? And in villages today, what are the underlying dynamics of the competition between Protestantism and Catholicism?

The purpose of this volume is to provide a kind of explanatory backdrop to such questions. Written from the pinpoint perspective of a single village, this book analyzes the secular conditions that have given rise to Protestantism.

It may strike some readers as odd or disappointing that, beyond this first chapter, most of this work does not deal with the guerrilla war or Guatemalan politics. The key figure here is not the zealot missionary or the Protestant president. If there is a central figure at all, it is not even a person: it is the village Indian's tiny plot of corn and beans, known as the *milpa*. The thesis here is that religious behavior is rooted in economic production—and that production is both an idea and an expression of social circumstance. As will be explained, the *milpa* is not only an economically elegant way to produce corn and beans, it is an elegant expression of what is here called "Indianness."

It will be argued that "*milpa* logic" evolved as an expression of the Indian's place in Guatemalan colonial society, and that, by deep historical association, *milpa* logic is "Catholic." In the twentieth century, a complex set of forces—some environmental, some social—undercut the relative cultural stability that had evolved from the long colonial era. Though missionaries may have helped articulate Protestant identity and such crises as war and earthquakes may have sped conversion, the central point here is that the rise of Protestantism is an expression of the "anti-*milpa* forces" taking gradual hold upon village life. Undramatically, Protestantism makes its entry at the frayed edges, where stable systems of economic production, culture, and social relations are beginning to come apart.

The present work describes this process in a single town, San Antonio Aguas Calientes. The work is organized in the following manner: Chapter 2 reviews the historical origins of San Antonio and its neighbors (the "Quinizilapa towns"), showing where these particular Indians (and, more important, Indianness) came from. Chapter 3 examines in greater detail the economy of a "rich" Indian town—in particular, the logic of *milpa* versus cash crop production. Chapter 4 examines some of the cultural implications of rising wealth inequality and social differentiation, showing how economic stresses and strains create incentives that underlie (though they do not completely explain) why Indians convert to Protestantism. Chapter 5 looks in

more detail at the missionaries and the nature of village Protestantism and Catholicism; it then examines differences in the economic
behavior of Protestants and Catholics. Chapters 6 and 7 look more
closely at a nonagricultural extension of *milpa* logic: handweaving.
Chapter 6 examines why women weave, and more specifically, why
Protestant and why Catholic women weave. Chapter 7 focuses narrowly on textile entrepreneurship. The conclusion, Chapter 8, sum-
marizes the overall argument and returns briefly to the issues raised
in this introduction.

From the book's title, readers may be surprised that the book does
not say more about God, that it may seem lopsided on the production side of the *and*. Perhaps that is because of an overly intellec-
tualized bias to see religious and economic behavior as inversions of
each other and to write about what is easier to see and measure. But
beyond that, the simple truth is that I never did learn to talk very
well to Indians about God. So I am aware that Edgardo Robertson and
other missionaries might well be justified in saying that even with
benefit of ten years to think it over, I still missed the point.

Methodological Note

I lived in San Antonio for nearly a year from September 1977 through
July 1978, though this research was conducted on and off between
late 1976 and mid-1980. During those years I was usually employed
as a contract researcher for international development agencies. Although that livelihood was a constant diversion from the San Antonio field research, overall the experience broadened and enriched
this study, since it brought me to many villages other than San
Antonio.

Since leaving Guatemala I have made several return visits to San
Antonio—in November 1982, October 1984, and August 1985. My
strong impression is that, apart from a precipitous drop in the early
1980s in income from tourism, which is now reviving, life in the
town goes on pretty much as described here.

Many of the data in this study were derived from a survey designed to quantify the minutia of production. The seventy-four-
household sample represents about 11 percent of the San Antonio
population.[17] A questionnaire was developed after more than a year
of participatory fieldwork. Its language, categories, and organization
were field tested extensively, including a twenty-five-case pre-test
that caused us to discard most of the original questionnaire. Interviewers, including myself, were foreigners who had lived in the town
for several months to a year. I worried over the respective advantages

of foreign versus local interviewers but finally decided that sensitive outsiders are granted greater latitude in asking nosy questions than would be allowed of locals (much less *ladino* university students or trained Indian interviewers from other villages). No family ever refused to be interviewed; however, three completed interviews were thrown out because of doubts about their reliability. Respondents were paid a small fee "for their time," which a few people politely refused. Data were initially analyzed in Guatemala City with a statistical package developed by the Instituto para Nutrición para Centroamérica y Panamá (INCAP), and then reworked at the University of Chicago using SPSS and SCSS statistical packages. I believe the data are generally reliable, and have tried to flag where I think they may not be. Until 1983, and for many years before, the Guatemalan *quetzal* was on 1 : 1 par with the U.S. dollar. During that time, inflation was generally low and prices were relatively constant. Since then, inflation has taken off, so some dollar amounts may seem improbably low to some readers.

This research was not guided by an initial hypothesis on religion. Much time in the field was spent doggedly trying to understand the social impact of tourism as viewed through the semiotic window of textile production. In graduate school at the University of Chicago, "What does it mean?" seemed like a perfectly good question; but my two elderly weaving teachers, Doña Paola and Doña Victoria, never quite seemed to understand what I was talking about. Instead, they preferred to answer "How is it made?" As it happened, Doña Victoria is devoutly Catholic, and her sister-in-law, Doña Paola (to whom she does not speak), is devoutly Protestant. The focus of this research began to shift while, sitting at the loom to learn how it is made, I came to understand that the same activity had far different meanings for each of them—and then, that that difference had something to do with their religions.

Ríos Montt came to power and was overthrown after I left Guatemala. What I had observed about Doña Victoria and Doña Paola began to make more sense. Fortunately, I had included Protestant/Catholic as a descriptive variable on my questionnaire, so post hoc, I began to reanalyze the data with new questions in mind.

As a final note, I should add that I never saw Edgardo Robertson after the incident described at the beginning of this chapter. I understand, however, that he was forced to leave the country several years ago under threat from the guerrillas.

2

Colony of a Colony

A Thumbnail History of San Antonio and the
Lake Quinizilapa Towns

THE MODERN town of San Antonio Aguas Calientes is one of Guatemala's best-known and most accessible Indian towns. It lies in the crook of a usually green, crescent-shaped valley, about seven kilometers by an all-weather gravel road from Antigua and another thirty-five kilometers by four-lane asphalt to Guatemala City. Tourists from all over the world know and visit San Antonio. The image of the San Antonio woman at the loom—clad in her *huipil* of blue and red and orange and a dozen other colors—has become a national icon for use on tourism and export promotion brochures.

The quaint beauty of the town itself was probably permanently lost in the earthquake of 1976 when most dwellings were knocked down. Though the town was rebuilt, the patina was lost as the old tile and thatch roofs, covered with flowering vines, were replaced by galvanized tin; brick and board replaced the more graceful adobe walls.

Yet the setting, if not the town itself, is still spectacular. The curve of the valley is formed by a sharp, low volcanic ridge. At its southeast corner rise the first elevations of the slopes of the massive, inactive Agua volcano. At the southwest edge begin miles of coffee fields, ascending toward the twin peaks of Acatenango volcano, and just beyond that—about three kilometers as the crow flies from crater to crater—is the active Fuego volcano. Fuego erupts irregularly, lighting up the sky and hurling volcanic grit and ash miles into the air. In San Antonio, nestled at the foot of the three volcanoes, it is said that the rumbling and eruptions are caused by "Jews," mythic creatures who were swallowed into the earth and imprisoned for their role in the Crucifixion. There they restlessly twist and struggle, shaking the ground and spitting fire as they try to escape eternal damnation.

Excavations and systematic archaeological analysis have not been carried out in this region, so no one knows for certain whether this

Figure 3. View of San Antonio from a ridge to the southeast of the town.

particular valley was inhabited when the Spaniards invaded in 1524 and located their capital in the neighboring Almolonga Valley in 1527. Today, a walk through a freshly turned field during the rainy season is likely to turn up a handful of pottery shards, so it appears that *someone* lived there in earlier times. But who and when is difficult to determine. Archaeologists familiar with the area suggest that shard samples are of Late Classic origin,[1] supporting the generally held view that the valley was unoccupied when the Spaniards arrived several hundred years later at the end of the Postclassic Maya era.[2]

As shown in Figure 4, six towns are today located in this valley: San Antonio, Santa Catarina Barahona, San Andrés Ceballos, Santiago Zamora, San Lorenzo el Cubo, and San Miguel Dueñas. Each of these towns was founded along the shores of what was once a lake, known long ago as Lago Quinizilapa.[3] Elders recall hunting for ducks and fishing in the lake during their childhoods. The lake, however, was a health menace. In the early years of this century, yellow-fever epidemics killed as much as a third of the population. In 1927, villagers petitioned the government to drain the lake, diverting the natural springs into the Nima Yá River. The following year the lake was drained, and the rich bottomland was equitably divided among town members through a "lottery." What remains of the lake today is

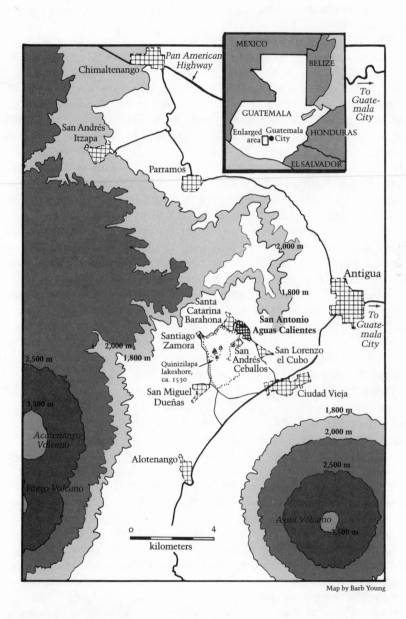

Map by Barb Young

Figure 4. Map of the Quinizilapa region.

a small marsh, still referred to locally as the *laguna* (meaning "lake," not "lagoon").

The six towns of the former shores of Lake Quinizilapa were all founded within a few years of the Spanish Conquest, between 1524 and 1530. *Milpas,* as these settlements were then called,[4] were initially land grants with which Conquistador Pedro de Alvarado rewarded his lieutenants, who settled a few miles off in Santiago en Almolonga, the site of modern-day Antigua.[5] The towns were named after their soldier-owners and supplied with a workforce of slaves who had been rounded up during the Conquest. The *"Milpa* of Juan de Chávez" (renamed San Antonio Aguas Calientes two centuries later) began as such a slave colony, but was legally given to its inhabitants about 1550, when slavery was juridically abolished and the founder, Juan de Chávez, returned to Spain.[6]

The Indians who were forced to settle the six Quinizilapa towns circa 1530 were generally picked up as Alvarado fought his way south from Cortés' headquarters in Mexico City. He gathered the future settlers from an extensive geographic and a highly diverse linguistic area. The heterogeneous origins of these Indians is suggested by a letter to the Spanish Audiencia Real in 1567, in which the inhabitants of Santa Catarina Barahona indicate to the king that their ancestors (relocated on the lake just forty years before this petition) came from five cultures: Chameltecos (probably San Juan Chamelco in present-day Alta Verapaz, an area where Kekchí is now spoken), Utlatecans (from Utatlán, capital of the Quiché state, i.e., Quiché speakers), Atitlán (Santiago Atitlán, capital of the Tzutujil state), Chontales (from Tabasco or Oaxaca in modern-day southern Mexico, i.e., speakers of Chontal Maya), and Pipiles (from the Pacific coast of Guatemala, possibly the area around Escuintla).[7] In a similar letter to the king in 1567, Indians from the neighboring Panchoy Valley refer to their ancestors as Tlecuiciahtecas (Tlacuiciahtlecas?), Xalanan (?), and Nauatlacas (Nahuatl speakers, probably but not necessarily from central Mexico).[8]

Because of the cultural and linguistic diversity of the Quinizilapa and Panchoy areas, one might suppose that the *ladino* language, Spanish—rather than the Indian language, Cakchiquel—might have emerged as the lingua franca. With no common indigenous language or root serving as a cultural core, the region could have been expected to have "ladinoized" rather than "Cakchiquel-ized" over the following centuries.[9] But that did not happen. To the contrary, the Spaniards were not interested in assimilation. They wanted unequal separation. They created a new class of beings: *indios,* an identifiable work force, tribute payers, potential soldiers, and the usually pliant objects of the civilizing, missionary, and charitable impulses of the conquerors. The Indian-*ladino* ethnic division reinforced a social order in which the Spanish colony's agricultural labor requirements were met, property rights were defined, and political authority was allocated. As Rodolfo Stavenhagen succinctly puts it, such "colonial relations" were characterized by "ethnic discrimination, political dependence, social inferiority, residential segregation, economic subjection and juridical incapacity."[10] That met Spanish colonial needs.

It also gave rise to the closed "corporate" Indian community,[11] a defensive but internally dignified indigenous response to social and economic discrimination. Supplying their own ideologies and institutions to govern local affairs, Indian communities created adjunct economies, appropriate technologies, and cultural boundaries to mark off that which was Indian and that which was *ladino*. If these spheres were unequal in power, at least communities maintained the prerogative to shape life within the limited spheres that they themselves controlled.[12]

Between 1550 and 1581, beginning just twenty years after the initial Hispanic settlement, the Quinizilapa population was already in decline as Indians fled or died from hunger, disease, and epidemic. In addition to the devastating regional pandemics that swept Mesoamerica in the 1540s and 1570s, local epidemics broke out in the Quinizilapa towns during every decade (except the 1580s) for the next two centuries.[13] These successive levelings of original population probably hastened the pan-Indian acculturation process. Then, during the long, relatively stable colonial and early independence periods, the lake towns acquired the features that have today come to be associated with "traditional" Indian society.[14]

The newly forged Indian identity (which genetically included even black slaves imported from the Caribbean[15]) was reinforced by a succession of export economies: sugar, indigo, cochineal dye, and coffee.[16] The principal crops of successive export economies changed, but the social organization of "colonial relations" did not. Although slavery was formally abolished shortly after the Conquest, forced payment of tribute or labor, which amounted to much the same thing, continued until just forty years ago. That stability formed the basis of what is here called "Indianness," meaning a particular cultural identity that took its form as much or more from the Spaniards as from the root characteristics of the Maya themselves.

The Town and Its Hinterland

Just as the Spanish colony (Guatemala) maintained its own form of colonial relations with its economic and political exteriors (Europe, and later the United States); and the colony's colonies (larger Indian towns like San Antonio) maintained colonial relations with the Hispanic overclass; so too, the colony's colonies developed *their* colonies, poorer, dependent hamlets in the rural hinterlands—these also distanced and protected from their exteriors through locally specific religious practice, language, and dress.

The colonial legacy of San Antonio can be read today in its physical characteristics and muted urban development. The combined, contiguous population in San Antonio/Santa Catarina in 1987 was approximately six thousand persons, which is a sizable urban concentration by Guatemalan standards.[17] Yet the "town" does not exhibit most of the traits that are normally associated with a settlement of this size. To the contrary, it is conspicuously "underdeveloped." There are no paved streets. There is no gas station, no mechanic, no welder. There is no doctor, lawyer, or government office, and no hardware or agricultural supply store. Apart from two or three families who vend food from their doorsteps on Sunday mornings, there is no public eatery, not even a *comedor* (a rustic restaurant). Despite forty or so years of tourism, there is no *pensión*, much less a hotel. And, perhaps most unusual by Guatemalan standards, there is no marketplace (marketing takes place in nearby Antigua).

In outward appearance, the richest and poorest homes in San Antonio are not greatly dissimilar. There is no "prestige" *cantón* or neighborhood that can be identified with some particular social group (e.g., rich people, *ladinos*, Protestants, weavers, craftsmen).[18] With few exceptions, all San Antonio homes are more or less alike: a cornstalk fence separates extended family compounds (called *sitios*) from the dusty public thoroughfare. Each *sitio* contains several rectangular, freestanding rooms, usually constructed from cornstalks and mud-daubing. Normally one nuclear family occupies each *sitio*, although there may be as many as three nuclear families as well as renters. Domestic groups that share a hearth usually operate as a discrete economic unit—that is, they share not only cooking but also land, income, labor, food, and child care. As space permits, most families raise animals (generally poultry), "kitchen crops" (herbs, fruit, and vegetables), and some commercial crops (especially coffee) within their compound.

With so little external physical differentiation, the town appears to be an "overgrown village," impressing most visitors as being

Figure 5. Interior of a San Antonio household compound.

smaller than it actually is. Aside from minor topographic variations, only three features break the homogeneity of appearance:

The plaza. This dusty open space in front of the church is delimited by the four *capillas* (small "chapels") of the respective *cantones* (quarters of the town), a public *pila* (laundry area with standpipes for drinking water), recently constructed municipal buildings, and several tourist *tiendas* (makeshift structures for the sales of handweavings), including one which has preempted the small gazebo at the centerpoint of the plaza. Unlike the charming town plazas of southern Mexico and elsewhere, the plaza of San Antonio has no fountains, benches, grass, shrubbery, monuments, sidewalks, or artistic ornaments to define or reflect its public use.[19]

The "main street." No streets in San Antonio have formal names. The main street, such as it is, extends from the "bus-stop corner" (one block from the central plaza) to nearby Santa Catarina Barahona. It is a meter or two wider than other streets, allowing two-way vehicular traffic to pass—though slowly and very carefully. There are several one-room *tiendas* (in the sense of "general stores," usually no more than a wall and counterful of goods), a rustic *cantina*, a room for billiards, and several tailors' workshops.

"Tienda Row." As many as fifty to sixty tourist stalls extend along

Figure 6. Young woman weaving as she tends the store.

Figure 7. Children offering a textile to passing tourists.

the access road from the outskirts of town to the plaza.[20] These *tiendas* are usually three-walled buildings with hard dirt floors, cornstalk walls, and galvanized sheet-metal roofs. As shown in Figures 6 and 7, woven goods are hung on open display and hawked loudly to passing tourists.

The apparent under-urbanization belies the economic importance of San Antonio within the microregion. As will be discussed in the following chapter, the town is a center for high- and mid-altitude vegetables such as carrots, cabbages, beets, and lettuce. San Antonio farmers are not only growers but also intermediaries. With a tight control over the flow of produce from their own hinterlands, they provide produce to the wholesale markets of Antigua, Guatemala City, and the lowland towns of the Pacific coast.

The town has been an economic "success" for over four hundred years. Yet what seems remarkable is how little of the agricultural or touristic wealth that passes through the town sticks there. As elsewhere in Guatemala (best described by Carol Smith in her various studies of marketing in the western highlands),[21] the region's agricultural produce flows up and out through a complex, tiered arrangement; and manufactured goods flow down and in. This happens without neighboring communities developing strong lateral linkages. Locally owned economic institutions (markets, restaurants, agricultural supply stores, welders, mechanics) that would divert the flow of capital and resources into physical development tend not to emerge.

Largely because of its favorable location, San Antonio has become preeminent among the Quinizilapa towns.[22] It organizes a sparsely populated hinterland that bears much the same relationship to San Antonio that San Antonio bears to Antigua and Guatemala City. That is, the rural hamlets channel agricultural produce and human labor to the higher-order centers—in effect, they are colonies of the colony's colony. In all, there are four subsumed towns and an extensive rural hinterland, described briefly below.

Santa Catarina Barahona

Though there is no natural or physical boundary marking where San Antonio ends and Santa Catarina begins, the two towns are distinct. Santa Catarina is the *cabecera municipal* (seat) of a separate *municipio*, with a territorial extension of thirty-one square kilometers and a 1987 population of about 1,700 residents.[23] Although no demarcation is visible to the outsider's eye, townspeople in both communities are well aware of the difference. Santa Catarina has its own churches and its own fiesta and ritual calendar. There is a subtle variation in Cakchiquel dialect between San Antonio and Santa Catarina. More importantly, San Antonio has been able to benefit economically from its slight locational advantage—more-direct access to produce markets and, in recent years, first shot at incoming tourists. Gradually, San Antonio farmers have gained land that Santa Catarina farmers have lost, and as a result, many Santa Catarina farmers now work as day laborers (*mozos*) for the generally more prosperous San Antonio farmers. Similarly, women in Santa Catarina frequently work as commissioned weavers or as wholesale textile suppliers for vendors in San Antonio.

San Andrés Ceballos

Also physically contiguous with San Antonio is the *aldea* (hamlet) of San Andrés Ceballos (1987 population, about 500). Though it has its own church, fiesta, and separate oral history, San Andrés has been under the administrative jurisdiction of the San Antonio *alcaldía* (mayoral office) since 1935.

In the early 1950s, INCAP field researchers described San Andrés and its residents as being at a "lower economic level [than San Antonio] . . . and not much interested in the betterment of their community."[24] Today, however, the town is a tightly knit and widely envied pocket of affluence. Most of the agricultural land belonging to the present-day community is former bottomland that was once Lake Quinizilapa. In recent years, these fields have been converted from corn to intensive vegetable and coffee production. Some San Andrés families have made further transitions from vegetable-growing to truck-farming, from buying pickups to offering transportation services. The relatively few San Andrés families now operate two small bus lines and several trucks.

Santiago Zamora

At the other end of the local spectrum is the *aldea* of Santiago Zamora, about three kilometers to the west. Of the six former lake towns, Santiago is today the most disadvantaged in natural resources and access to external opportunity. The village is located at the base of the jutting volcanic ridge, just *above* the bottomland of the former lake. This higher land is generally dry, seriously eroded, and unproductive. The bottomland that does belong to Santiago is not fully drained and is therefore suitable only for the production of marsh reeds (*tul*). These reeds are woven into flat mats called *petates*, and provide serious employment for only the poorest of the poor (see Chapter 3).

Over the years, Santiago has lost much of its once extensive holdings. Today, few families farm as much as ten *cuerdas* of their own land.[25] Most men work on nearby coffee plantations (*fincas*) or in recently opened nurseries that grow ornamental flowers for export. Many families trade their labor for the right to harvest an agreed-upon quantity of reeds from the nearby *fincas* or from the San Antonio landowners. For example, in exchange for *tul*, a man agrees to clean fifteen *cuerdas* of bottomland owned by the *finca*. Thus, the family is assured of raw material that will produce supplemental income, and the landowner is assured of laborers during times of peak demand for workers.

San Lorenzo el Cubo

The *aldea* of San Lorenzo el Cubo lies less than a kilometer from San Antonio along the road to Antigua. The town belongs to the administrative jurisdiction of a larger nearby city, Ciudad Vieja. It is the only one of the original towns not settled literally on the shores of the former lake.

Like its neighbors, San Lorenzo was founded as an Indian-slave agricultural community, the *Milpa* of Diego Monroy, Señor of San Lorenzo. The land grant to Monroy was converted to a tribute-paying *encomienda* in the late sixteenth century. However, despite its origins identical to those of the other Indian settlements, the town is now considered to be purely *ladino.*[26]

Why San Lorenzo lost its "Indianness" while San Antonio, a stone's throw away, became all the more Indian, is an intriguing question. Within this region, San Lorenzo is the only community that is today nearly landless. Land was lost mainly to upper-class Guatemala City families who built coffee *fincas* in the late nineteenth and early twentieth centuries,[27] and the remainder was lost piecemeal to encroachment by the better-off farmers from San Antonio and San Andrés. It is therefore tempting to conclude that the accelerated ladinoization process in San Lorenzo was caused by a weakening of Indian cultural institutions that could not survive in the absence of a land base. However, the ladinoization of San Lorenzo apparently was well underway in the mid-nineteenth century and predates the incursions of the large coffee *fincas.* More than a century ago, José María Navarro remarked of the people in San Lorenzo, "their dress, language, and customs are identical to the other [Quinizilapa] towns, with the difference that these people are much taken by ladino dress and the Spanish language."[28] So perhaps there is a more subtle reason than loss of land. (It should be noted that in nearby San Miguel Dueñas, the sixth Quinizilapa town, ladinoization also occurred rapidly. Today the town has few remnants of its earlier Indian origin. In this case, the influence may be a more-biological *mestizaje* [through the incorporation of a larger number of blacks and mulattoes] rather than a more-cultural *mestizaje.*)[29]

San Lorenzo now subsists on income from wage labor, mostly in Ciudad Vieja and in nearby Antigua. Every morning a stream of workers departs from San Lorenzo—the men on bicycles, the women walking. During periods of peak agricultural demand, the landless San Lorenzo *ladinos* frequently work as *mozos* for San Antonio Indian farmers, a highly unusual ethnic role reversal for Guatemala, a society strictly stratified by race.

The Hinterlands

In the hinterlands to the north and west of San Antonio is a sprinkling of remote, named places, often merely fields or a cluster of houses. Little infrastructure is found here—only crisscrossing footpaths and one all-weather gravel road. Much, if not most, agricultural produce is still hauled by human portage. It is not uncommon for a San Antonio farmer to carry his family's supply of firewood from his own land to town (a distance of seven to eight kilometers) two or even three times a week. Carriers generally use the *mecapal*, or tumpline (see Figure 8), to transport crops from the fields to the road. Produce is then carried into San Antonio by foot or hired pickup truck, then to Antigua on a truck or public bus.[30]

Over the years, San Antonio has expanded its land base through purchase and, to a lesser extent, through a government land redistribution project implemented during the 1950s (see Chapter 3). Today San Antonio–owned lands extend well into the Department of Chimaltenango, abutting and reaching into the *municipios* of Parramos and San Andrés Itzapa. In some areas (particularly the *aldeas* of Chimachoy, Chicasanga, Pampay, and Chicarona) the former local owners have virtually been forced off their land by San Antonio farmers. Most have left for the coast or the capital; some are living on their former lands as renters or day-laborers; many have migrated to the *cabecera municipal*, where they work as laborers or intermarry with San Antonio families; and a few have maintained their ownership and continue to farm—but within the orbit of the San Antonio economy.[31] Unlike Indians in midwestern and western Guatemala, farmers in the Quinizilapa towns do not seem to prefer full-time rural residence; instead, they live in town and, when necessary, temporarily reside on the land. There is, however, a need for resident rural laborers. Landless peasants from San Antonio and the neighboring towns fill this need. They migrate to the countryside to live in these tiny hamlets and work the vegetable fields that are owned by nonresident farmers. There the migrants become full-time *mozos*, *peones*, or *colonos*.[32] Poor couples frequently have no choice but to begin their married lives in this fashion. As a result of this ongoing exchange of population between San Antonio and the hinterlands (with corresponding intermarriage), the whole area has come to be dominated by San Antonio. Symbolically, this cultural and economic hegemony perhaps is reflected in the adoption of the San Antonio *traje* (dress style) throughout an area well beyond the boundary of the actual *municipio*. The immediately identifiable colors and designs of the San Antonio woman's blouse (*huipil*) have become regionalized, absorbing and supplanting heretofore distinct local styles in the "colonized" hinterlands.

Figure 8. Man with *mecapal* carrying cornstalks.

Literacy and Language

San Antonio is exceptional for an Indian town—in fact, for any rural Guatemalan community—because of its high rate of literacy, particularly its high rate of female literacy. In the late 1970s, John Early found that San Antonio had the highest female Indian literacy rate for any *municipio* with a population more than 90 percent Indian.[33] According to both my field data and the 1973 census,[34] about three-fourths of the adult population is literate. The median is about four years of school, with of course much higher rates for the younger people.

The uniqueness of San Antonio's high literacy can be appreciated by comparison to other Indian regions. For example, the Department of Alta Verapaz—with a 1973 population of more than 250,000 (including urban and *ladino* as well as Indian populations)—had an estimated overall literacy rate of only 14 percent. In El Quiché, the overall departmental literacy rate was only 22 percent.[35] A cross-tabulation of available census data indicated a literacy rate among adult, rural, female Indians of only about 2 percent in 1973.[36] In other words, the town of San Antonio, with a population of about 5,000, had about three times as many literate Indian women as the entire Department of El Quiché, with a population of nearly 300,000.[37]

High rates of literacy and school attendance are not recent phenomena in San Antonio. Navarro glowingly described San Antonio's *two* schools in 1874,[38] a hundred years before many small Guatemalan Indian towns had *any* schools. Today there are three schools: a government public school, a recently opened, foreign-supported Catholic parochial school, and the Protestant Nima Yá school.[39] Graduates of the primary schools may go on to *básico* in Antigua, and many children have continued through secondary schools and even the university.

San Antonio is also unusual in its longstanding bilingualism. Unlike many communities in western and northwestern Guatemala, San Antonio never experienced a period of predominant monolingualism. A hundred years ago, Navarro described San Antonio Indians speaking Spanish "as if it were their native language." In the late 1940s, field researchers from the Instituto Indigenista Nacional estimated about three-fourths of the population was bilingual. In the early 1950s, two INCAP field workers noted, "All the inhabitants (of San Antonio and San Andrés) speak Spanish and Cakchiquel, except a few women in San Andrés who do not understand Spanish."[40]

During the past generation, two important shifts in language have taken place. First, Spanish has become the more widely used of the two languages.[41] Second, an almost total reversal has occurred from Cakchiquel to Spanish as the first language of children. In my field survey, none of the present group of one- to four-year-olds were learning Cakchiquel as their first language, while almost all children in the generation now over forty learned Cakchiquel first.

What may be somewhat more surprising about language is that higher levels of education and income correlate with bilingualism—not monolingualism in Spanish as might be expected. To "make it" socially and economically requires facility in both Indian and non-Indian spheres. As the formerly Indian *ladinos* of San Lorenzo illustrate, one does not cast off Indian identity and then move up. Language represents a social boundary, not an obstacle.

Conclusion

The strong Indian identity of San Antonio has maintained itself in the face of influences that might be expected to be strongly acculturating—the proximity within ten kilometers of a major *ladino* center, four hundred years of intense interaction with *ladino* society, no common indigenous roots, a high level of literacy, and longstanding bilingualism.

As the next chapter will discuss, San Antonio is unlike most other Indian towns in its degree of economic "success." Yet what "success" means is replication from one generation to the next of colonial relations. What is replicated is Indianness, a permanent state of unequal separation. Acculturation occurs not because of cultural or physical proximity but because of breakdown in the smooth, generation-to-generation transfer of Indianness. Latter chapters will elaborate more fully how the Indian economy, Indian identity, and colonial relations are all intimately linked—and how that knot is unraveling, loosened by those individuals who are either too successful economically or not successful enough to fully accept Indianness. And it is here, at the margins of Indian cultural stability, that Protestantism has emerged as a force.

3

The Economy of a "Rich" Indian Town

FOR A TOWN of rural Guatemala, San Antonio is fortunate in its generous endowment of resources and its wide range of economic opportunity. Indians from neighboring communities often say that San Antonio is "rich."[1] And indeed it is—at least by Guatemalan standards of relative poverty.

According to calculations from the late 1970s based on a survey of seventy-four households, the median annual family income in San Antonio was $1,115 (mean, $1,254)—a per capita income of $214, or $.59 per day per person.[2] Median family wealth—that is, the total cash value for *all* family assets—was $2,037 (mean, $4,006),[3] and the median per capita wealth, $407. By contrast, documents from government and international development agencies generally report "average" family incomes of $400 to $500 or less for other highland Indian communities.[4]

Yet an informed walk through the town reveals that though San Antonio may be less abjectly poor than other villages, it is still poor.[5] Homes are built of the most rustic of Guatemalan construction materials: cornstalk (*caña*) and mud daubing.[6] All but a few families prepare food as does the woman in Figure 9: on an unraised, open, wood fire with *comales* for heating tortillas and her cooking pots propped upon three rocks—smoke filtering upward through the walls and roof. During the earthquake of 1976, all the older clay-tile and thatch roofs crashed down; they have been replaced with corrugated panels of galvanized sheet metal. Quinizilapa houses virtually never have formal, suspended ceilings—just the underside of the sheet metal. Although concrete floors are becoming common, most homes, like the one shown in the photo, still have hard-packed dirt floors.[7]

Like most towns in the Sacatepéquez area, San Antonio has potable water.[8] Only about a quarter of the families have a pipe and spigot actually inside their household compound. But for the most

Figure 9. Elderly woman at hearth grinding corn.

part, they do not have to walk very far to reach water. Only about a third of the families have to walk more than a long block to reach a standpipe.[9]

No family has pipe drainage or closed indoor plumbing. No family has flush toilets, of course; but unlike those in many less-advantaged areas of the country, most families do have rustic, covered latrines.[10] In contrast, in the departments of Sololá, Totonicapán, and San Marcos, I found that only 40 percent of rural or village families have latrines, sanitary or not; and in rural Quiché, only about 17 percent.[11] Although I have no recent, reliable medical data, I know— from living in the village for a year—that chronic diarrhea regularly kills or contributes to the death of San Antonio children, despite the nominal presence of latrines and potable water.[12] For the year 1974, Julia Marina Arreola Hernández estimated that infants under one year of age had a mortality rate of 87 per thousand (a neonatal rate of 24 per thousand plus a postnatal rate of 63 per thousand).[13] By comparison, U.S. rates are generally 12–15 deaths per thousand. For a developing country, rates of over 100 per thousand are considered to be extremely high.

Child mortality is closely associated with chronic diarrhea and malnutrition, each of which has a compounding, exacerbating effect on the other.[14] And income, or lack of it, is obviously related to incidence of malnutrition.[15] Yet even with the relatively high incomes that San Antonio families enjoy, Arreola Hernández estimates that only 30 percent of children under five are unaffected by malnutrition. She estimates that 55 percent of children suffer from relatively mild, Grade I malnutrition, and 13 percent from Grade II malnutrition. However, only 2 percent suffer from clinically severe, Grade III malnutrition.[16]

So, indeed, the "wealth" of San Antonio is a relative matter. Although the town is certainly poor, it is at least less poor than most others. Although there is hunger, there is less hunger; and despite the constant anguish from child death, there is less child death than elsewhere.

Sectors of Economic Opportunity

What accounts for the Antoneros' fortune to be not-so-poor Indians? The easy answer is: good land, a mix of crops, access to markets, education, convenient opportunities for wage labor, tourism, and, more recently, moderate insulation from political violence. Compared to other towns, San Antonio offers a wide range of economic alternatives. While I lived there, I studied ten distinct economic activities: *milpa* agriculture, cash-cropping, small family business, animal husbandry, wage labor by men, wage labor by women, wage labor by children, *petate*-making, small-scale vegetable marketing, and textile production for sales to tourists.[17] In each "sector," I found San Antonio families to be shrewd and energetic in exploiting every shred of opportunity. In general, I believe the key to their "success" is their practical capacity to match labor and investment capabilities to the endlessly shifting permutations of opportunity. Yet there are also subtler reasons. The remainder of this chapter explores these reasons by more closely examining the character of several economic "sectors."

Milpa Agriculture

The *milpa*[18] is the cornerstone of food production for most families in the Quinizilapa towns. Virtually all families who own or rent any land grow corn[19] as their first crop. As it has for at least four millennia, the cycle of corn production serves to organize the use of time and resources for a large majority of San Antonio families.

What seems odd is that corn production appears to have a low rate of return compared to virtually any economic alternative. Studies of

Table 1. *Costs, Yields, and Profits from One Cuerda of Corn Production*

Labor Costs[a]	Days	$/Day[b]	Cost ($)
Prepare soil	7.1	2.17	15.40
Plant	.9	1.84	1.66
Weed/"clean"	1.1	2.20	2.43
Apply fertilizer	.8	1.88	1.50
Calzar la mata[c]	1.6	1.89	3.03
Doblar la mata[d]	1.3	1.83	2.38
Harvest	2.4	1.61	3.86
Subtotal			30.26

Nonlabor Costs	Weight (Lbs.)	Cents/Lb.	Cost ($)
Fertilizers	53	9	4.78
Seed	3.7	8	.31
Transportation	61	5	3.10
Subtotal			8.19
Total costs			38.45

Yield[e]	Weight (Lbs.)	Cents/Lb.	Value ($)
Good crop	579	7.4	42.85
Bad crop	366	7.4	27.08

Profit (value of yield minus total costs)

Good crop	($42.85 − $38.45)	$ 4.40
Bad crop	($27.08 − $38.45)	−$11.37

[a] Completely accurate labor costs are difficult to determine because of (1) variations in planting techniques and land characteristics, (2) the practice of responding to questions with ranges (e.g., "Oh, it takes me about two or three days to do that"), (3) the difficulty of calculating inputs of family labor, and (4) the difficulties in translating a farmer's thinking from his actual land (perhaps work on several plots, all of different sizes) to a hypothetical one-*cuerda* plot.

[b] The going rate for agricultural labor was $1.75–$2.00 per day when this survey was carried out. These estimates reflect the value of that labor even though some or all labor may have been provided by the family. Variations from row to row reflect a tendency to "over-report" paid versus family-provided labor—that is, a paid laborer is likely to do the hard manual labor of preparing the soil, while the wife and children are likely to help out during the easier work of the harvest.

[c] *Calzar la mata* is to build a "boot" around the stalk at its base, thus protecting it from wind and directing the water flow.

[d] *Doblar la mata* is to bend over the stalks, just below the ears, after they reach physiological maturity. They are then left inverted in the field to dry and await harvest in the dry season.

[e] A "good crop" was defined as (1) a crop grown in a season of optimal growing conditions, (2) a crop harvested from rich or recently fallow soil, or (3) a well-fertilized crop. A "bad crop" was defined as (1) a crop grown under poor growing conditions, (2) a crop from high-clay or exhausted soil, or (3) an unfertilized crop. See also endnote 21 for this chapter.

Figure 10. Stored corn drying in the sun.

agriculture in this region generally show that dollar output per unit of land is about four times higher for commercially grown vegetables than for corn.[20] The gross cash value of one *cuerda* of corn with a "good crop" is only about $43; with a "bad crop," $27 (see Table 1). When the farmer's costs are deducted from the value of the yield, a "good crop" comes to about $4 a *cuerda*, while a "bad crop" represents a theoretical loss of about $11.[21] And poor crops are far from uncommon.[22]

Why, then, continue to produce corn? Why doesn't everyone just grow vegetables instead?

The continued reliance on corn despite its ostensibly low rate of return represents, first, a pragmatic response in which very poor people avoid the worst-case nutritive risk. The hardiness of corn is remarkable. Despite misuse of the land, neglect, insufficient rotation, lack of fertilizers, drought, and eroded topsoils, corn survives. By planting corn a family might assure itself of poverty, and possibly even hunger—but it will *not* face starvation.[23]

Not only is corn agronomically reliable, but when consumed with beans and modest supplements of fresh vegetables, it makes a nutritionally complete diet. Marina Flores and Emma Reh reported in 1955 that cereals (almost exclusively corn) accounted for about 77 percent of total caloric intake for San Antonio families and 62 percent of all their protein intake. (Beans provided another 9 percent of caloric intake and 19 percent of all protein intake. Meat, milk, and eggs together were sources for only 15 percent of protein intake.) In addition, cereals accounted for 52 percent of all fats, 83 percent of all calcium, 53 percent of all iron, 63 percent of all thiamin, and 66 percent of all niacin.[24] Thus, when asking why people don't plant vegetables instead of corn, the true comparison is not between the cash value of corn versus the cash value of vegetables but between an almost-certain guarantee of minimal family nutrition versus a possibility of better nutrition. Understandably, the poorer the family, the more likely they are to be cautious and pro-corn in making this choice.

The *milpa* has survived as the dominant form of peasant agriculture despite more than two decades of efforts by the Ministry of Agriculture and international development technicians to persuade small farmers to shift to the seemingly more lucrative production of vegetables. As a development technician myself, I initially shared the bias against the *milpa*—or at least held the view that *milpa* agriculture would inevitably decline as "development" proceeded and more farm families reached a threshold of nutritive security.

But in fact, the issue is far more complicated. The *milpa* persists not only because of its nutritive reliability; beyond that, it also serves as the physical and intellectual "suprastructure" of a versatile and surprisingly practical productive system. Like "Indianness," the highland *milpa* is in many ways a place-particular legacy of colonial relations (see Chapter 2). Its key characteristic is that it "produces" by absorbing the low-cash-value "spare inputs" that a poor family is likely to have in abundance and transforming them to higher value. Moreover, this occurs in a way that is socially stabilizing: by optimizing input rather than maximizing output, the *milpa* produces nothing that can be extracted; thus, it reinforces the internal sphere (village society) without increasing vulnerability to the extractive external sphere (the *ladino* overclass).

Agronomically, it is easy to misread what is happening in a seemingly simple, half-*cuerda*-or-so plot of corn. During my early fieldwork, I consistently misunderstood both the quantity and the character of *milpa* production. Most often, I overlooked intercrops— even after I was well aware of their importance. In early stages, I frequently mistook tuberous and vine crops for weeds. Farmers often casually described plants by saying *"solo es monte"* (just weeds) even though such "weeds" can be sold as herbs, medicinal plants, dyestuffs, or can be fed to the turkey. In field inventories I frequently

Figure 11. Fields above the town toward the end of the dry season.

did not see or failed to ask about crops of very rapid maturation, usually ornamental flowers and occasionally radishes. I misunderstood that plants which seemed inedible can at some times or during some seasons be prepared in edible forms.

The point here is that the *milpa* is an agronomic system that operates by producing a very large number of very small quantities. In many instances, the intercrops can be more important than the primary corn crop. Because of the biotic diversity and seasonal variability, the precise output defies quantification. Since most *milpa* inputs require no direct outlay of cash, a farmer is unlikely to have a corresponding notion of what is produced. Upon being asked what is being grown in a particular field, a farmer is likely to simply respond *"milpa"* or *"maíz"* (in some senses, the words are interchangeable). The ambiguity arises because the farmer conceives a cornfield as a place with corn, beans, some carrots, a few *guicoy*, a half-dozen-or-so *ayotes*, a row or two of radishes, several kinds of *chiles* for cooking, a couple dozen *pacayas* for Easter, three coffee bushes, two *gravilea* trees for shade and firewood in the northwest corner, fodder for his brother-in-law's cow, dried cornstalks to be used for a new kitchen wall, and so forth. The alternative to asking a farmer what and how much he produces from a given unit of land—on-site case studies of individual plots based on field observation during a full agricultural cycle—is inordinately time-consuming and does not lend itself to aggregation of statistical data for more than a few cases.[25]

While population in the Quinizilapa towns has increased dramatically over recent generations, land ownership has become increasingly skewed. The majority find themselves with more and more family members to support on smaller and smaller plots of land. For them, the *milpa* is ideally suited for crop intensification. Because of its reliability and dietary importance, corn is the logical choice for the primary crop. Because of its nutritive and agronomic complementarity to corn, either a ground or climbing variety of beans is generally planted as a second crop.[26] But beyond that, a farmer's selection of intercrops can be based on a complex range of agronomic, spatial, demographic, and social factors. What varieties are best suited to the land, slope, water, available light? What are the interactive effects among combinations of crops? If his *milpa* is distant, for example, or if he has other employment, a farmer is less likely to choose intercrops that require daily care. Who is available to tend secondary crops? Is there a young son who can be sent daily to weed vegetables and watch for pests? Crops can be more or less processed (e.g., sorted, cleaned, cooked, bundled) before being sold at market. Is someone available who has the time and skills to do the process-

Figure 12. View of an intensely intercropped San Antonio field.

ing—someone, moreover, who cannot earn a higher rate of return at some other occupation during that unit of time?

What is remarkable about the *milpa* is its capacity to absorb "inputs" that might otherwise be wasted—microquantities of resources that the family may have in abundance but have no use for without the transformative suprastructure. The *milpa* utilizes "resources" that may be abundant but are otherwise unusable: dawn weeding hours, after-school hours, knowledge of flower-growing, a particular style of food preparation, waste water, human and animal feces, the fact of an upcoming fiesta. What is more important socially is that because the *milpa* is built upon the principle of optimizing inputs rather than maximizing outputs, it yields little that can be extracted. *Milpa* product, for the most part, is consumed by the family or traded within the village. That means that no one can get rich or make someone else rich by farming a *milpa*. Since it works against capital accumulation, it is antithetical to entrepreneurship.

In short, planting a *milpa* optimizes resources in a very particular way. First, it works to assure nutritive security, even, ironically, if that means ensuring material poverty. Second, it "tidies the household environment." In a sense, the *milpa* acts as the horticultural equivalent of a pig—a biological transformer which recycles table scraps into pork—only in this case, the scraps include loose bits of unproductive time and pieces of miscellaneous information, as well as material and human wastes.[27] Third, it reinforces the family and household unit as the basis for social organization by optimizing "resources" that exist largely as a result of the sociodemographic fact of the family (e.g., a grandmother's availability for weeding and her knowledge of herbs is a tangible resource within the context of a family-operated *milpa*). And fourth, because of its fundamentally anti-entrepreneurial character, it reinforces the egalitarian character of the village (discussed more fully in Chapter 4), a cultural trait which came to be central to the Indian society that evolved during the postcolonial period.

Nevertheless, despite the agroeconomic versatility of the *milpa* and its conservative social character, there are practical, physical limits to a form of production that is based on input substitution and crop intensification. The most obvious constraint is land. Landless families can still operate within this traditional productive system by renting land in exchange for labor—and therefore preserve the lifestyle and ideology that has evolved along with that system—but only if *some* land is available.

San Antonio has maintained, even improved, its landholdings relative to its neighbors; yet the absolute availability of land has decreased substantially over the last century. In 1874, Navarro reported a population of 1,340 persons (264 households) and landholdings of 16 *caballerías* (approximately 6,400 *cuerdas*), about 24.2 *cuerdas* per family.[28] I estimate that 5.9 *cuerdas* are necessary to provide an average family with corn for one year (5.1 persons per household × 1.1 pounds of corn consumed per person per day × 365 days per year ÷ 350 pounds of corn per *cuerda*).[29] Assuming a reasonably equitable distribution of village land one hundred years ago, each family would have had roughly four times the amount of land needed to assure self-sufficiency in corn. Today, the population is roughly four times greater than in the 1870s, and according to calculations from my survey results, San Antonio's landholdings today total about 16,000 *cuerdas*, or about two-and-a-half times the amount that was available one hundred years ago.[30]

The difficulty is not only that there is relatively less land per person; what is more important, land ownership within the community is considerably less equitable than it used to be. Fully 40 percent of the families in my sample of households owned no land (though some had access to land through rental, parcels borrowed from parents, or labor exchange, as discussed in the next chapter). The top five landholding families owned nearly half the total land in the sample.[31] Among those families who owned *any* land, the median holding was 4.7 *cuerdas*—that is, considerably less than the minimum 5.9 *cuerdas* needed for subsistence in growing corn.

There are limits to adaptiveness. As land becomes more scarce, a subsistence equilibrium can be re-established up to a point through intercropping, multiple cropping, and increased use of nominally marginal inputs. But the incentives to keep re-establishing that equilibrium begin to break down for people in two categories: those without minimal land or hope for land and, at the other extreme, those with abundant land (i.e., those who do not have to farm by the logic of intensification). What actually happens is examined and explained in Chapter 4.

Cash-Cropping

Poverty of material resources, nutritive threat, and cultural subjugation have each worked to reinforce the stability of an egalitarian, internally self-sufficient, self-regulated culture. The *milpa* embodies the technology of that culture and is in turn at the core of the particular ideology that has come to be identified with the Indians of the highlands. Yet commodity production—growing cash crops for external markets—is nothing new in San Antonio. In a very real sense, connection to the external world through markets is as fully "indigenous" as is the *milpa*. To view the *milpa* as "traditional"— and therefore more indigenous—and commodity production as modern—and therefore alien or foreign—is to misunderstand Indian history and society.

Production for outside markets is as old as the town itself and, in fact, was one reason why Juan de Chávez founded the town in the first place. Whether through forced labor, tribute, or the marketplace, the town has always been an exporter—though of course, it has always tried to improve its terms of trade. The earliest known document concerning the *Milpa* of Juan de Chávez, "Los indios que eran esclavos . . ." (from the mid-sixteenth century) is a formal protest to the king of Spain in which the newly freed Indians argue against having to provide fodder for the Spaniards' horses and having to sweep the streets of Antigua on fiesta days.[32]

The zone has always been a center for commodity production. For four centuries San Antonio and the Quinizilapa towns were stable because they adjusted to each of the successive export booms—in sugarcane, indigo, cochineal, and coffee—upon which the colonial export economy was based. In the late nineteenth and early twen-

tieth centuries, large tracts of prime coffee land were taken over by
wealthy *ladino* coffee growers. Today, medium and small plots are
farmed intensively, and sometimes extensively, by Indian vegetable
growers. The area has evolved into an important regional center for
the bulking and distribution of commodities. Among just the seventy-four families in my sample, the following crops, among others,
are grown for sale outside the town: corn, beans, cauliflower, carrots,
cabbage, turnips, beets, radishes, sweet potatoes, squash, potatoes,
watercress, onions, peanuts, coffee, cut flowers, ornamental ferns,
marsh reeds, firewood, palms, oranges, lemons, and avocados.[33]

As in most peasant societies, production for consumption (versus
production for the market) is determined more by the needs and resources of the family than by the price of equivalent commodities.
As previously explained, the family first produces corn, then beans,
and then whatever crops nutritively complement corn and beans and
optimally "absorb" surplus inputs of space, sunlight, children's weeding hours, and so forth. Total output is dictated first and foremost by
the utility of a particular crop mix to the household, balancing the
nutritional and psychological security of those crops against the dis-
utility of not having and having to produce or buy them. Beyond
that, the key question is the availability of land and other cash-
related inputs, such as purchased labor. Generally, the greater the re-
sidual resources available to the family, the more likely they are to
engage in commodity production—and if not agricultural commodities, then nonagricultural, commodity-like business enterprises.

Table 2 illustrates the incentives and some constraints to growing
cash crops instead of *milpa*.

The first two rows of Table 2 illustrate that the classic "*milpa*
crops," corn and beans, have similar labor and cash requirements
(Columns A and B) and about the same rate of return (Column E). At
the risk of oversimplification, I have aggregated information for several crops (such as carrots, cabbage, and cauliflower) as "garden vegetables" in the third row of the table. These crops can serve as *milpa*
intercrops or, on a larger scale, can be semi-commercial cash crops.
In this collection of data, I was not able to distinguish between, say,
cabbage for household consumption planted in the *milpa* and cabbage planted strictly for the market. Nevertheless, a marked difference still emerges in both inputs and profitability between these garden vegetables and the standard crop of corn and beans. To better
illustrate a "true" cash crop, I have included potatoes on the fourth
row of the table.[34] Thus, the table should be understood as follows:
corn and beans represent traditional *milpa* output; garden vegetables
represent an intensified *milpa* (or alternatively, an underfinanced

Table 2. *Corn, Beans, Garden Vegetables, Potatoes:*
Comparative Data (per **cuerda***)*

	(A) Labor Input ($)	(B) Cash Input ($)	(C) Total Inputs (A + B) ($)	(D) Selling Price ($)	(E) Profit (D − C) ($)	(F) Profit as % of Input (E/C)
Corn	12	13	25	34	9	36
Beans	14	9	23	31	8	35
Garden vegetables	32	32	64	101	37	58
Potatoes	42	102	144	225	81	56

Note: This table is derived from my field data, supplemented by information provided by the regional office of BANDESA in Antigua. The discrepancy in corn production between this table and Table 1 is accounted for by changes in market prices and
labor costs between the years 1977 and 1979 and by BANDESA's slightly different
method of computing the value of family labor, which I have adopted here in order to
make the table internally consistent.

commercial crop); and potatoes represent an extensively planted
cash crop.

Column E shows that the garden vegetables generate four times
the net income of corn or beans—and potatoes, about eight times
the net income of those two staples. The semi-commercial garden
vegetables require three times the cash input and at least double the
labor input (there is the additional practical difficulty of finding as
well as being able to pay supplemental workers). On the other hand,
although inputs are more expensive for the garden vegetables and potatoes, they yield not only much better selling prices and profits, but
also returns to scale, i.e., a much higher ratio of profits to inputs
(Column F).

The other side of the coin is that the higher-yield cash crops also
entail higher risks—principally because of variation in market prices,
and also because of bugs, worms, molds, mildew, and the weather.
San Antonio farmers are fully aware of the disadvantages of a cash
crop like potatoes. They realize that potatoes are many times more
expensive to plant than corn or beans, that there are no readily available storage facilities, that market prices fluctuate unpredictably, and
that potato blight is a constant threat. So despite the incentive of relatively generous, low-interest bank loans and encouragement from
government agronomists, I found no San Antonio farmers planting
potatoes during the 1977–1978 agricultural season.

The key to a farmer's decision-making in crop selection is largely a matter of his willingness to make these trade-offs between safety and gain. I certainly never discerned any mystical attachment to corn for its own sake. Government technicians and popular books with chapters like "Corn Is King" and "The Mystery of Maize" commonly propound the notion that Mayan farmers have either an obdurate or a mystical attachment to corn. In my experience, this is nonsense. Farmers do not grow corn because they like to, because they can think of no other alternatives, or because their ancestors did it that way; they grow corn because it is an efficient and practical response to restricted resource opportunities. And by extension, those factors that reduce risk and improve gain work to shift choice in the direction of the more lucrative commercial crops.

In San Antonio, a number of factors, discussed below, have been at work during this century to improve the reliability of returns on higher-yield cash crops—at least for some farmers. These are what I am calling the "anti-*milpa*" forces, because they tend to push and pull at the social equilibrium of the community. Although they are not the only forces that undercut the stability inherited from the colonial era, by widening opportunity they challenge and disrupt both the harmony within the internal culture and the relationship of that culture to the powerful external sphere.

Windfalls of High-Quality Land

During the late nineteenth and early twentieth centuries, San Antonio farmers withstood land-grabs by *ladino* coffee entrepreneurs far more successfully than did those in the five other Quinizilapa towns. The town lost relatively less land and then gradually recouped losses at the expense of its neighbors. In addition, some families benefited from two communal land acquisitions. First, in the mid-1920s, municipal and public health officials agreed to drain the lake, leaving potentially rich bottomland available for agriculture (see Chapter 2). Town authorities surveyed the bottomland and divided it into equal plots. A "lottery" was then held to determine who would receive each plot. As a result, nearly one hundred winners (according to one elderly informant) each received several *cuerdas* of prime land. In the nearly three generations since, the original plots have been divided and subdivided, bought and sold, lost and gained. Many microplots of one-fourth or even one-tenth of a *cuerda* (the size of a large room) are passed from father to son. On the other hand, some growers have been able to consolidate these microplots into choice *finquitas* for vegetables and coffee.[35] The unusually high world coffee prices between 1976 and 1979, in turn, provided an un-expected cash boon to many families with coffee land.

A second windfall occurred during the land reforms of Jacobo Ar-benz's presidency, from 1951 to 1954,[36] when many San Antonio fami-lies obtained highly productive lands in Calderas, an area on the slope of the volcano Acatenango. Most lands expropriated during this pe-riod were returned to their previous owners after the CIA-engineered overthrow of Arbenz in 1954.[37] However, one large Calderas *finca,* apparently expropriated during World War II,[38] was eventually sold inexpensively and with favorable financing by the Instituto Nacional de Transformación Agraria (INTA) to San Antonio families in 150-*cuerda* plots. For the most part, those families who were fortunate enough to acquire and hold on to these generous tracts are today the wealthiest farm families in the town and include many of the people engaged in larger-scale, commercial vegetable production.[39] Seizing upon their advantage, these families typically have acquired addi-tional small plots from marginal producers, further skewing intra-village land distribution and exacerbating wealth differences. The land-gainers, though still marginal by the standards of agribusiness vegetable production, now own more land than they can work with family-supplied labor (and of course face no constraining nutritive threat). With excess land, they possess ample collateral for borrow-ing capital to hire labor, purchase chemical fertilizers and pesticides, store crops, and control marketing. That is a far different proposition than struggling to upgrade *milpa* production through more intense use of pre-dawn weeding hours, feeding weeds to the family's two turkeys, and so forth.

Access to Agricultural Inputs and Development Programs

William Cameron Townsend, the evangelical missionary who ar-rived in San Antonio in 1917 (and later founded the Wycliffe Bible Translators; see Chapter 5) was the son of a failed Oklahoma tenant farmer. With the memory of early poverty, he grew up in the lushness of Orange County, California. As someone who had been "saved" himself, Townsend believed in and promoted "modern" agriculture.[40] Confronted with the *milpa*—tied to a cycle of fiestas, debt, and forced labor on the southern coast of Guatemala—he inveighed not only against the witchery of the "Romish church," but against what he viewed as economic enslavement and primitivism of daily life. In Townsend's view, economic and spiritual liberation were inseparable, the Indian's passport to independence. As entry points for prosely-tization as well as means for projecting their vision of the Indians' future, the missionaries not only built a church but also established the Nima Yá school, an "agricultural store," and a small coffee-processing plant.

The coffee-processing plant was established with the help of a St. Louis coffee manufacturer, A. E. Forbes, who read of Townsend's work in the *Christian Herald* and sent money for a turbine and a coffee sheller. With a sheller in operation and the Forbes company to buy all the products, Townsend was able to help set up a production and marketing cooperative, which must have been one of the first such cooperatives for Indians in Latin America.

The farm store, like the Nima Yá school, was open freely to the community. According to elderly informants, the religious message did not discourage patronage. As a result, all farmers had access to pesticides, fertilizers, wire, tools, pumps, and improved seeds. Such a farm store must surely have been rare in an Indian community sixty years ago, and indeed, one like it does not exist in San Antonio today. Recently, imported agricultural inputs have become generally available from hardware and farm stores in nearby Antigua. So, one way or another, for more than half a century San Antonio vegetable farmers have known about and could purchase materials that facilitate experimentation with cash crops.

As Charles and Geraldine Katy have pointed out about the allocation of health services by private voluntary agencies, the density of development projects tends to be highly correlated with the attractiveness and convenience of the setting for development technicians.[41] Thus, it is not surprising that picturesque San Antonio, only fifteen minutes by bus from colonial Antigua and less than an hour from Guatemala City, has attracted more than its share of post-sixties development programs. And since San Antonio farmers have a reputation for being technically progressive, literate, and willing to innovate, they have frequently been selected for pilot rural development programs. For example, the first regional office of the national agricultural development bank, BANDESA, was established in Antigua, and San Antonio farmers were among its first and most consistent borrowers.[42] For a great many San Antonio vegetable and coffee growers, BANDESA loans are as regular a feature of the agricultural cycle as they are to the wealthy *ladino* agroexporters of the Pacific coast. Similarly, AID-financed programs in soil conservation, forestry, marketing, nonformal education, and agricultural extension have actively sought out participants from San Antonio.

Interestingly, the cooperative movement (in textile handicrafts as well as in agriculture) is relatively weak in San Antonio, despite the missionary history and the organizational groundwork laid by two generations of Peace Corps volunteers and other cooperative promoters. Probably cooperatives failed to take root here because so many coop services (marketing, credit, agricultural supplies, technical assistance with new crops) are already relatively available. Farmers have little incentive to invest the considerable time and energy required to make cooperatives work, particularly since the key middle-income small farmers (those who are typically most attracted to cooperative services) can individually obtain these services on the open market.

Surplus Cash

Because of the proximity of wage-earning opportunities and the additional money derived from tourism, occasional cash surpluses within families are not uncommon. When that happens, a family either reinvests in expanded agricultural production or "diversifies" by shifting resources to a sector that yields a higher rate of return on capital investment. Often a land-owning farmer and members of his family will work as *mozos* on a neighbor's land or as day laborers in Antigua during their agricultural slack season. With cash in hand, the farmer will then hire *mozos* during his own peak seasons—quite possibly, the same farmers for whom he and his family recently worked. Through this mechanism, every farmer tries to ratchet up his entrepreneurial activity. Obviously, the more cash that a family can mobilize, the more it can withstand crop failure, afford risk, and enhance its productive capacity through returns to scale.

High Educational Level

Although there is much debate as to the precise causal connection between education and market-oriented agriculture,[43] in Guatemala—and in San Antonio—there is certainly a *positive* association.[44] As pointed out in Chapter 2, the town has exceptionally high rates of education and literacy. Virtually all adult men, all school-age children, and most women know how to read.

The relationship between education and agricultural income is suggested in Table 3, which shows correlations between the number of family school-years (among persons over fifteen) and income from corn and beans, from cash crops, and from all (including non-agricultural) sources. As shown in Column A, there appears to be no association between number of years of schooling and corn and bean production—that is, *milpa* farming may require a high level of skills, but those skills are not related to school learning. Column B,

Table 3. *Correlation of Years of Schooling with Milpa, Cash Crop, and Total Income*

	(A) Income from Milpa Corn & Beans	(B) Income from Cash Crops	(C) Total Income
Years of schooling			
Correlation (r)	.07	.23	.43
Significance (p)	(.55)	(.05*)	(.000***)

*p ≤ .05
**p ≤ .01
***p ≤ .001

however, shows a positive and statistically significant association between years of formal education and income from cash crops. The relationship is doubtlessly not so simple as "more years in school equals greater ability to read the instructions on a can of pesticide." Column C indicates that years of schooling are strongly associated with overall family income, and as suggested in the preceding section, the availability of surplus cash and the capacity to make lateral income transfers strongly affects a family's propensity to invest in cash-crop agriculture. The high level of education in San Antonio probably affects agriculture indirectly rather than directly, yet it certainly is a factor that undermines *milpa* stability.

Location

In many parts of the Guatemalan highlands, marketing presents a far greater obstacle to commercialization of vegetables than does actual production. The frequent lack of roads, storage, and processing facilities makes sales to nonlocal markets a high-risk venture at best, and flatly impossible at worst.

In this regard, San Antonio enjoys a locational advantage. Not only is the town within convenient access to the daily market in Antigua, but it also has relatively easy access to the large Bus Terminal Market in Guatemala City, the highland regional market in Chimaltenango, and the coastal markets of Escuintla and nearby towns. As have the farmers of Almolonga, Zuñil, and San Pedro Sacatepéquez (Department of San Marcos), the Indian vegetable growers of San Antonio have capitalized upon their initial locational advantage by purchasing transport vehicles.[45] In turn, reliable access to transport strengthens their hand as intermediaries and their control of the production and flow of commodities from the hinterlands.[46] The corresponding cash gain and the reduction of a significant risk factor—benefiting some families far more than others—has in turn prompted further shifts toward cash crops.

Locational advantage, land windfalls, and the other factors discussed here have not created a transformation from *milpa*-farming to cash-cropping. They are simply factors that encourage and enable such a change—for some families. There is no inevitable substitution of one system for another, but rather a simultaneous widening and constriction of opportunity. Since the "rich" farmers and roadside textile entrepreneurs are highly visible to outsiders, it is tempting to expand upon the "San Antonio is a rich town" theme. Yet, on balance, accumulation of wealth has been highly selective, and most people are as poor as ever, if not poorer. Probably families are becoming poorer at a faster rate than they are becoming richer.

The following section examines how a poor person operates in San Antonio. It is a short case study in "*milpa* logic." It illustrates the range of choices and how decisions are made in weaving *petates* (mats), a non-agricultural economic activity for those who are very poor.

Petate Making

The weaving of mats from dried, flattened marsh reeds almost certainly predates the backstrap loom in Middle America. Fossilized mat impressions, usually occurring on burned adobe fragments, have been found at many early archaeological sites.[47] At the Late Preclassic site of Kaminaljuyú (today the location of Guatemala City), a substantial number of impressions have been found in the hard-packed fill of the Miraflores-Arenal tombs (300 B.C. to A.D. 200). Viewing these mat impressions in museums or on bookplates, one can see that they are virtually identical in construction to the *petates* that are woven in San Antonio today.

Contemporary San Antonio *petate* makers gather reeds, called *tul* (*Cyperus* sp.),[48] from the swampy bottomland of the now-drained lake. The reeds are cut with a machete, dried in the sun, and stored in tall bundles. Weavers say that the reeds are more pliable and easier to work at early dawn and dusk or during the rainy season. Apart from a heavy, round pounding-stone (much like a *metate* for grinding corn) to flatten the reeds, no tool, loom, or stabilizing device is used in making *petates*. The weaver simply sits on the reeds to hold them in place and creates a twill by interlacing the strands at right

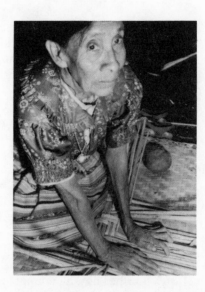

Figure 13. Elderly woman seated on reeds with her pounding-stone.

angles—over-two, under-two, over-two, under-two (see Figure 13). He or she begins with the long reeds to make large, "bed-sized" *petates* and then uses the leftovers to make smaller sizes. Three to four hours of weaving are required to make a large mat. Though more common among women, the work is not strongly associated with sex roles, as is farming (male) or backstrap weaving (female).

It has often been observed that artisans in peasant societies frequently come from the poorest groups, especially from among the landless poor.[49] This is certainly true in the Quinizilapa zone, where in this sense, *petate*-making—and not handweaving—is the true artisanal occupation. Only the very poorest families engage in full-time *petate*-making. A typical *petate*-making family is an elderly couple: she, eyesight failing, with arms and joints too weak for weaving; he, landless and too old to rent land or work as a day laborer. Or a very young couple: she, illiterate and caring for one or two toddlers; he, the landless son of a landless family, helping out with *petates* between stints as a day laborer. In the nearby *aldea* of Santiago Zamora and occasionally in San Antonio, these families subsist largely on *petate* income—the elderly family until death, the young family until they find something better.

More commonly, however, *petate*-making is a complementary, fill-

Figure 14. ". . . failing eyesight, with arm strength and joints too weak for weaving."

in activity among poor*er* but not the poor*est* families. For most, *pe-tate*-making is one element of a larger set of activities, at the heart of which is the *milpa*. Each of these activities improves the overall efficiency of the household by absorbing (with minimal cash inputs) labor or skills from the least economically productive workers (the elderly or older children) or improves the output of the primary wage earners by upgrading the value of their normal "down time" (dawn, dusk, the rainy season). Accordingly, *petate* income among San Antonio families correlates positively with the number of elderly persons (ages sixty-five and over) in the household ($r=.27$, significant at the .021 level), not because it is a particularly archaic or "traditional" craft but because younger persons can usually find more lucrative work elsewhere.[50]

None of the families in my seventy-four-family sample subsist solely on full-time *petate* income, which accounted for less than 1 percent of total income earned by all the families in the sample. Only twenty-two of the families (30 percent) reported any *petate* production.[51] The highest annual *petate* income in the sample— which is to say, one of the poorest of the seventy-four families—was $200. The mean value of their production was only $47; the median, only $36.[52]

Is $47 a significant contribution to household income, even by standards of relative poverty? Yes, at least for some people. Assuming that the mean of $47 were a complete per capita income, it would be sufficient to provide the barest maintenance—the equivalent of 500 person-days of *tortillas* (1.1 pounds of ground corn per day at 6.5 cents per pound) and not much else. In other words, an elderly couple with both husband and wife working regularly at *petates* and planting a small but intensive garden could survive, if just barely; or an elderly parent living with adult children could "pay her own way."[53]

Although *petate*-making is an occupation of the poorest—within the region, within the community, and within the family—it is by no means an uncomplicated activity. In order to optimize his or her meager output, the *petate* maker must weigh an extraordinary range of choices before making each "microdecision." As shown in Table 4, there are dozens of possible "routes" which can lead from acquisition of raw material to sold *petates*. Each step is partially dictated by resource advantage at that point; each step has costs associated in cash, time, and entrepreneurial effort. These must be balanced against likely variations in rate of return. At nearly every decision point judgments must be made: the resource advantage can be further enhanced . . . or cashed in.

Wage Labor and Doorstep Businesses

Though it accounts for less than 2 percent of San Antonio's total economic output, I have elaborated upon *petate*-making in order to illustrate the nature of decision-making under the normal conditions of greatly restricted opportunity. The key point to this illustration is that the colony-of-the-colony's historic legacy is not a physical artifact (a "Mayan vestige," such as the *petate* or *huipil*), or even a technology (handweaving or the *milpa*), but an approach to production, a way of handling resources that both ensures survival under the colony's terms and sends up the flags of cultural identity.

On the other hand, the situation is complicated by the fact that opportunity and access to resources have selectively widened during this century. For all its political and economic problems, Guatemala has sustained the strongest and most diverse economy in Central America. Although oppression and exploitation have been constant, twentieth-century Indians have nonetheless encountered a widening set of economic, entrepreneurial, and educational choices (though always within limits established and condoned by the larger *ladino* society).

At the village level, this "widening" is most apparent in opportunities for wage labor outside the household and village. Today, wage labor is the largest single source of cash income in the town. According to my calculations, it accounts for nearly 40 percent of total income; indeed, it surpasses agriculture, which accounts for only a quarter of all income. The total value of this wage labor among seventy-four households was more than $34,000, roughly $460 of supplemental income per family.[54]

Table 5 illustrates the range of wage opportunities found within this sample of households. As shown, there were eighty-three distinct outside-the-household "jobs"—that is, an average of 1.1 jobs per household.

One might ask whether domestic agriculture is being displaced by wage labor. The answer is no. There are basically two categories of farmers in San Antonio: those with enough land and those with insufficient land to meet their subsistence needs. Table 5 shows that the largest job category—representing fully 35 percent of all jobs and 24 percent of all wage income—is accounted for by agricultural day laborers (*mozos*). Relatively few San Antoneros are full-time, permanent *mozos*. Rather, *mozo* labor allows families with insufficient land to generate supplemental income that stabilizes their *milpa*-centered livelihood. And it allows families with more than enough

Table 4. *Choice and Decision-Making in* Petate *Production*

IN REGARD TO RAW MATERIAL (*TUL*), YOU
Own your own land in the lake bottom, so you (or someone in your family) can
—cut your own *tul*, which you
  —sell to a neighbor for his or her use.
  —keep for your own *petates*.
  —give to the *mozo* for his work on your land.
—rent out the land, for which you receive
  —cash.
  —payment in kind (*tul*).
  —labor.
—hire a *mozo* to harvest your *tul*, paying him
  —in cash.
  —in *tul*.
—not bother with it, since the return is not worth the distraction from other activities.
Do not own land in the lake bottom, so you (or someone in your family) can
—rent a piece of lake bottom, which is worked by you, a family member, or a *mozo*.
—buy cut (or cut and dried) *tul* from a neighbor.
—buy cut *tul* from a nearby *finca* or, more likely, exchange labor on the *finca* for right to harvest *tul*.
—receive *tul* in exchange for several finished *petates*.
—receive *tul* which you will work on a wage or piecework basis.
—receive *tul* as a gift which contributes to your support (from an adult son or daughter, for example).

IN REGARD TO MANUFACTURE: HAVING ACQUIRED RAW MATERIAL, YOU
Make the *petates* yourself,
—working steadily and regularly as a primary occupation.
—working between other tasks as time permits.
Delegate the work to your family, i.e., to an aged parent, a school-age child, a spouse who has "free" hours at dawn or dusk.
Hire someone, whom you pay
—a wage.
—a piecework fee.

IN REGARD TO MARKETING: ONCE *PETATES* ARE MANUFACTURED, YOU
Consume them through use in your household.
Store them for future sale.
Sell them to a neighbor for his or her consumption.
Sell them to a middleman, someone who
—comes to town regularly with a truck and purchases in bulk from you and your neighbors.

Table 4. (*continued*)

—has a steady purchase arrangement with you (e.g., a vendor in
  Antigua).
—is a neighbor who will sell them in outside markets.
Collect several bundles of *petates* (perhaps buying more from neighbors)
and take them by bus to a regional market (Antigua, Chimaltenango,
Tecpán, Guatemala City) for sale in bulk; and while you're at it, you
purchase regional products for
—your own consumption.
—resale in San Antonio.
—a regional market, where you spend the day selling one-by-one in order
  to get the best individual prices.
—isolated hamlets for door-to-door or local market sales.
Collect a large number of *petates* which you transport in your own or a
rented truck to a distant town (probably on the south coast); you return
with a load of tropical fruit.

---

land to make up the labor deficit that constrains cash-cropping.[55] In
other words, wage labor reinforces rather than supplants the agricultural basis of the economy.

The man shown in Figure 15 is a reasonably typical example of
someone who works outside the town in order to stabilize rather
than abandon his primary occupation as a *milpa* farmer. This man
works as a gardener and caretaker of a large home in Antigua. His
elderly father, wife, and daughter care for the *milpa* while he takes
advantage of the wage opportunity made available by an American
employer.

Similarly, the mason shown in Figure 16 is able to obtain lucrative
but irregular work in Antigua. Masons account for eleven of the
eighty-three jobs (and most of the ten "helpers") listed in Table 5.
The large number of masons is accounted for by the construction
boom that followed the 1976 earthquake. The reconstruction of
Antigua generated sharp demand for rural masons. By the time that
work tapered off, many San Antonio families had the money to invest in local reconstruction. For some, occupational mobility may
result: a few of these semi-skilled, rural masons may eventually become master craftsmen whose sons may then become university-
trained civil engineers. But as the earthquake reconstruction boom
waned and political violence slowed new building, most San Antonio masons simply returned to their land—or more accurately,
they had never left it and returned to relying upon it. If too little land

Table 5. Men's Income from Wage Labor[a]

Job Type	(A) Number of Jobs	(B) % of Total Jobs	(C) Range of Incomes ($)	(D) Mean Income ($)	(E) Total Income from This Job ($)	(F) % of Total Wage Income
Mozo	29	35	6–540	275	7,975	24
Mason	11	13	185–1,130	532	5,852	18
"Helper"	10	12	60–720	342	3,420	10
Carpenter	6	7	510–1,680	700	4,200	13
Musician	6	7	120–720	426	2,556	8
Weaver	5	6	96–753	285	1,425	4
Tailor	4	5	240–560	419	1,676	5
Driver	3	4	540–1,050	755	2,265	7
Slaughterer	2	2	24–45	35	70	<1
Rugmaker	1	1	192	192	192	<1
Teacher	1	1	300	300	300	1
Caretaker	1	1	77	77	77	<1
Public works construction	1	1	720	720	720	2
Civil servant	1	1	780	780	780	2
Radio announcer	1	1	1,105	1,105	1,105	3
Woodcutter	1	1	684	684	684	2
Total	83	100	6–1,680	477[b]	33,297	100

[a]Data from survey of 74 households.
[b]The mean of the sixteen means, not the total of the means or the overall average of this sample.

Figure 15. San Antonio farmer who works as caretaker for an American family in Antigua.

Figure 16. Part-time mason working in Antigua (Agua Volcano in background).

means that more family labor cannot be reabsorbed, they must shift to something else. So they may temporarily become paid tailors or carpenter's helpers or trumpet players in a *marimba* band. In relatively few cases do these *milpa*-farmers-cum-wage-earners find stable, full-time occupations (teacher, civil servant, bus driver) that allow them permanent independence from agriculture.

The sharp business acumen of Guatemalan Indians has been frequently described in the anthropological literature. My own view is that the nature of small business in San Antonio, like the nature of wage labor, has more to do with the fact and logic of the *milpa* than anything related to the U.S. concept of business entrepreneurship. As shown in Table 6, there is a wide range of "business activities" in the town. Just under half the families in the sample operate some sort of enterprise. Families with almost any spare capital will find some microbusiness in which to invest.[56] A farmer may start selling corn and beans from his doorstep, then supplement his own two-sack inventory with a purchased sack and a few cases of soft drinks on a fiesta day. With a favorable cash flow and a wife or teenager to mind the "store," his doorstep business may evolve into a more complex enterprise—or decapitalize and disappear when cash becomes short.

Table 6. Earnings from Family Business Enterprises [a]

Business Type	(A) Number of Businesses	(B) % of Total Businesses	(C) Range of Incomes ($)	(D) Mean Income ($)	(E) Total Income from These Businesses ($)	(F) % of Total Business Income
Tailor	9	22.0	32–2,040	820	7,380	40
General store	8	19.5	54–720	327	2,616	14
Dollmaking workshop	5	12.2	260–720	475	2,375	13
Petate business	4	9.7	32–650	291	1,164	6
Agricultural processing	3	7.3	36–128	66	198	1
Vegetable wholesaling	2	4.8	480–720	600	1,200	6
Drawing designs for weavers	2	4.8	180–900	540	1,080	6
Butcher	1	2.4	345	345	345	2
Barber	1	2.4	240	240	240	1
Corn-grinding mill	1	2.4	540	540	540	3
Rugmaking workshop	1	2.4	330	330	330	2
Electrician	1	2.4	900	900	900	5
Sausage maker	1	2.4	40	40	40	1
Needle carver (for weaving)	1	2.4	70	70	70	1
Selling maize & soft drinks	1	2.4	60	60	60	1
Total	41	100	32–2,040	376[b]	18,538	100

[a] Data from survey of 74 households.
[b] The mean of the means.

Figure 17. Washing carrots and making clothing in home tailor's workshop.

The close relationship, literally, between household agriculture and small business is illustrated in Figure 17, which shows the interior of a family-run tailor workshop. The family in this photo owns four sewing machines and hires tailors on a daily wage basis. Yet the family is still primarily agricultural, as evidenced by the carrots on the floor that are being washed and bundled for market. The fact that the family can extend its production into a cash crop such as carrots is directly related to the fact that it can also afford and operate four sewing machines.

Conclusion

The previous chapter showed how San Antonio formed a stable relationship with the dominant colonial society and, in turn, replicated that relationship with its neighbors and its rural hinterland. The present cultural character of the town is a reflection of that relationship, not a vestige of pre-Conquest Indian tradition.

This chapter has looked at San Antonio as a "rich" Indian town. San Antonio's relative "success" lies not so much in its unusual endowment of resources (though that has certainly helped) as in its long-term stability vis-à-vis the dominant society. Historically, the town has played a role in each of the "export booms" of Guatemala's colonial and independence eras. In addition to labor, it has supplied sugar, indigo, cochineal, and coffee. That participation, while creating no real excess local wealth, has allowed a secure, relatively uninterrupted evolution of Indianness based on family-centered *milpa* agriculture. Unlike many towns, San Antonio held on to its lands during the coffee incursions of this century, though the former egalitarian pattern of landholding has become markedly skewed. Moreover, nearby markets in Antigua and Guatemala City and on the south coast have provided opportunity for outside-the-village wage labor and for petty commerce in agricultural commodities.

The *milpa* remains the cornerstone of San Antonio's economy. As illustrated by the case of *petate*-making, the logic of the *milpa* transfers even when land ownership ceases. Similarly, wage labor and small business entrepreneurship are in some respects complementary to rather than substitutes for the *milpa*.

Yet at the same time that both the *milpa* and its logic remain in place, so too, a series of anti-*milpa* factors tug in the opposite direction. In farming, those factors that favor higher output—land windfalls, agricultural technology, locational advantage, access to capital—favor externally directed cash-cropping. The same holds true in non-agricultural activities where, in a sense, the radio announcer is a cash-cropper while the *petate*-maker, even though landless, is a *milpa* farmer. The anti-*milpa* forces do not work just in favor of the better-off families: educational opportunity can work to the advantage of the poor, or the jackpot opportunities created by tourism can be pursued aggressively by the landless.

As a result of these forces, the economic equilibrium that was the basis of cultural stability for four hundred years is unraveling. The next chapter takes a closer look at that unraveling: it examines how growing wealth differentiation undermines *milpa* stability and its corresponding ideology.

4

Milpa Logic and Wealth Differentiation

Background: The Ideology of Indianness

THOSE CULTURAL traits of Indianness that today are often called "traditional" evolved during the long, relatively stable post-Conquest period. For nearly four centuries, towns like those around Lake Quinizilapa provided, first, forced labor in one form or another; second, usufruct payments known as *terrazgos*, since the Spaniards owned virtually all the land;[1] and third, commodities that stoked the colonial export economy. In return for their forced labor, land rent, and cheap commodities, Indians were "given" a certain measure of autonomy within clearly defined behavioral spheres (parameters of acceptable religious practices having been set by Spanish educators during the mid-sixteenth century). Year after year the towns exported their payments to the outside, making few demands and receiving no services or return payments from the larger society. The fact that Indians could do whatever they wanted—so long as they were passive, powerless, and kept themselves in penury supporting the Spaniards—led to a kind of cultural stability.

With cash-cropping to "pay the rent" and symbols of Indianness to define the boundaries, one response to external exploitation was to turn increasingly inward. The *municipio* became the principal unit of cultural integration. Within *municipios*, Indians shared a language dialect, a distinct costume and a weaving idiom, a fiesta schedule, a cast of saints and *espíritus*, and usually an economic specialization such as garlic-growing or pottery-making. Within regions, communities were linked horizontally through shared participation in the revolving "solar" marketing economy, but such linkages were generally weak and did not form a basis for national political power or even supravillage cultural identity.

Within the Indian sphere, the *milpa*, not commodity production, was the basis of local economies and social organization. At the family level, the *milpa* was the processor of household resources and the allocator of labor. The brilliance of the *milpa* was that as a productive system it generated a relatively fixed output that was pegged to consumption rather than the largest possible yield (the point to commodity production). As discussed in Chapter 3, the *milpa* operates by transforming abundant noncapital inputs into a secure subsistence. It is not particularly amenable to capital intensification or greatly expanded output. In other words, no matter how well he farms a *milpa*, a farmer cannot achieve an economy of scale, which is the essential difference between *milpa* production and cash-cropping. Practically, this means that at the end of a year the *milpa* farmer is unlikely to be able to purchase his neighbor's land. In a good year he will have produced a certain measure of security and little excess cash. Through the pooling of household labor and resources, the farmer's family will be bound more tightly together—and they will be at a safe and friendly distance from the resources of their neighbors.

According to most Mesoamerican ethnographers, Indian values found their fullest expression in the *cofradía*, a civil-religious cargo system that served to integrate the lives of individuals with the life of the community. Ostensibly the *cofradía* operated as a cult to venerate particular village saints. Its purpose, literally, was to celebrate; but in organizing celebration, it also directed communal life. The *cofradía* translated into practice a spiritual ideal of communalism that lent dignity and significance to a life of material exploitation.

In part, *cofradía* participation helped rationalize the *milpa*—and the logic of the *milpa* in relation to commodity production. *Cofradía* participation imposed on the individual a progressively burdensome obligation for communal service and financial contribution. Through the escalation of religious expenditure, the *cofradía* acted to level wealth within the village. To the extent that any surplus product was formed and not externally appropriated, it was consumed locally in celebration—or perhaps more subtly, in celebration of willingness to celebrate. If legal, class, military, and ethnic constraints operated at the national level to prevent Indians from seizing wealth and power, so too, at the village level, the *cofradía* enforced—but legitimized—a life of material poverty.

As Kay Warren has pointed out, Indian religion reversed external *ladino* values: poverty became purifying and good; material riches were a result of evil.[2] Since Indians could not realistically translate wealth into economic and political power in the *ladino* sphere, the accumulation of wealth was morally rejected in favor of reinvestment in a kind of social currency negotiable only at the village level.

In a sense, religion rationalized the Indian brand of economic production by creating something of value for wealth to purchase.

Indian religious generosity may have been the basis for local stability. Wealth in the hands of a few was dangerous to the many in that it could be used to purchase land and thereby undermine the egalitarian and corporate nature of the community. As Manning Nash described the resulting regulatory process, "a set of concrete social organizations [evolved] which directly channel economic choice, on the one hand, and a set of sanctions which operate to keep economic deviants in physical as well as moral jeopardy on the other."[3] In lieu of the hope for long-term material gain, the *cofradía* participant-celebrant gained a lifetime of prestige, honor, and stability—with certain poverty and probable cirrhosis thrown into the bargain.

In most areas of Guatemala, the administrative and then the moral authority of the *cofradía* began breaking down decades ago. In the aftermath of the Revolution of 1944, a clear juridical separation was established between religious and civil office. Of particular importance, the Arbenz government in the early 1950s instituted local electoral procedures and encouraged the formation of opposing parties. Naming young men as candidates for elective office had the effect of undermining a *cofradía* structure that conferred special authority on the aged.[4] And more deeply, it undercut a *milpa*-based economy that allowed Indians to make sense of life in an Hispanic society whose convenience they were created to serve.

Even when the Arbenz reforms were significantly reversed after 1954, electoral politics continued to secularize the countryside. During the late 1960s and in the 1970s, development projects favored the emergence of community organizations led by younger, better-educated, outward-looking men—a kind of local meritocracy that further undercut the religious gerontocracy. Today, the *cofrades* have faded from authority. They are left mainly to struggle against the younger activists of the Catholic Action movement, or they are relegated to organizing fiesta celebrations in only the narrowest sense.

Though much can be made of the differences between the older generation of *costumbristas* and the new generations that have largely replaced them, there is nonetheless a common ideological ground between the old and the new: a behavioral ideal of communalism based on individual sacrifice to the collective good, a notion embedded in four hundred years of shared history and an essentially unchanged position vis-à-vis the larger society. This means that in a community like San Antonio, where four *cofradías* survive, the crosscurrents are strong from shifting values and changed patterns of authority; but despite that, some core ideas—in this case, the code by which an individual relates to a larger community—remain more or less intact. Even without strong *cofradías*, the ideal of communalism survives.

A Typology of Peasant Producers

Taking into account Guatemala's propensity for natural and unnatural disaster, the difficulties of production under the best of circumstances, exploitation, the leveling of wealth through social pressures, a war, and the productive limits of the *milpa*, it is not surprising that most Indian farmers have had no difficulty in achieving no more than the social-spiritual ideal of subsistence. Nevertheless, widespread changes that have expanded economic opportunity have occurred in the highlands, perhaps beginning with Jorge Ubico's modernization of communications systems in the 1930s. Since then, cooperatives, roads, marketing schemes, agricultural extension programs, health programs, primary schools, communications links, and new farming technology have penetrated heretofore inaccessible backwaters as discussed in Chapter 3.

In most respects, the economic situation is worsening. Intense population pressure upon land that is already in short supply and inequitably distributed leads to environmental degradation, which in turn undercuts agricultural productivity.[5] National balance-of-payments difficulties have fueled inflation and led to currency devaluations, which have pushed up local prices for agricultural inputs and consumer staples. Years of repression and political violence have taken a heavy economic as well as social toll.[6] Thus, even with the best *milpa*-optimizing strategies, subsistence has become unattainable for a large and growing proportion of the population. Looking at both ends of the spectrum, the situation has never been better for some and has never been worse for more.

With disequilibrium at both ends, the cultural stability that evolved during the colonial period is under strain. What happens, one might ask, when the institutions promoting egalitarianism are no longer capable of providing at least a secure poverty and a stable, sustaining ideology? And what would happen if the long-restricted horizon of economic opportunity were to open, and offer incentives other than investment in local ceremonial wealth? Particularly in the mid-1970s, ethnographers investigated how the *cofradía* system broke apart under conditions of rapid economic and cultural change.[7]

As a heuristic device for illustrating the implications of this kind of differentiation and its effects upon Indian ideologies, I have adapted

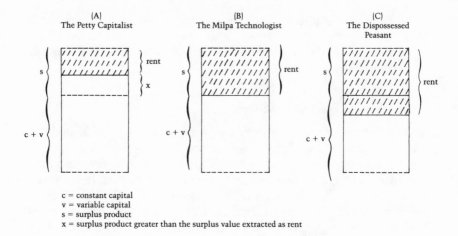

c = constant capital
v = variable capital
s = surplus product
x = surplus product greater than the surplus value extracted as rent

Figure 18. A typology of San Antonio peasant producers. Adapted from William Roseberry, "Rent, Differentiation, and the Development of Capitalism among Peasants," *American Anthropologist* 78 (1976): 52.

a simple typology from William Roseberry. Roseberry uses this typology to illustrate "possible outcomes for particular peasant units in a given year after the extraction of rent."[8] He implicitly assumes that if village cultural institutions are not directly caused by these rent (i.e., exploitation) outcomes, at least they are highly responsive and adaptive to them. While my own view is somewhat less deterministic, I find the modified typology useful in showing how wealth differentiation within a changing economy undercuts traditional religious-cultural stability.

In Figure 18, the three vertical bars represent three hypothetical "types" of peasant family, which I have called "petty capitalist," "*milpa* technologist," and "dispossessed peasant" households. In the middle position, the *milpa* technologist household best illustrates the production situation of the "traditional" Mayan peasant family: at equilibrium. The quantity $c + v$, representing their annual investment of constant and variable capital,[9] is equal to the replacement and consumption cost of subsistence. The family produce a surplus, s, that is equivalent to rent. If at the end of the year, they find themselves no richer, neither are they poorer.

One might question whether ritual expenditure should be considered as a kind of rent or as surplus product. Most anthropologists would argue that ritual expenditure should be distinguished from true rent because of its voluntary character. My own view is that ritual expenditure, though not forced in the same way as, say, tribute or formal land rental, is nonetheless nearly obligatory in a system that offers no social or political incentives for investment of surplus beyond the village. Since the *milpa* technologists' opportunities are bounded not only by the productive limits of the *milpa* itself, but also by caste and ethnicity, it is reasonable for them to reinvest their output into a form of wealth that may be non-negotiable outside the community but that confers a coherent framework of psychological reference (including stability, prestige, pleasure) within the local milieu.

As shown in Column C of Figure 18, "the dispossessed peasant" household is economically much worse off: their annual replacement/consumption cost, $c + v$, exceeds surplus production, i.e., their rent is greater than their surplus product. If losses accumulate year after year (which they probably will), then they must be paid at the expense of fixed capital or through reduced rent. Typically, they are forced to sell land—or, as more frequently is the case, they simply inherit none. As their bargaining position vis-à-vis the larger economy progressively deteriorates, they are increasingly forced "below" the point where they can generate subsistence, in either a biological or a cultural sense.

Once elasticity in consumption is exhausted, the dispossessed peasants essentially have two choices. One is to further cut rent, though at this level of impoverishment only ritual expenditure is expendable. In doing so, they may give up full participation in community life, marginalizing themselves socially as well as economically. If so, the *milpa*-based household economy becomes a steadily less-compelling way to earn a living. The other choice is greater intensification of production. The family must find some way to restore production to its former equilibrium (most commonly by renting land), or they must find some higher-yield source of income (a permanent, outside-the-village job) that does not operate by the low-output rules of *milpa* logic. The former solution draws the family back into the village; the latter pushes them out. But even renting land is a stopgap measure. In the long run, it worsens while temporarily stabilizing their condition. Although their rent (in the real-estate sense of the word) increases, they may at least be able to maintain their nominal participation in community life by preserving *milpa* production and its associated lifestyle.

At the other end of the spectrum is the "petty capitalist" household (Column A in Figure 18)—"capitalist" not only in being price conscious and entrepreneurial,[10] but also in the more technical sense: they produce a surplus (s) *and* manage to hang on to it (s is greater than rent) *and* use that surplus to earn more capital (x is re-invested, usually in c). Frequently, the San Antonio "petty capital-ists" are land rich but cash poor. To exploit their land advantage they need laborers. To get them, they must either acquire scarce cash or forego use of some land.

Like the "dispossessed peasants," the "petty capitalists" are faced with two alternatives, one which pulls them closer to and one which pushes them away from traditional values and behavior. On the one hand, they may adjust the household economy by exchanging the use of some land for a labor obligation—most likely, passing on "free" use of their land to adult children. They may then grow corn extensively, a relatively easy crop that will meet household needs, absorb the remaining land, generate little surplus, and provide ade-quate time and income for investment in communal life. In a sense they divest surplus and profit but hang on to the security that land ownership provides. Alternatively, they may respond aggressively to the opportunity that surplus land provides. They can borrow from the bank and intensify the production of cash crops,[11] reaching a point at which labor can be flexibly purchased as needed. If so, they are likely to be more concerned about giving their children an educa-tion than binding them to the land and family-centered production. They may even take the radical step of selling (some) land in order to shift into new kinds of high-output investments—for example, buy-ing a bus. Obviously, ritual consumption competes directly with other uses of surplus capital, and the more they are inclined to maxi-mize, the less inclined they will be to make anything other than a token ritual contribution.

Applying the Typology in San Antonio

In order to look more concretely at the relationship between wealth and the ideology that underlies production, I have broken down my sample of seventy-four households into an approximation of the three peasant types. This was done by summing the dollar value of all material assets for each family and calculating a value for each family's total wealth, an approach that assumes that per capita wealth is a fair proxy for surplus. Presumably, the families with high per capita wealth would correspond to the "petty capitalists," and those with lower per capita wealth correspond to the "*milpa* technolo-gists" and "dispossessed peasants."

As explained in Chapter 2, the total wealth for each family was

Table 7. *Absolute Wealth Differences among the Three Peasant Types*[a]

	(A) Average Number of Cuerdas Owned	(B) Average Land Value ($)	(C) Average Value of Machinery & Vehicles ($)	(D) Wealth per Capita ($)	(E) Range of Wealth per Household ($)
Petty capitalist	42.6	7,706	307	2,390	5,879–31,417
Milpa technologist	6.7	1,179	74	534	1,070–5,767
Dispossessed	1.2	66	4	150	117–1,014

[a]Data from survey of 74 households: 15 petty capitalist, 37 *milpa* technologist, 22 dispossessed.

calculated by summing the value of all material assets (i.e., land, tools, machinery, business inventory, textile inventory, vehicles, animals, and the value of the house and plot). In the survey, informants were asked only whether or not they possessed these assets; they were never asked to ascribe numeric values to possessions. Standard values were determined in separate mini-surveys. For example, a separate study determined that a *cuerda* of land in Pampay was worth $188, a *cuerda* of prime vegetable land in the lakebottom was worth $525, etc. Thus, individual informants were only asked whether they had land; if so, where; and how large the individual plots were. With separate information on land value by location, the computer then calculated the dollar value of each family's total landholdings. Similarly, the value of the household plot (*sitio*) was calculated with a formula that multiplied the dollar value of a *cuerda* of land in town times adjustment factors for the locational desirability of that plot, the number of rooms on the plot, the construction material of each room, the presence of fruit trees, the access to electricity, and the convenience of potable water. In this manner, all assets were converted into dollar equivalents, then summed for each family and further broken down to a wealth-per-capita basis.[12]

Table 7 illustrates the magnitude of difference in absolute wealth among the three different peasant types.[13] A striking maldistribution in wealth separates San Antonio's petty capitalists from its dispossessed. Despite the appearance of shared poverty suggested by the physical homogeneity of the town and the social pressures that supposedly level wealth, there is sizable discrepancy between the assets of the richest and the poorest families. On the average, the richest families own over six times as much land as the middle families; and the poorest families, as a group, own almost no land at all.[14] On a per capita basis, the richest families have almost sixteen times as much total wealth as the poorest families.[15] Although I have not made careful comparisons, I would speculate that wealth within the supposedly homogeneous Indian community is probably as maldistributed as is wealth within Guatemala as a whole, and without doubt more maldistributed than wealth in a developed country like the United States.

Table 7 acquires additional significance when interpreted in terms of labor requirements for *milpa* production. The "*milpa* technologist" households own an average of seven *cuerdas*. Local farmers report that a man whose primary occupation is agriculture can work approximately six *cuerdas* by himself.[16] Thus, if six *cuerdas* were adequate to generate subsistence for a normal-sized family, the average *milpa* technologist head-of-household would appear to have just the right amount of land to comfortably farm by himself without recourse to purchased labor.

With an average of only 1.2 *cuerdas*, however, the dispossessed families have enough land to absorb only about one-sixth of the labor of the heads-of-household. And even if each family actually owned this hypothetical average, it would hardly be sufficient to produce enough corn and beans to supply minimal nutrition for a normal-sized family.

At the other extreme, the "petty capitalist" families own on the average approximately six times the amount of land (42.6 *cuerdas*) that a head-of-household can actually work by himself. As might be expected, since the land-rich "petty capitalists" need labor and the "labor-rich" dispossessed families need land, there is a redistributive transfer—in this case, through the mechanism of land rental.

Four distinct kinds of rental arrangements are to be found in the Quinizilapa zone, as shown in Table 8. First and most commonly, elderly parents rent land (for cash, labor, or gratis) to their adult sons or sons-in-law. This arrangement helps assure the father of a reliable labor force; it promotes filial deference; and it establishes moral rights to inheritance. Second, the land-rich "petty capitalist" families rent out land in exchange for labor obligations or for the cash that can be used to hire labor. Third, nearby and some distant Pacific coast *fincas* which are owned by urban *ladinos* rent land in exchange for labor obligations. And fourth, the community-owned *astillero*, though much reduced in size and now fairly distant from the community, is still freely available for firewood and is rented inexpensively to very poor families by the community.

Table 8. *Land Rental Arrangements*[a]

Type of Rental Arrangement	Number of Plots	% of Total
Intra-family rental		
Lent by parents (free)[b]	13	26
Lent by in-laws (free)[b]	5	10
Rented from parents (for cash, payment in crops, or labor)	1	2
Rented from in-laws (for cash, payment in crops, or labor)	1	2
Subtotal	20	40
Rich neighbor (petty capitalist) rental		
Rented from neighbor (for cash)	11	22
Rented from neighbor (for work)	5	10
Subtotal	16	32
Finca rental		
Rented from nearby *finca* (for work)	9	18
Rented from nearby *finca* (for cash)	1	2
Subtotal	10	20
Astillero rental		
Rented from *astillero* (communal land belonging to the municipality)	4	8
Total	50	100

[a] Data from survey of 74 households.

[b] The high percentage of plots classified as "free" is probably an error in the data due to ambiguity in questionnaire wording. Many informants interpreted "free" to mean "requiring no cash payment." They wished to imply a greater sense of voluntarism and flexibility than is found in a labor obligation to a *finca* or neighbor. Nevertheless, though cash is seldom exchanged within the family and the term *arrendar* (rent) is not normally used, obligation is still implicit: usually a sharing of the harvest or labor. There is a fine line between rent and a binding gift; and, in this case, I suspect that a substantial portion of the 36 percent of plots reported as "lent free" would in a more technical sense be considered as rented.

About 35 percent of the individual plots and about 16 percent of total agricultural land in the San Antonio sample are rented.[17] The apparently small percentage of total land that is rented should not belie its importance to the majority of producers or to the smooth operation of the regional agricultural system. This is illustrated in

Table 9. As shown in Column C, "dispossessed peasants" rent 70 percent of the land that they farm, and even the *"milpa* technologists" rent 41 percent of their total land.

Complementing their holdings through land rental, the average household of "dispossessed peasants" now have at their disposal about four *cuerdas* of land, but even so, this represents only about half the land that could be potentially farmed by relying solely on the head-of-household's labor. Even if he wanted to, he would still be unable either to absorb his own labor or completely support his family from this tiny amount of land. Therefore, additional sources of outside income must be found (see Chapter 2), even after paying rent for land.

Through the addition of rented land, the average family of *"milpa* technologists" now possess about 1.5 times the amount of land that the head-of-household can farm with his own labor. However, the mean number of males over fifteen years of age per household is also 1.5. In other words, through rental the hypothetical average farmer brings his landholdings up to the average adult-male laboring capacity per household.[18]

The practical consequences of this land-labor redistribution are shown in Table 10.

After renting out or fallowing land, the average "petty capitalist" household will actually plant 26.2 *cuerdas* of land. The 44 percent of their land *not* planted can be used to generate the labor beyond the household's capacity or the cash needed to support a commercialized mode of farming (see "Cash-cropping," Chapter 2). In this manner, the household's total agricultural income is equal to about $700, of which $576 represents cash-crop production.

With the addition of rented land (41 percent of their total), the *"milpa* technologists" bring their average landholdings up to 11.4 *cuerdas.* They plant 82 percent of this land, leaving some fallow or possibly renting out a plot to a neighbor or relative. Altogether, they plant 9.4 *cuerdas,* generating $280 in agricultural income. Average corn production is equivalent to 1.49 pounds per person per day, an amount comfortably in excess of the minimum 1.1 pounds per person per day that are needed for consumption.[19] In addition, $183 worth of cash crops are produced. Realistically, the *"milpa* technologists" have neither the land, the labor, nor the capital to shift easily toward a more intensive output (bearing in mind that on the average they already obtain 41 percent of their land through rental). Nevertheless, they are at least in a stable and temporarily sustainable position. Although they may only be slightly above the subsis-

Table 9. *Land Available for Farming (Rented and Owned) by Peasant Type*[a]

	(A) Average Number of Cuerdas Rented	(B) Average Number of Cuerdas Owned & Rented	(C) % of Total Land Rented
Petty capitalist	0	46.6	0
Milpa technologist	4.7	11.4	41
Dispossessed	2.8	4.0	70

[a]Data from survey of 74 households: 15 petty capitalist, 37 *milpa* technologist, 22 dispossessed.

Table 10. *Average Agricultural Production by Peasant Type*[a]

	(A) Number of Cuerdas Planted	(B) % of Total Land Planted	(C) Agricultural Income ($)	(D) Lbs. of Corn per Person per Day	(E) Income from Cash Crops ($)
Petty capitalist	26.2	56	700	4.37	576
Milpa technologist	9.4	82	280	1.49	183
Dispossessed	4.7	118[b]	123	.58	73

[a]Data from survey of 74 households: 15 petty capitalist, 37 *milpa* technologist, 22 dispossessed.

[b]Total greater than 100% as a result of intense intercropping and multiple cropping (more than one planting per year).

tence level, they are still producing a small surplus for ceremonial expenditure.

With the addition of rented land, the dispossessed peasant head-of-household has brought the amount of land that he plants up to 4.7 *cuerdas*. Necessarily, he farms as intensively as possible by intercropping and minimal fallowing (i.e., 118 percent of his total available land). Still, his agricultural income is only $123, and his corn production is only .58 pounds per person per day, about half what his family needs per person for consumption. Thus, even though his position has been somewhat improved through rental, he still must find some supplemental source of income—if he and his family are to *survive*, much less accumulate surplus income for ceremonial expenditure.

Table 11. *Average Wage Labor and Business Income by Peasant Type* [a]

	(A) Male Wage Labor ($)	(B) Family Business Income ($)	(C) Total Family Income ($)
Petty capitalist	360	477	1,804
Milpa technologist	496	212	1,220
Dispossessed	518	148	935

[a] Data from survey of 74 households: 15 petty capitalist, 37 *milpa* technologist, 22 dispossessed.

The most common means of making up the shortfall in income is through wage labor outside the household or by operating a family business, as shown in Table 11.

There is a positive, statistically significant correlation between wealth and income in San Antonio. Yet taking into account that "petty capitalist" households have, on the average, about sixteen times the per capita wealth of the dispossessed (see Table 7, Column D), it is perhaps surprising that the discrepancy in total family income between the "petty capitalist" and the "dispossessed peasant" is only a factor of two (Table 11, Column C). Why doesn't the "petty capitalist" family have sixteen times the income of the "dispossessed peasant," or even more?

This is a complicated matter, taken up in part in the next chapter. Briefly, there are two aspects to the explanation. The first is that not all wealth in San Antonio is "income-generating." Some wealth, particularly land held by traditional Catholic families, is used to purchase or maintain social position rather than to earn money. Although generational income-leveling via *cofradía* participation has lessened, a deeply rooted Indian-Catholic tradition against displaying wealth still exists (another reason for the physical homogeneity of the town). Catholics with significant resource advantages have little real social incentive to use their wealth to maximize their earnings. The other aspect is that some of the poorest families are so poor that, in a sense, they are driven to break the mold and live by a new set of rules. For example, the son of a landless farmer may be driven off the land—he may go to school, become a tourist guide, or join the Antigua labor pool—and in doing so, he often earns much more than he would from the *milpa*-based livelihood for which he was otherwise destined by tradition. Both these trends work to equalize income, though not necessarily wealth.

Conclusion

Two sets of forces simultaneously tug the San Antonio economy in opposite directions, and in doing so they recast the economic foundation of cultural identity. On the one hand, there is the *milpa*, the productive engine of colonial Indianness. The pro-*milpa* forces support a low-output economy based on constant reshifting of scarce material inputs for ever-greater productive efficiency. The system is reliable and relatively impervious to outside exploitation. In earlier times, the *cofradía* may have operated in tandem with the *milpa* to regulate community life and confer meaning upon the lives of individuals—in a sense, knocking off an economic, an existential, and a political problem with a single stone.

Yet there is also a set of anti-*milpa* forces that is acting to unbalance colonial Indianness. The chief destabilizer is growing inequity in the distribution of land. This chapter has described how the institution of land rental enables the system to accommodate land maldistribution and perpetuate itself. As shown, each of three peasant types is in a somewhat more stable position because of land rental. First, the capitalist peasants obtain cash or a work obligation with which they can obtain the outside labor or the agricultural inputs that will allow intensified production and thereby produce a greater surplus. In practice, some households reinvest this surplus to continue intensifying production; others invest in cultural celebration—a sort of "cultural tax" that is an investment in the idea of community. Second, through land rental the *"milpa* technologists" command a critical mass of land that can absorb most of the available household labor, allow production of most family nutritional needs, and, after payment of "rent," produce a small surplus for investment in celebration. Third, the "dispossessed peasants" (like the "peasant capitalists") tend to be pushed in two directions. Since their resources remain inadequate to support a family in the *milpa* lifestyle—even *after* acquisition of additional land through rental and optimizing scarce inputs with the utmost ingenuity—they must seek outside employment. If they wish to remain within the traditional framework, they can become full-time renters or distribute their time between farming rented land, working as day laborers, making *petates,* and handweaving. If they also have the expectation of inheriting land (particularly if they are renting from parents or in-laws), this may be a sustaining strategy.

Yet if the son of the "dispossessed peasant" has no reasonable hope of obtaining land himself—and particularly if he has some education or personal experience that prompts him to reject the prospects of a lifetime as an agricultural day laborer—then he may be impelled to think more boldly—perhaps more desperately. He is likely to look outward, ready for change.

As one travels through Guatemala today, these outward-looking sons—and daughters—are not hard to find. In every village, young men stand watchfully around the town square. They talk of migrating to Guatemala City, or perhaps of slipping into the United States. Antennae out, they are ever ready to receive those who come with their clipboards and projects. When the *centro* or *comité* is set up, they are there to register for the training courses in tailoring, family planning, soil conservation, or carpentry. They are quick to volunteer to be the community promoter for health or bilingual education. One or another young man plays trumpet in a marimba orchestra and longs to learn to drive a car. He has tried to learn English through home correspondence and a long-playing record. On the street, he is ready to be the host: he rapidly makes friends with the tourist (he wants to be more than a guide); he is the informant to the researcher; he collaborates with the Peace Corps volunteer. Or, young and with every good reason to be angry, he is recruited by the guerrillas. Spiritually restless and drifting from his parents' values, he is at loose ends, watching, listening, waiting for a message.

5

The Production of Christians

THE CULTURAL stability of the past four hundred years has been fractured during this century, on the one hand, by population pressure, growing landlessness, environmental deterioration, and military repression; and, on the other hand, by land windfalls, new technology, development programs, and expanding primary education. Both kinds of pressures have contributed to a surprisingly skewed distribution of wealth within the ostensibly homogeneous Indian community, and that growing maldistribution of wealth has, in turn, undermined the cultural rationale for production.

In a sense, two different types of productive systems have emerged— one an extension of the "*milpa*-promoting" forces, the other an extension of the "anti-*milpa*" forces. A key difference in these two systems lies in how campesino families choose to handle surplus product. In the first instance, they are willing to invest surplus product in symbolic acts that celebrate and reinforce communalism. Doing so provides an anchor in a dual sense: it *secures* in that it ties them into a stable and coherent cultural system, but it *restrains* in that production of local prestige precludes the purchase of significant power outside the village.

In the second instance, the families either have no surplus product to invest or choose to invest in expanding their economic opportunity. They reject the "cultural tax" and subordinate village-communal identification (and security) in exchange for a different set of rewards that can confer prestige, familial well-being, or spiritual gratification on a personal, nonvillage basis. In effect, they alienate themselves from the village-centricity that the *milpa* reinforces. Alternatively, their poverty may have already so marginalized them from full communal participation that the village alienates them. One way or another, their anchorage is lost and they must find new moorings.

In San Antonio, these distinct choices are manifested through and associated with religious affiliation. Very approximately: being

Catholic is to be of the first system; being Protestant is to be of the second.

About 80 percent of the population in my survey called itself Catholic and about 20 percent Protestant. Yet seemingly clear-cut distinctions between who is Catholic and who is Protestant—and what a Catholic believes and does, versus what a Protestant believes and does—are obscured for two reasons. First, nominal church affiliation may not be a reliable indicator of how someone behaves. As elsewhere, a chasm often separates professed belief from action. In terms of behavior, San Antonio is filled with Catholic-like Protestants and Protestant-like Catholics.

Second and perhaps more important, there are many contemporary Guatemalan branches of both major religions, and though I have tried to concentrate here on what I consider the two trunks rather than the branches, the branches are not unimportant. In San Antonio and Santa Catarina alone, three distinct Protestant denominations are active.[1] Each has its own church, pastor, and separate affiliation to U.S., European, and Guatemalan umbrella groups. Similarly, as will be discussed, Catholicism in Guatemala today is by no means monolithic; indeed, its branches brush over upon the Protestant tree.

Bearing in mind these caveats, there still *are* deep differences between Protestant and Catholic, and I believe that these differences are more fundamental than intra-group variation. As the final section of this chapter and the next two chapters show, these differences extend far beyond religious practice. They carry over into such secular matters as farm production, handweaving designs, and political behavior.

Missionaries and the Growth of Protestantism in Guatemala

Although the term "Protestant" is used here—to distinguish it generically from "Catholic"—the term more commonly used in Guatemala and throughout Latin America is *evangélico* ("evangelical"). This usage is generally understood to exclude such groups as Jehovah's Witnesses, Mormons, and Adventists. It does include both the extreme and the moderate Pentecostal groups found in Guatemala.

The first Protestant missions to Guatemala—the Presbyterians, the Central American Mission, the Church of the Nazarene, and the Friends Mission—arrived within a twenty-year period beginning in 1882. They were encouraged, in part, by the liberal reformer, President Justo Rufino Barrios, who saw the missionaries as useful allies in piquing the Catholic Church and weakening its political power.[2] Under the liberal regime, most foreign Catholic clergy were expelled from the country, all Catholic Church property was expropriated, and the Church's power to act as a legally recognized entity was revoked.

By the first decade of the new century, Protestant missions were well established and actively proselytizing among the highland Indian population. As early as 1900, an evangelical and medical ministry was operating in Chichicastenango in the department of Quiché. Indeed, within a few years the four "pioneer missions" had ambitiously divided up the entire Indian territory by language and cultural group—in much the same manner as had the Spanish religious orders four hundred years earlier.[3]

In their first fifty or so years, the missionaries barely dented the entrenched Catholicity of Guatemala, despite the fact that severe restrictions on the Catholic Church begun by the liberals in 1871 marked probably the longest and most severe anticlericalism in all of Latin America. As late as 1967, *Protestant* sources estimated baptized membership to be no more than 1.6 percent of the total population.[4] Yet the missionaries were not easily discouraged. Bred and loyally supported by thousands of small-town churches in the North, they inched forward patiently. They expected, perhaps even welcomed, adversity. Through the decades of rejection, expulsion, and occasional violence they persisted—with a resoluteness that government workers, soldiers, Peace Corps volunteers, or development technicians seldom maintain. The missionaries thought in terms of lifetimes of work, not months. Supported by virtually inexhaustible funding and motivated by God rather than careerism, they came . . . and stayed.

Foreign colporteurs and itinerant preachers took on Indian assistants, and together they worked the periodic Indian ("solar") markets as shrewdly as did the ambulant vendors of Chichicastenango.[5] Wherever they went, they sought to "plant" a congregation—a group of believers meeting first in a home, soon in a rustic church. Each rescued soul was greeted as a miracle; and in a sense it was, for within each tale of personal salvation was the obligation to give public witness, and therein lay the seed for geometric membership expansion.[6]

The missionaries concentrated not just on salvation, but also on edification. That meant fortifying the new believers to the faith and keeping them spiritually renewed. Those edified souls were the key to success and the reward for patience, for they were to become witnesses to the Word and the real foot soldiers of the divine army. In short, the Protestant laity became an army of evangelists.

As the missionaries were replaced on the front lines by a second and third generation of national preachers, the foreigners began the more sophisticated work of institutionalizing support systems. First, they set up Bible-training institutes, then theological seminaries. They organized thousands of camp meetings, revivals, and retreats. Later they launched publishing houses, radio stations, and private-aircraft services. In a Sunday afternoon white elephant sale back in Akron, Ohio, a suburban Baptist congregation could raise enough money to build a country church in faraway Guatemala. And through mission headquarters in Guatemala City, the sister congregation could easily send down a retired farmer or electrical contractor to help out with the construction. Some of their everyday skills in Ohio (they could easily build a garage or remodel a rec room) were not necessarily everyday skills in Guatemala. It was not trivial to be able to rewire a generator, install a loudspeaker system, set a window frame, treat anthrax, or land a light plane on a country road.

Bible translation was a key to what became known as the Mayan Evangelical Ministry. Following William Cameron Townsend's rendering of the Bible into Cakchiquel, Wycliffe/Summer Institute of Linguistics (SIL) missionaries went on to translate the Bible into virtually every Indian language and major dialect.[7] In 1931, the politically astute Townsend presented the first copy of his New Testament in an Indian language not to the Cakchiquel Indians, but to Jorge Ubico, the *caudillo,* who then asked Townsend to repeat the good work among the Kekchí.

When the Revolution of 1944 overthrew Ubico, that too boosted Protestantism because the new liberal government fostered a clear separation of religious and civil office. While the *cofrades* tended to fear and oppose the reformist Arévalo and Arbenz governments, Indian Protestants were active participants in the newly formed peasant leagues and agrarian committees.[8] By the late 1950s and early 1960s, the number of converts was still not large, but a foundation for future growth had been laid through a half-century of missionary work.

As the fact of a deep cultural change became evident, anthropologists started to document the process of conversion.[9] As the rate of conversion increased, they took up the more subtle questions of why and under what conditions Indian culture was receptive to the evangelists' message. Several categories of explanation have been discussed. These include: Protestant acceptance of individuals who are otherwise socially, economically, or psychologically maladjusted;[10] help in dealing with urban social isolation;[11] support in coping with alcoholism;[12] the spread of literacy;[13] the desire for economic gain;[14] the curing of disease;[15] and help in allaying the frustration of those who are experiencing "status incongruency."[16]

For whichever reasons—external promptings from the missionaries or internal changes within "modernizing" Maya culture—Protestant church growth did begin to take off. By 1976 Julian Lloret calculated that the overall evangelical population in Guatemala had risen to 4.5 percent, including 3.7 percent of the Indian population, and was growing by about 6 percent annually.[17]

In the late seventies and early eighties, three external events hastened the pace of conversion, as earlier linear growth began to expand toward its geometric potential. First, the earthquake of 1976 (which killed 20,000 and injured another 100,000 people) caused massive physical dislocation in the highlands. Some ninety villages were almost or completely leveled within a one-hundred-mile radius of Guatemala City. The physical fracturing of villages, the primary units of Indian cultural integration and economic activity, dramatically disoriented rural life and increased the number of "dispossessed peasants" (see Chapter 4). At the same time, it provided the missionaries an opportunity to enter new communities, to preach on God's wrath, and to build new churches. Second, the war that brutally escalated during the Lucas García regime caused another kind of dislocation. Indians were the chief victims of the widening violence that for many became a maelstrom. The "hot" apocalyptic religion offered by the Protestants—a gospel of tears, shouting, and speaking in tongues—was sustaining and seemingly appropriate for the times. And third, during the tumultuous Ríos Montt regime, from March 1982 through August 1983, Protestantism was simply safer than Catholicism. Whether through prudence or religious revelation, the pace of conversion steadily quickened—until now, in the mid-1980s, probably a fifth or more of the Guatemalan population is Protestant.[18]

The Creed of the Village Protestant

How do people in San Antonio conceptualize and practice Protestantism? In the first place, many of the doctrinal distinctions that are familiar to U.S. Protestants are of no great consequence to Mayan Protestants. Whether, for example, the wafer is substantiated or transubstantiated is something I have never heard discussed in San Antonio.

When local people explain what being a Protestant means, they usually do so by contrasting Protestantism with Catholicism. They usually define in terms of a series of negatives. Generally, they make the following points, more or less in this order:

- Protestants do not drink, smoke, dance, or gamble. (Considerably more importance is attached to not drinking than to not smoking, dancing, or gambling.)
- Protestants do not venerate saints, and they flatly reject as idolatry all artifactual representations of saintly or demonic personages.
- They do not participate in any *cofradía*-related ritual.
- They reject *compadrazgo*, ritual godparenthood.
- They reject communal celebration of saints' days (*fiestas*), which involve the parading of religious images through the streets or the re-enactment of holy drama.

What do Protestants do? As elsewhere, Protestants in San Antonio focus on Christ the Savior. The key notion that Christ is a *personal* savior is ceaselessly repeated at meetings and in teachings. Salvation is through the personal Christ, who is the Son of God and who died and rose from the dead for the remission of sin. Protestant doctrine stresses that there is one God, creator of all things, and that everyone is created with direct responsibility to Him. The death and resurrection of Christ were the divine solution to sin and the purest expression of God's love. To sin is to reject that love, to betray—personally—God's gift.

Religious practice for the Mayan Protestant centers around personal testimony and personal prayer rather than group liturgy. To most, Satan is as real as a rock—but alive and slathering for souls, hunkering at the door of the home, the cantina, and the church. Lust is a badgering reminder that he is out there—waiting, tempting, reaching out to regain what he has lost. The stronger the temptations of the flesh, the greater the struggle. The stronger the resistance, the greater the ecstasy.

Probably half of all Guatemalan Protestants belong to Pentecostal sects.[19] Like the storefront Pentecostal church in Chicago, the Mayan church is filled with shouts of anguish and exclamations of praise. The rhythms of guitars, tambourines, and handclapping pick up the currents of emotion and spread the pain and joy.

As Robert Redfield pointed out, the response by Catholic natives to Protestantism may be conditioned by the extent to which the new religion resembles syncretic Catholicism in structure, belief, and values.[20] Certainly, the Protestant missionaries have understood this principle, and wherever possible, they have offered "functional substitutes"[21] to ease transitions. Church elders replace *cofrades*; camp days replace fiesta days; singing replaces the Mass. Contemporary evangelical preachers discuss the nature of angels as "created spirits." But in this case, the spirits are subject to the will of one all-powerful God, as if the complex Mayan pantheon were not entirely depopulated but rather brought under the control of central authority.

The believer's transition from the old to the new religion is not easy. Even though conversion may be facilitated by apparently familiar functional analogs, the new meanings that invest old activities must still be placed upon emotional layering that is hundreds of years old and at the core of Mayan identity. I recall, for example, sitting in the home of a small congregation of evangelicals during the long fiesta days of Semana Santa (Holy Week). For San Antonio, the liturgical Easter drama is the most compelling and emotionally charged fiesta of the year.[22] Day by day, the community re-enacts in the streets the story of the crucifixion and resurrection. From dawn, the *chirimía* and *tambor* (Figure 20) have been playing their eery, snake-charmer music on the steps of the Catholic church. Each Catholic family has constructed an *alfombra* (rug; see Figure 21) of pine needles, colored sawdust, and flowers in front of its home (the children love the custom, like setting up a Christmas tree). Throughout the day, mournful processions kick through *alfombras*—destruction and renewal, destruction and renewal.

The small group of Protestants are far from immune to the high drama that is taking place within earshot. From their point of view, the streets are given over to Satan. The believers huddle together, their guitars and tambourines in hand, as if clutching to sides of a lifeboat. The approaching procession is at once innocent, yet as seductive as childhood memories. It is their common past and their own symbols that wind toward them, calling from the street.

So as the *anda*-bearers (Figure 22)—clouded in a somnolent haze of incense and sweating beneath their purple robes—approach the Protestant home, the believers inside are finely tuned. The monster outside is hypnotic, and they begin to break its spell with jubilant exclamations. By the time the procession reaches the Protestant house, it is met with heretical cacophony: on the street, the baleful sounds of trumpet, trombone, and bass drum; from the house, a rising chorus of hallelujahs and shouts of praise. As the procession passes, angry eyes glare from the purple robes outside; but inside the house there is noisy rejoicing. It has been, in a dual sense, a *rite of passage*.

The Holy Trek: *Del suelo al cielo*

The notion that there is an entrepreneurial "Protestant ethic" has, of course, advanced to conventional sociological wisdom since Max

Figure 19. Young boys in a Holy Week procession, Antigua.

Figure 20. Street procession in nearby village, Santo Domingo Xenacoj, led by *chirimía* and *tambor* (drum).

Figure 21. Admiring an *alfombra* before the procession arrives, Antigua.

Figure 22. *Anda*-bearers in Holy Week procession, Antigua.

Weber's classic statement on the subject, *The Protestant Ethic and the Spirit of Capitalism*. From the foregoing section, it should be clear that conversion to Protestantism among Guatemalan Indians is considerably more complex than simply rationalizing economic gain. Yet on the other hand, there *is* a Protestant ethic; and the draw of the new creed at the village level is closely related to the fact that it encourages personal rather than collective use of wealth.

As Chapter 4 showed, the fact or lack of surplus capital is particularly important for those two groups of producers who are at the margins of *milpa* stability: the "petty capitalists" and the "dispossessed peasants." This section will examine the theological dimension of economic activity in greater detail; and the final section of this chapter and Chapter 7 will show some empirical differences between Protestant and Catholic economic behavior.

By all accounts, it is "cheaper" to be a Protestant than a Catholic. San Antonio Protestants do not hesitate in explaining the practical advantages of a religion that venerates a god who is inexpensive to serve. Expanding upon this theme, missionaries have unabashedly promoted the material benefits of surrender to Christ. This is so much the case that the accusation "He just did it for the money" is frequently leveled by both Protestants and Catholics at converts of dubious spiritual sincerity.

William Cameron Townsend, the founder of Wycliffe Bible Translators/Summer Institute of Linguistics and the first missionary in San Antonio, was the son of a poor tenant farmer. He grew up in Orange County, California, where citrus-grove owners provided a helping hand to the Townsends in the form of a minister's scholarship to the poor but worthy youth. Townsend was deeply affected by his father's struggle with indebtedness and the family's escape from poverty.[23] Possibly because of this family history, debt deeply offended Townsend. From his point of view, the ritual extravagance of the Maya paved the way to their economic, spiritual, and biological enslavement; and Townsend worked against it with all the passion, instinct, and ego of a liberator.[24] He excoriated the "Romish church," which he invariably linked rhetorically to "the saloon keeper and witch doctor," for perpetuating the bondage of Indians through promotion of alcohol-related debt.

In his prolific writings for missionary publications, Townsend frequently recounted conversion stories of individual Indians. The path to salvation typically was linked to explicit economic motivation.[25] One such story is "A Rich Chief's Family Getting 'Saved,'" which Townsend published in 1926:

Don Jacinto was the wealthiest chief in San Antonio, and in keeping with the position he had occupied during his lifetime, his funeral was the longest celebrated and with the most rum. The drink feast lasted for over a month and, indeed, his sons did not let up except for brief breathing spells until they had finished the fortune their father had left them. At different times they would try to brace up and call a halt. Upon these occasions they would often come to the mission station and ask for some medicine to cure them. Time and again we would explain them the Gospel and assure them that that was the only sure remedy. They were fearful, however. Their old father had instilled into them something of his own hatred of the Gospel. On the other hand was the desire to reform in time to save a little of their inheritance from being lost. This very financial interest seemed to make it necessary for the Lord to let them come to the end of their rope. And the eldest son, don Teodoro, quickly arrived there. Poverty stricken and alone, a virtual tramp away on the hot lowlands, he breathed his last. . . . A short time after his death his oldest son accepted Christ and is now a faithful and prosperous member of the San Antonio congregation. Then a daughter of the old chief, a bright young woman, one of the few in her tribe who can run a sewing machine, accepted the Lord.

Don Apolinario was the favorite of his father. He was given every opportunity to get an education and came to be a school teacher. Several times he was principal of the government school in San Antonio. For two years he ran a school of his own, which the children of the principal families of the town attended. But his terrible enemy, drink, was continually after him until he finally lost his home, his lands, and the respect of all. Barefoot, and with ragged clothes, the once proud son of the rich old chief had barely been able to eke out a living for his family with his hoe. His nephew and half sister kept pointing him to Jesus until finally at a special service he made a profession of faith. A different look came into his eyes. He testifies that since then he has had no desire for liquor. The townspeople soon saw the change. The Mayor went to him and asked him if it were so that he had been converted. When don Apolinario replied that it was, the Mayor offered him the position of the public school. Pray for him.[26]

This notion that economic advancement is a sign of spiritual grace is an endlessly reiterated theme in Protestant evangelism. *"Del suelo al cielo,"* said Florentina Carmona reflectively. A now-prosperous textile merchant (Figure 23), she recalled her family's fifteen-year rise from dirt poverty to relative wealth. She uses the phrase as a double (triple) entendre.[27] The sense of it is, "from dirt floor to the sky; from rags to riches; from earth to Heaven."

During the course of fieldwork, I collected about half a dozen "*suelo al cielo*" stories from successful Protestants. The stories inevitably resemble the one from the Carmona family. The accounts begin with the teller in ignorance or in a fallen spiritual state. There has been some loss, usually through profligate behavior that the narrator later will come to recognize as sin. Typically, the family fortune has been squandered, frequently through a practice associated with traditional folk Catholicism. The crucial moment comes when the reprobate finally recognizes as vice what he or she previously regarded as virtue—or if not virtue, at least as innocuous. This moment of recognition is described as an emotional, divinely guided, revelatory experience.

Frequently such accounts involve sexual profligacy or alcoholism. The bonds of the family are stretched to the breaking point. Often there is a crisis, such as an illness, that brings events to a head. The sufferer has been to a local curer, possibly to the *ajitz'* (shaman) in Santa Catarina, the shrine of Maximón in San Andrés Itzapa, or the image of Don Diego in San Miguel Dueñas. He or she is disillusioned, depressed; the doors of life seem to be closing.

At this point, a guide appears—a tract, a radio sermon, an evangelist, or counsel from a converted relative. The sinner hears and understands what was previously shrugged off; goes to church, where God is revealed; and, in a bolt of understanding that will later be acknowledged as the most profound experience of life, repents, makes a decision for Christ, and is saved.

This spiritual struggle parallels an economic struggle. Economic gain is both the path and the reward. Investment in economically unproductive social institutions is not only a waste; it is a sin. Typically, the ensuing economic-spiritual struggle stretches through years of trial, temptation, backsliding, and rededication. Many informants describe an anorexic-like compulsion to save, i.e., "We got up at four every morning, dressed in rags, only ate beans and corn for a year until we could buy the truck . . ."

In its basic elements, this story has probably changed little in this century. Writing more than sixty years ago, Townsend recounted the story of his first convert in San Antonio, Silverio López:

One day, Silverio's little daughter took sick, or rather it came on to her gradually. Her little stomach swelled up all out of propor-

Figure 23. Florentina Carmona, whose family has risen *"del suelo al cielo."*

tion while the rest of her body became thin and she lost all desire to work or play. The age-long custom of his people dictated that he consult a witch doctor. The sage instructed him to buy candles and burn them before certain images at different Romish shrines. For two weeks he labored, spending 200 pesos, the sum total of his capital. In spite of all the father's efforts and the medicine man's best enchantments, the child died. One hundred pesos was required for her burial. These he borrowed from the witch and later paid them back by 18 days of hard labor. He was a disgusted Indian, but later when another child took sick in the same way, he went again to consult a witch doctor, only this time he sought out a different one [to no avail and at further expense]. . . .

Silverio then went to a saloon keeper who rubbed the child's stomach with oil [also to no avail]. . . . so he returned to the first shaman who advised that he buy more candles. On the road to Antigua to buy the candles, he discovered a scrap of scripture with the words, "My house shall be called the house of prayer, but ye have made it a den of thieves (Matt. 21:13)." . . . Surely it referred to the witch doctors and their co-conspirators, the priests. They certainly had robbed him and he was only one of the multitudes of victims . . . He would look elsewhere for help . . .[28]

One contemporary *"suelo al cielo"* family now operates a heavy-duty, four-ton, Mack diesel truck on the Pacific coast and a three-quarter-ton Ford pickup in the region. Since 1958, the family has variously owned four trucks, two buses, and an automobile. Their path, which began with conversion and two small inherited plots of land in the mid-1950s, has not been smooth. The elderly head-of-household experienced one devastating loss after another with his vehicles—a twenty-year roller-coaster ride with alcohol, accidents, temptations of the flesh, bus route licensing difficulties, thrown rods and blown gasket heads, the loss of faith and family, and seemingly endless confrontations with police and motor vehicle bureaucracies.

Watching his grown sons unload his *second* vegetable crop of the year (his was the first mechanical irrigation system in San Antonio) from the bed of his truck, he told me about his first vehicle. For three years he had risen to work in the fields before dawn and saved every penny, denying himself and his family all but the most meager diet. Finally, with the income from two successive, successful carrot harvests and the sale of half his land, he was able to make a down payment on a truck—only to be wiped out a few short weeks later in "about twenty minutes" when he failed to understand the seriousness of an oil leak. He smiles ruefully at the memory. But he reminds himself, ever the optimist and Christian philosopher, "It is through rectification of our ignorance that we are redeemed."

A Catholic Cultural Tax

The extravagant and nearly obligatory nature of ritual-related drinking has lessened considerably since the time when Don Jacinto's mourning sons consumed their inheritance. As it has throughout Mesoamerica, the financial burden of formal *cofradía* participation has decreased substantially in recent generations;[29] and what I refer to as "Catholic" in these pages should not be taken too narrowly as meaning "*cofradía*-related ritual"—much less should it be assumed that this element describes the large and complex contemporary Catholic Church in Guatemala.

To set the context of Catholicism in San Antonio, it may be helpful to distinguish at least four variants that have *not* taken strong root in the town.

1. The revolutionary Catholic Church. Particularly since the Second Vatican Council (1962–1965) and the Bishop's Conference in Medellín, Colombia, in 1968, the theology of liberation has of course evolved into a major force. In Guatemala and throughout Latin America, religious workers have become increasingly involved in political struggle.[30] In light of Guatemala's history of violence and repression, philosophical questions such as "Is investment in celebration as worthy as investment in land?" may have become trivial, or at least do not describe the cutting edge of Church thinking. Yet in San Antonio, liberationist issues have not fired the local imagination. As far as I know, in the immediate San Antonio area there has been almost no significant Church-led political activity in recent years. (One notable exception was the death of Father Hermogenes, a priest in the nearby Quinizilapa town of San Miguel Dueñas, who was killed about 1978 for his involvement in a land-water dispute.)

2. *Costumbrista* sects. Elsewhere in Guatemala, communities have sometimes been bitterly divided between Mayan traditionalists (where there are strong *cofradías*) and apostolic groups who are more in line with central Church authority. In Aguacatán, the struggle of various religious sects (including Protestant as well as Catholic factions) is brilliantly described in Douglas Brintnall's *Revolt against the Dead*. In well-educated, already "modernized" San Antonio, however, the traditionalists are not strong, influential, or well organized. When people cannot cure illness by a visit to the pharmacy or health clinic, they occasionally seek out a shaman in Santa Catarina or

nearby towns, but shamanism as an institution is not deeply entrenched as it is in, say, the Quiché area.[31]

3. Charismatic sects. Several years before my fieldwork, a priest who briefly promoted a sect of *carismáticos* worked in the town. That experience involved much handclapping and singing and probably was intended to compete directly with the robust evangelical cults. Although there is still a small group of Catholics who call themselves *carismáticos,* the sect is much reduced (the proponent priest having been driven out) and is not a serious rival of either the mainstream Catholic or the evangelical churches.

4. Catholic Action. About 25 years ago, a new apostolic sect known as Acción Católica (Catholic Action) began missionizing within the Church itself. This movement now represents "modern Catholicism" in most parts of rural Guatemala and elsewhere in Latin America. Catholic Action incorporates features of Protestantism and inverts many traditional Catholic values. In an important sense, just as Protestantism borrows from Catholicism and incorporates "functional substitutes" to ease transitions, so too Catholic Action borrows from and incorporates Protestantism. For example, Catholic Action recasts the traditional notion of spiritually purifying poverty into an opposition between the sacred and the material, with economic advancement being good and both *ladino* domination *and* the wealth-dissipating *cofradía* being exploitative.[32] Although Catholic Action exists in San Antonio, primarily through the effort of several activists, it is nevertheless not a major force in the town as it is in other Guatemalan communities.[33]

The Catholic Church in San Antonio might be described as the "garden variety"—that is, the community is tended by a diocesan priest who lives in the parochial seat of San Miguel Dueñas and visits the town regularly to celebrate Mass and fiestas. Without a resident pastor, religious practice is dominated by *catequistas* whom the priest instructs and organizes, and by heads-of-household. Most prayer and religious practice takes place within the home (Figure 24).

Three *cofradías* are active in San Antonio today, but they are no longer controlling institutions. They are viewed primarily as fiesta-organizing committees and have little actual authority beyond that specific responsibility.[34] On the other hand, although formal *cofradía*-directed expenses have declined, active participation in Catholic ceremonial life still requires substantial investment of resources. The magnitude of this investment is suggested by Table 12, which lists the ceremonial expenses of a family of two adults and five children over the course of one year.

Figure 24. Elderly *petate*-maker in her home in front of altar for home prayer.

Table 12. *Fiesta Expenses for One Catholic Family*

January: Fiesta de Dulce Nombre de Jesús	
Husband's participation in Baile de los Moros (Dance of the Moors)	
Rents horse for procession	$5.00
Rents saddle	1.50
Buys mask for dance	2.00
Buys material for costume	5.00
Contributes to fiesta committee	3.00
Buys sword	2.00
Subtotal	18.50
Family's expenses	
Food, special meals, entertaining relatives	10.00
Liquor	5.00
New clothes for 5 children[a]	20.00
Contribution to fiesta committee	2.50
Firecrackers and skyrockets	5.00
Flowers	2.00
Candles and church offerings	2.00
Subtotal	46.50
April: Semana Santa (Holy Week)	
Offering in church	3.00
Special meals (bread, honey, vegetables, etc.)	25.00
Liquor	5.00
Flowers (including *alfombras*)	5.00
Candles	2.00
Subtotal	40.00
June: Fiesta de San Antonio (titular fiesta)	
Offering in church	3.00
Offering in canton chapel	2.00
Special meals	15.00
New clothing for 2 adults[a]	20.00
Liquor	8.00
Flowers	3.00
Candles	2.00
Bullfights and entertainment	1.50
Palos de monte (Easter palms)	3.50
Toys, gifts for children, treats at the street fair	5.00
Subtotal	63.00
August: Asunción (Assumption)	5.00
September: Virgin of Dolores and National Independence Day	5.00
November: Día de los Santos (All Saints' Day)	4.00
December: Pascuas (Christmas season)	17.50
Total	199.50
[a]Minus adjustment for purchase of clothing	−40.00
Adjusted total	159.50

As it happens, this young, exceptionally poor family owns neither land nor any other substantial material assets. The household *sitio* on which the family lives and the twelve *cuerdas* that the husband works are borrowed from his father. Total family wealth is equivalent to only $297, placing the family in the seventh percentile among the seventy-four families in the sample. Their income (as opposed to their assets) is derived entirely from what the family grows on the borrowed land, the husband's day labor, the occasional sales of textiles, and the wife's irregular weaving lessons for foreigners.

Although the husband theoretically has twelve *cuerdas* at his disposal, he is unable to farm the entire amount. He plants only three *cuerdas* in corn and one *cuerda* in beans (his family's nutritive subsistence base)[35] and three *cuerdas* of carrots and one *cuerda* of *camote* (his two cash crops). He does not plant his other four *cuerdas* or farm more intensively because he can neither afford hired labor nor rely on his wife (who cares for a seven-year-old, a five-year-old, a three-year-old, a two-year-old, and a six-month-old baby) to help him in the fields. Lacking funds to buy sufficient fertilizer or pesticides, he cannot afford to grow potentially more profitable vegetable crops, much less afford the nutritive risk to his family if these crops should fail. Furthermore, in exchange for usufruct, the harvest from a portion of "his" land is pledged to his father, and he must also work for several days without pay on his father's land. So despite the evident need to grow either more food or more cash crops, he would be hard pressed to handle more than the eight *cuerdas* that he presently plants. Because he lacks the capital to purchase the inputs that would justify the investment of time, he uses his "spare time" (i.e., intervals between his own peak demands of labor) to work as a mozo on his neighbor's land. Sometimes he can find work as an unskilled helper for a local mason. All in all, he works about eighty days per year as a wage laborer.

Taking into account his financial situation, the $159.50 per year in ceremonial expenses shown in Table 12 represents a significant investment—indeed, nearly a quarter of the family's total income. Moreover, this is probably a conservative calculation. First, this budget assumes no major crisis or family passage, e.g., a death and burial (about $100–250), a birth and baptism ($20–30), or a marriage (roughly $200–400). Second, it includes no ritual-related curing for illnesses that go beyond the pharmacy, health post, or a physician in Antigua. Such items might include prayers, consultations with curers, the purchase of candles, food, and *guaro* (a local, clandestine alcoholic beverage) for offerings, or supplicatory visits to religious shrines. Considering that this is a family with five undernourished

Figure 25. Mother of Catholic family (Table 12) and four of her children.

children under eight years of age, health problems are a regular and predictable expense. Third, the budget includes the fulfillment of no special religious obligations, participation in minor fiestas, or visits to fiestas in neighboring towns. San Antonio families are well aware of fiesta days in a dozen or so nearby towns and religious shrines; when money is available, they enjoy traveling to venerate special saints or religious patrons. (This family has not been able to afford the major pilgrimage to the shrine of the Black Christ of Esquipulas, near the Honduran border.)[36] Fourth, it includes no *cofradía* expense. Though this male head-of-household has not served in the *cofradía* and expresses no interest in doing so, he estimates that prodded participation would cost about $40 for himself and his wife. Finally, but

Figure 26. Vendor selling toys at a village fiesta.

Figure 27. Village children on hand-cranked swing during fiesta.

perhaps most important for judging the veracity of the budget, this estimate includes a ceremonial alcoholic consumption expense of only $18. Knowing the family well, having drunk with them, I am quite certain that this is a genteel understatement,[37] though I have not taken the liberty of adjusting the data to match my suspicions.

In short, the $159.50 estimate, which amounts to about 24 percent of this family's total income, is probably not unrealistic.[38] Is a quarter of their income, particularly in the face of grinding poverty, a bad investment? Though the family is financially poor, it certainly is not without resources or hope. Apart from the spiritual rewards and psychological security derived from firm beliefs, the family also knows that the system will eventually work to improve their fortune. The father someday will inherit the tiny household plot and the twelve *cuerdas* presently borrowed from his father. At about the same time, the sons will be old enough to help work the land; and the wife, with three adolescent daughters to assist her, can look forward to expanded weaving production and sales. In the meantime, life has a sense of orderliness—the family can accept the present and feel a certain assurance about the future. No shame or social stigma is attached to their poverty. It would not occur to this family that their privation is caused by sloth or moral turpitude or that they are not good people. Positioned within a society that does not measure life by material standards, their lives ebb and flow within an orbit larger than ambition. In fiestas, they celebrate the subsumption of self-identity within community identity. Just as they accept the Catholic paradox of the Trinity—that there can be more than one in One—so too, in celebration, individuals are one and more than one. Celebration punctuates daily life: it orders the random flow of events into cycles, but more important, it renders the trivial significant.

Whether such punctuation is a sufficient return on economic activity is an existential question to which I have no answer. But from the Protestant point of view, that question is easy to answer: no. The $159.50-a-year ritual expenditure by this family is not only "waste"; it is "sin." Because village Catholicism supposedly encourages such vice, the Protestants view the priest and the Church to be flatly guilty of theft. The sum of $159.50, a Protestant would likely point out, is adequate to buy a fairly good *cuerda* of *milpa* land. By changing priorities, a family such as the one described above could theoretically "advance" from its present poverty, landlessness, and "dispossessed-peasant" status to nutritive self-sufficiency and the ownership of five *cuerdas* in about five years. The husband could hire one or two seasonal helpers and boost his carrot output . . . and then reinvest that return on an even more profitable mix of crops the following year. Or, with nutritive self-sufficiency guaranteed in five years (and no rental obligation), he could begin investing ceremonial savings in a household business—for example, in a sewing machine to boost the productivity of his wife's nascent textile operation.[39] Or if after several successful harvests the family sold its accumulated land, it would be able to make a down payment (about 30 to 40 percent is required) on a small, used four-cylinder pickup truck. Whether or not they are successful in achieving such goals, this is more or less how Protestants think and try to act; and it is certainly how they like to pejoratively describe Catholics as *not* thinking and *not* acting.

Comparing the Economic Performance of Protestants and Catholics [40]

I do not wish to imply that all Catholics are happily and innocently impoverished and that all Protestants are compulsive savers who become financial super-achievers. That isn't the case. And even from an economic point of view, the marginally greater amount of money that Catholics invest in communalism is not necessarily a "bad investment." The $159.50 that the family described above invests in celebration might be fairly described as a "cultural tax," but it is not

Table 13. *Correlation among Wealth, Income, and Land, by Religion*

		Total Wealth		Income
Income	(C)	.50***		
	(P)	.12		
Value of land	(C)	.92***	(C)	.47***
	(P)	.71**	(P)	.13

C: Catholic (61 households)
P: Protestant (13 households)
 *$p \leq .05$
 **$p \leq .01$
 ***$p \leq .001$

necessarily non-utilitarian. In light of Guatemala's overarching class barriers, reinforced by ethnicity and enforced by political oppression, investment in community rather than personal gain, as Waldemar Smith argues, does not seem unreasonable.[41]

Yet the larger confluence of "anti-*milpa* forces" that are undercutting traditional communal stability also works to make personal gain both more attractive and more necessary. As argued elsewhere, ideological rationalization of personal gain is not the only—and probably not even the most important—incentive to conversion; yet, by and large, Protestants do seem better geared and far more motivated than Catholics to pursue lifestyles that will either lift them out of poverty or protect hard-won financial gain.

The most fundamental dissimilarity between the Protestant and Catholic economic positions is suggested by Table 13, a correlation matrix for three variables: land, wealth, and income.

As would be expected, there is high intercorrelation among the variables. Among Catholics, all three variables are highly and significantly correlated with each other at the .001 significance level. For Catholics, it is almost literally true that land *is* wealth ($r = .92$). "Income and land" and "income and wealth" are both highly positive, about .5. The implication, simply, is that the economic performance of Catholics, measured by either total income or total wealth, is highly associated with how much land they have.

For Protestants, land and wealth are still highly correlated, though less so and at a lower level of statistical significance. More interesting, however, income is *not* significantly associated with land value, nor is it significantly associated with wealth. The implication is that

Table 14. *A Comparison of Elements of Household Wealth, by Religion*[a]

	(A) Average Catholic Wealth from This Source ($)[b]	(B) Average Protes- tant Wealth from This Source ($)[c]	(C) Catholic/ Protestant Ratio
(1) Land	2,245 (61)	1,825 (40)	1.23
(2) Household plot	858 (23)	987 (22)	.87
(3) Textiles	428 (12)	673 (15)	.64
(4) Animals	44 (1)	205 (4)	.21
(5) Machinery, tools, vehicles, business inventory	119 (3)	866 (19)	.14
Total	3,694 (100)	4,556 (100)	.81[d]

[a]Data from survey of 74 households: 61 Catholic, 13 Protestant.
[b]Figures in parentheses are percentages of the Catholic total.
[c]Figures in parentheses are percentages of the Protestant total.
[d]The ratio of the Catholic and Protestant totals.

Protestants, unlike Catholics, create livelihood strategies that are not necessarily dependent on land. Probably this is because most Protestant converts come from the ranks of "dispossessed peasants." Most are from families pushed to the point at which rent exceeds their consumption-maintenance costs, that is, families driven to a state of landlessness. Those whose spiritual-economic paths follow the "*suelo al cielo*" route tend to pick up land on the way *or* find potentially more lucrative means of investment that are not necessarily land-based.

This lessened Protestant dependence on land as a source of wealth and income is further illustrated by comparing the elements of household wealth among Protestants and Catholics (Table 14).

Here, family wealth is broken down into five elements, ranked according to the descending order of the ratio of Catholic to Protestant values. The average Catholic family owns 1.23 times as much land as the average Protestant. However, for every other element the value of Protestant holdings exceeds that of Catholics. Overall, the total average Catholic wealth is only .81 of the average Protestant wealth, despite the apparent Catholic advantage in the critical land variable.

The most striking discrepancy between the two groups is in machinery, tools, vehicles, and business inventory. Catholic wealth in this category equals only .14 of Protestant wealth. The presence of one bus-owning household (that of Florentina Carmona [Figure 23]) among the thirteen Protestant families greatly inflates the average

Table 15. *A Comparison of Elements of Household Income, by Religion* [a]

	(A) Average Catholic Income from This Source ($) [b]	(B) Average Protestant Income from This Source ($) [c]	(C) Catholic/ Protes- tant Ratio
(1) Small-scale vegetable marketing	61 (5)	3 (<1)	20.33
(2) *Petate*-making	17 (1)	1 (<1)	17.00
(3) Children's wages outside household	14 (1)	1 (<1)	14.00
(4) Male wages outside household	486 (40)	424 (29)	1.15
(5) Total agricultural income	311 (26)	353 (24)	.88
(6) Textile sales	64 (5)	111 (8)	.58
(7) Female wages outside household	42 (3)	90 (6)	.47
(8) Business income	205 (17)	445 (30)	.46
(9) Animal production	11 (1)	43 (3)	.26
Total	1,211 (100)	1,471 (100)	.82 [d]

[a] Data from survey of 74 households: 61 Catholic, 13 Protestant.
[b] Figures in parentheses are percentages of Catholic total.
[c] Figures in parentheses are percentages of Protestant total.
[d] The ratio of the Catholic and Protestant totals.

values in this category; nevertheless, despite the statistical distortion, it is certain that many Protestants have turned toward transportation as an alternative to traditional farming. In a separate survey of vehicle ownership in San Antonio and San Andrés, I identified forty-three vehicles belonging to thirty-five different households. Of these, 49 percent of the families, who owned 51 percent of the vehicles, were Protestant, while only about 18 percent of the general population is Protestant.

The propensity of Protestants to develop nonfarm sources of income is reflected in Table 15. This table shows, first, the mean values for Catholic and Protestant subincomes for each of the nine major elements of total household income, as well as the percentage of total income for either group that each of the nine represents. Second, it compares the Catholic and Protestant values and ranks the elements in descending order of the ratio of values.

As in Table 14, the elements are ranked from "most Catholic" to "most Protestant." Several points concerning Table 15 require explanation. First, almost no Protestants engage in small-scale vegetable marketing or *petate*-making. These two activities are largely extensions of the production logic of the "*milpa* technologist"; and, not surprisingly, as economic alternatives they are not particularly attractive, even to poor Protestants. Second, although there is almost no reported wage income for children among Protestants, and children's wages account for only 1 percent of total income among Catholics, it should not be inferred that children do not work. Rather, most families find their children to be more productive as workers within the household, not as wage earners.[42] Children are ideal *milpa* laborers: they weed, they harvest small quantities of crops for domestic consumption, they carry messages and meals to and from the fields. Protestant children, however, are less likely to assume these roles because, first, their parents' lives are less likely to be organized around *milpa* production and, second, their parents are more likely to emphasize education. Third, Catholic males earn more from wages outside the household than do Protestant males, both absolutely and as a proportion of total income. However, the broad category "wage labor outside the household" tends to obscure the more significant difference, that is, *how* this income is earned. For Catholics, wage labor is most often *mozo* labor. It supplements *milpa* income as land per family declines and more land must be rented to bring total planting up to subsistence size. Protestant wage laborers, on the other hand, tend to seek higher-paid, upwardly mobile occupations that lead to small businesses—like, for example, the tailor in Figure 28, who is the son of a landless farmer. The items in Rows 6, 8, and 9 of Table 15—textile sales, business income, and animal production—all reflect the greater Protestant disposition toward business activity. In each case, the business-related income is both absolutely and relatively more important for Protestant than for Catholic families.

A typical maximizing Protestant "*suelo al cielo*" family optimizes resources within the "newer" sectors of the San Antonio economy, but carries over the logic and ingenuity of *milpa* management. For example, one of my neighbors was fortunate to have acquired land during the agrarian reform of the late 1950s. Instead of buying more land, he branched into new ventures, utilizing family members as managers and operators. For instance, one adult son, who maintains a separate household, operates the family truck. The father continues to work the land, principally with hired *mozo* labor; the son makes regular runs to the southern coast to sell produce, purchasing additional vegetables from his neighbors or charging a fee for transport to the higher-paying, distant market. While on

Figure 28. Protestant tailor.

the coast, he buys or transports loads of mangos, papayas, and melons; and he also picks up fodder for his two cows from a small piece of land that his neighbor rents from a *finquero*. When the oldest son returns, the father and his youngest son (a twelve-year-old whose primary obligation is school) drive a load of cow manure to the family's nearest vegetable plot. Meanwhile, the daughter-in-law has set up a small butcher shop. She sells fresh meat, without refrigeration, over the counter two or three times a week from the front room of her house. When a cow is slaughtered, part is retailed in the family shop, and the rest is wholesaled in Antigua. The son also uses his frequent trips to and from Antigua and the coast to buy additional fresh meat. Keeping an eye on the tiny *tienda* and caring for her own small child, the daughter-in-law is assisted by one of the older children (her niece). Meanwhile, her mother-in-law operates a tourist *tienda* on the road leading into town. With the family truck at her disposal, she occasionally makes selling trips to Guatemala City. Although she is an expert weaver and *petate* maker herself, she buys or commissions all her stock from her neighbors.

Given the Catholic land advantage (Table 14) and the Protestant emphasis on nonfarm activity, it is not surprising that Catholics earn a relatively higher proportion of their total family income from agriculture than do Protestants. However, *despite the fact that Protestants own less land*, Protestant agricultural income actually *exceeds* Catholic farm earnings (a Catholic/Protestant ratio of .88). Table 16 takes a closer look at performance in agriculture. The several variables relating to agriculture are again listed in descending order of the Catholic-to-Protestant ratio.

The fact that Protestants have higher agricultural incomes than Catholics is all the more surprising given that Catholics own 1.41 times as much land and rent more than twice as much land. When owned and rented land are combined, Catholics have a total of one-and-one-half times as much land as Protestants. Nevertheless, Catholics do less well than Protestants in virtually every measure of agricultural productivity. Catholic agricultural income is only .88 and Catholic income from cash crops is only .79 that of the Protestants, underscoring the fact that when Protestants do farm, they are more likely to plant high-yielding commodities rather than corn and its typical *milpa* intercrops. Protestants also farm more intensively: they plant 96 percent of their land, compared to 70 percent for Catholics. As a result, the effective land gap is narrowed so that, overall, Catholics plant only an average of 11.5 *cuerdas* compared to an average 10.4 *cuerdas* planted by the Protestants. Protestants also seem to obtain the better land. As a result of frequent buying and

Table 16. *A Comparison of Agricultural Performance, by Religion* [a]

	(A)	(B)	(C)
			Catholic/
	Catholic	*Protestant*	*Protestant*
	Average	*Average*	*Ratio*
(1) Number of *cuerdas* rented	3.5	1.7	2.06
(2) Total *cuerdas* (owned + rented)	16.5	10.9	1.51
(3) Number of *cuerdas* owned	13.0	9.2	1.41
(4) Production of corn (lbs./person/day)	1.9	1.5	1.27
(5) Value of land owned ($)	2,245	1,825	1.23
(6) Number of *cuerdas* planted	11.5	10.4	1.11
(7) Income from *milpa* ($)	114	104	1.10
(8) Total agricultural income ($)	311	353	.88
(9) Average value of each *cuerda* owned ($)	172	198	.87
(10) Income from cash crops ($)	173	219	.79
(11) % of land planted	70	96	.73
(12) Value of output per *cuerda* ($)	24	38	.63

[a] Data from survey of 74 households: 61 Catholic, 13 Protestant.

reselling of plots, they own a disproportionate share of the higher-yielding vegetable and coffee bottomland from the former lake. This is reflected in Row 9, which shows that an average *cuerda* of Protestant land is worth $198, versus $172 for that of Catholics. Finally, because they own better land, plant more intensively, and plant a higher proportion of cash crops, Protestants achieve an overall output per *cuerda* of $38, versus $24 per *cuerda* for Catholics. The only agricultural variable in which Catholics outperform Protestants is corn production, which no doubt reflects the greater Catholic reliance on the *milpa*.[43]

Conclusion

In earlier chapters I tried to show how not only the economy but also, to some extent, the ideology of the town is a product of colonial relations. Separate but unequal spheres were established that allowed economic subsumption to be offset by a limited cultural autonomy. What we now think of as Indianness is less a relic of a more glorious, pre-Hispanic Mayan past than a cultural package that solidified Hispanic control.

Despite their frequent right-wing political identification today, in at least one sense the early Protestant missionaries were grassroots revolutionaries. They viewed Indians as being spiritually, biologically, and economically enslaved. In their eyes, the Church, alcohol, and debt were the instruments of that enslavement—and they, the missionaries, were the liberators. Unlike the contemporary liberationist Catholic Church—which considers Indians to be *politically*, and from there, economically enslaved—the missionaries did not attack or even necessarily question the organized structure of oppression. They did not challenge the *finca* owners or the government; rather, they attacked the culture.

The missionaries saved and edified relatively few Indian souls during their first half-century of proselytizing. But they preached a strong message, oriented themselves upon the prevailing winds of cultural change, and laid the organizational groundwork for future mass conversions. In that "witness" and public testimony were key aspects of Protestantism, every convert had the potential to start a chain reaction. In the late 1970s and early 1980s, the process accelerated: an earthquake fractured the physical grounds of cultural unity, a counterinsurgency war created a nightmare of psychological insecurity, and a Protestant president gave the evangelistic message an official stamp of approval.

The evangelical chain-letter is in the mail. Today, well over 20 percent of Guatemalans are Protestant, and some missionary sources predict that the country will be half Protestant by 1990.[44] Yet, as this chapter shows, conversion may be nurtured but is not caused by foreign missionaries. Certainly the missionaries have toiled to liberate the Maya from their culture—and certainly they have been aided by earthquakes, war, and a zealot president—but the fact that the message has been heard in the village reflects a deeper, gradual erosion of the economy and ideology of colonial relations. In a sense, the forces that have undercut the replicability of the "*milpa* technologists'" world—the same forces that have replaced them with "dispossessed peasants" and "petty capitalists"—have prepared the ground for the conversion process. And then, the relatively better economic performance of Protestants, whether at the rich or poor end of the economic scale, has reinforced their spiritual choices with a material rationale.

6

Religion and Why Women Weave

PROBABLY NO element of Mayan culture is more emblematic and generally identified with Indianness than backstrap weaving. This chapter and the next examine contemporary weaving from the perspective of religion. Here I examine the general question why Indian women weave—and then try to show how the cultural rifts that express themselves as "Protestant" and "Catholic" are also manifest in weaving. Chapter 7 then expands upon the "religious character" of textile entrepreneurship, a topic in itself.

Background: What Is Backstrap Weaving?

Textiles have been woven, more or less as they are today, for at least three millennia in Mesoamerica. They are produced on a simple but remarkably versatile loom generally known as the "backstrap loom." In contemporary Guatemala, this device simply consists of six to eighteen loose sticks. The loom has no fittings, joints, connections, movable or manufactured parts—just the sticks held together by the tension of looped threads on a continuous warp.[1]

In order to weave, a woman must first stretch the warp taut. She takes one of the end sticks and attaches it to a tree or a house post; she then attaches the other end to her belt (the "backstrap"), which she wraps around her hips (see weaver in Figure 29). By leaning slightly forward or back, she finely adjusts the tension of the warp. By inserting additional sticks through the warp, she raises and lowers alternate sets of paired threads to create openings through which the weft thread, wound on a shuttle, is passed back and forth. That creates the basic structure of the fabric. She imparts the design and ornamental quality through techniques such as ikat and gauze weaves.[2]

In San Antonio, the most important design technique is brocading, which gives San Antonio's fabrics their characteristic thickness, richness, and texture. To brocade, the weaver interlaces supplementary colored threads into the structural warp and weft threads. This

Figure 29. Elderly San Antonio weaver at the loom.

creates a superimposed pattern. The weaver works in her designs row by row, as shown in Figure 29.

Virtually all locally born women (and a good number of men, about 5 to 10 percent I would estimate)[3] know how to weave. Nearly half the adult women in my sample reported that they weave every day for three or more hours. Only 4 out of 115 women reported that they do not know how to weave at all, and only 15 women said they know how to weave but never do.

Normally, little girls begin learning to weave at the age of six or seven by watching and imitating their mothers and grandmothers. By the time they are young adolescents, most girls are proficient and are able to produce small textiles (*telarcitos*) for sale. By late adolescence, daughters are generally as highly skilled as their mothers.

Why Women Weave

Why do women weave in the first place? What motivates nearly half the women in San Antonio to spend three or more hours a day at a backstrap loom? Why the sore fingers, and the hours of effort that could be spent at any of a thousand other activities?

This chapter briefly examines four reasons. First, women weave because it is a familiar way to produce objects that they need in their daily lives, that is, clothing and carrying cloths. Second, they weave because they enjoy the activity and the product. The activity provides pleasure and aesthetic satisfaction. That is, the women like the mechanics of the work, the social experience, and they take pride in the elegance and beauty of what they produce. Third, they weave to create "symbolic texts." As anyone who has ever held a weaving intuitively feels, richly colored and designed textiles are "expressive"— they "say something" in the silent, obscure language of color, pattern, and design. Last, but by no means least, San Antonio women weave because they can sell what they make—and they desperately need the money.

As it happens, both Catholic and Protestant women weave, and they devote about the same amount of time to it.[4] But while both groups may nominally be doing the same thing—weaving for three or so hours a day—they are increasingly doing the same thing for very different reasons.

The Manufacture of Utilitarian Objects

Women weave to make a particular kind of clothing that is appropriate to their needs and self-perceptions. The woman in Figure 29 is making the basic garment woven in San Antonio, a *huipil* (pronounced we-PEEL, sometimes spelled *güipil*), a slip-on blouse. *Huipiles* are made from two rectangular pieces of cloth that are taken directly from the loom without cutting or tailoring, joined lengthwise, and sewn together at the sides and top, leaving openings for the neck and arms. The skirt (*corte*) worn by virtually all Indian females consists of several yards of foot-loomed cloth (produced outside this village) that are wound round the waist and fastened with a long, tightly wrapped belt (*faja*). *Fajas* are of two types: a narrow ornamental band with intricate designs and stylized figures, or a wide, plain-striped sash. Although most women know how to make their own belts, a decreasing number actually do so. Instead, *fajas* are purchased outside the village (nearly identical, machine-made versions from Totonicapán cost about a third less than locally made belts) or from village women who are specialists in belt-making (see the weavers in Figure 5).

Only a handful of very old men still wear the traditional men's garb: a heavy woolen overgarment (*gabán*) worn over home-sewn underclothing, and a handwoven belt. The man in Figure 30 was encouraged to put on his *gabán* for this photo; he does not normally wear it in the streets. Indeed, relatively few men today wear even the modified version of traditional campesino clothing—baggy, hand-stitched pants; sandals; a light-colored handmade shirt; and a back-strap-woven *faja* (see Figure 31). Typically, young San Antonio men cannot be distinguished by dress from other Guatemalan Indians.

It is now generally cheaper for women to buy rather than weave their clothing. There are several reasons: the tourist market has forced up the price for handwoven goods; the relative cost of machine-manufactured clothing has declined; and the value of and demand for female labor has increased. As a result, making clothes for family wear should be viewed as non-utilitarian—or at least non-maximizing—behavior.

Apart from the *huipil*, the woven products most used by San Antonio women are square or rectangular cloths called *servilletas* in Spanish and *tzutes* in the Mayan languages.[5] The cloth is a kind of multipurpose tool, a thing virtually always at hand. In San Antonio, a woman is not fully dressed without a *tzut* or *servilleta* on her head, under her arm, or in her basket. Before sitting, she will use it to dust the ground and then spread it flat so that she can sit. If she has something to sell, she displays it on a cloth. Market purchases, coins, *cédula* (identification card), and lunch can be wrapped in a cloth and carried by balancing the bundle on her head. Or the cloth can be folded into a cushion for protecting her head as she carries a basket

Figure 30. Elderly man wearing his *gabán*.

Figure 31. Man in "traditional" campesino dress.

or a water jug. Her cloth serves as a sling in which to carry a child, and then at home she turns it into an infant's hammock. She swats insects, shoos chickens, and protects herself from the sun, the rain, and the early morning chill with these cloths. When they are finally worn and tattered, she cuts the rags into potholders and diapers.

Important differences emerge between Catholic and Protestant women in regard to how they use the textiles that they make. Although both groups spend about the same amount of time weaving, Protestant women are far less likely than Catholics to actually wear *huipiles*, the primary woven product and symbol of San Antonio identity. About two-thirds of the Catholic women wear a *huipil*, compared to only just over a third of the Protestant women. The discrepancy is most striking among women fifteen to twenty-nine years old. Nearly half of the young Catholic women wear *huipiles*, while only one in ten of the young Protestant women does so. In fact, *huipil*-wearing is confined almost exclusively to first-generation converts, i.e., women who developed the habit of *huipil*-wearing when they were Catholics. Certainly, no Protestant thinks of *huipil*-wearing as evil. But by extension, acceptance of Protestantism implies alienation from the cultural roots and the behavior that is linked to a Catholic past.

Weaving for Pleasure and Aesthetic Satisfaction

If asked why they weave, San Antonio women are likely to respond first in utilitarian or commercial terms. But weaving can also be physically relaxing and pleasing in its own right. Many—though by no means all—San Antonio women weave because they enjoy it. They like manipulating color and design, the mechanics and rhythm of the work, and social interaction in small groups. They are also well aware that outsiders know and admire them for their skill, and that is a source of pride. Many women are quite content to spend their day at the loom, all the more so if they perceive the alternative to be laboring in the fields with their husbands.

Beyond that, San Antonio women also weave because they have a sense of the beautiful. Nothing about weaving seems more obvious, yet is harder to understand, than its aesthetics. To run your fingers over row after row of elegantly stated designs is to touch—but not quite touch—a deeper logic and expressive intent. The logic of the visual language and its relationship to a sense of beauty is not easily deciphered. Weavers do not readily verbalize *why* one piece is more elegant than another. It just is. They "know" what forms belong where, what colors and threads are permissible in what positions,

Figure 32. Grandmother, wearing *huipil*.

Figure 33. Granddaughter, wearing machine-made blouse.

and what "looks good." But they do not necessarily have the categories or words to explain why. Their graphic compositions are the shared product of their collective consciousness. Essentially, one either shares that consciousness or doesn't.

In an attempt to penetrate at least the surface of weaving aesthetics, I "apprenticed" myself to an elderly weaver, and later to her sister-in-law. As it happened, one woman was Catholic, the other Protestant. And it was their respective approaches to aesthetics that led me to first wonder about the depth of cultural change implied by religious conversion. Each of my two teachers had woven nearly every day of her life for more than a half-century. Each wore her *huipil* as proudly as if she were a navy admiral in uniform. In teaching me, both had endless categories, classifications, and caveats on how (if not necessarily why) to do anything. Doña Victoria, the Catholic weaver, was the more reflective of the two. She would caution against extremes in color and would emphasize the need to balance what she perceived to be opposites—"*ni mas maq'an, ni mas tew,*" she would say, repeating the dictum "not too hot, not too cold" in her Cakchiquelized Spanish.

To Doña Victoria, all thread colors (and even thread types) are "hot" or "cold" in the humoral sense—just as are all foods, medicines, and illnesses. Wearing a *huipil* with imbalanced colors not only shows poor taste, it can endanger one's health. Hot colors lead to sore eyes, arthritis in the arms, and fevers. Too much cold can lead to psychic depression and even the chilling of a mother's milk.[6] In general, the two basic principles of hot-cold balancing—avoidance of extremes and selective use of opposites—are as valid for weaving as they are for curing.

To understand Doña Victoria's sense of harmony in color and thread, it is necessary to understand her deeper sense of what constitutes order. The issue is not attractiveness but balance. To maintain the right physical (and psychological) balance within the body, she combines hot and cold foods into her family diet with clinical precision. When a grandchild is sick, she boils water in a curative rather than a preventative fashion. She believes that the *microbios* that she has heard about are tiny particles of cold. She reasons that they must be cold, since boiling is widely said to neutralize them; and by the same token, she would not give refrigerated water to the sick child.

The way she chooses colors for a *huipil*, cures a sick child, and prepares food are all, figuratively, part of the same cloth. The principles for balancing opposites and avoiding extremes tell her how to position her bed vis-à-vis the night breezes and the door, and how to lay out a garden. (Her husband, too, sometimes considers his *milpa* in terms of the hot/cold appropriateness of specific intercrops to specific soils. As a farmer, he has his own sense of which crops belong together, and look good together in the field as well as in the cooking pot or on a plate.)

The Protestant weaver with whom I studied, Doña Paola (Figure 35), tends to discount color balancing. She does not concede that colors are "hot" or "cold"—at least not in any respect other than that "hot" colors are chromatically brighter. Years earlier, when she rejected the *ajitz'* (shaman) and *curandero* (traditional healer), she also rejected their logic for restoring psychic order and for healing. And, by extension, she rejected the subconscious logic that guides her sister-in-law's hand as she reaches for a hank of salmon-colored thread to complete a dot inside the third row of a *pie de chuchu* ("dog-foot") design.

In practice, the actual colors that both women select for their *huipiles* are not radically different. Doña Victoria and Doña Paola are, after all, members of the same generation. They learned together and share an inherited conception of what a *huipil* is. But even though their color combinations may be the same or similar by habit, they describe their choices very differently. To discuss color with Doña Victoria is to discuss First Principles: This is how the universe is constructed. Her sense of beauty derives from the sense that she has created a thing in harmony. With her, one senses antiquity—that one is touching the distant Mayan past, if only through a remnant of its ancient logic. With Doña Paola, in contrast, one is talking about . . . color. Though she is sentimental about her "mother's colors" and fondly uses "the old colors," she speaks of them as if she were a folklorist. The colors are her mother's, not hers. To her, the familiar combinations are largely a matter of brand-name identification for San Antonio products. If pressed to make classifications, she responds with a dichotomy used by younger women: *triste* and *alegre*, categories that do not exactly translate as "sad" and "happy" but that vaguely relate color to the age or mood of the wearer.[7] It is as if Protestantism has turned what is beautiful for Doña Victoria into something that is merely pretty for Doña Paola.

Weavings as Symbolic Texts

A San Antonio textile, particularly a *huipil* or a *tzut*, has the feel of text.[8] It *looks* as if it "says something"—row after neat row of stylized designs, a collection of signs recorded on a flat surface. Yet, if they are texts, what do they say? How do they translate?

Over the past anthropological generation, several investigators have discerned mythological and cosmological significance in contemporary textile design;[9] and pursuing the theme of textiles-as-texts, several have tried to "read" the designs. To date, the most comprehensive effort of this sort is by Walter Morris, who has compiled an extensive inventory of textile designs based on fieldwork in Chiapas.[10] Morris believes that some pre-Columbian costume elements and textile motifs were "glyphs" and hypothesizes that designs found in widely separated contemporary Mayan communities might be traceable to a common, Classic Mayan source.[11] Information from modern Mayan textiles might therefore be useful in interpreting pre-Columbian hieroglyphic writing. In Guatemala, Flavio Rodas has made a persuasive case for text-like pre-Columbian symbolism surviving in contemporary weaving.[12] More recently, Barbara and Dennis Tedlock have analyzed Quichean weaving in terms of *Popul Vuh* symbolism and extended that analysis to "such arts as instrumental music, storytelling, prayermaking, dream interpretation, divination, housebuilding, and horticulture" through the notion of "intertextuality."[13]

It should be kept in mind, however, that San Antonio, unlike Chamula or Chichicastenango, is a Mayan town created *after* the Conquest. As explained in Chapter 2, the original inhabitants were rounded up from throughout the area, and they were not necessarily even native Cakchiquel speakers. So, whether or not textile designs may be "glyphs" in other parts of Mesoamerica, it should not be surprising that San Antonio offers little evidence to suggest carried-over, much less self-conscious symbolism. Other than the occasional use of a crucifix motif or a representation of the Trinity, my own field experience is consistent with reports from those investigators, such as Hilda Pang,[14] who found no overt cosmological symbolism blended into the threads.

Nevertheless, absence of overt religious symbolism does not mean that textiles do not have semiotic purpose and utility. In fact they do, and this utility is subtly tied to contemporary religious difference. The following sections present two illustrations of symbolic function in contemporary weaving. The first section shows how textiles project locative information, and the second suggests the novel and altogether speculative idea that *huipiles* serve as "walking production function equations." In both cases, symbolism reflects differences in values that can be associated with religion.

Locative Information

Huipiles are a little like maps. Their graphic elements represent "spaces," but these spaces are not just geographic; they can also be social domains demarcated by race or class. The *huipil* does not express this information in linear relation as a map would; rather, it expresses the "spaces" and then establishes where within the expressed spaces the wearer belongs.

How is the map "read"? A knowledgeable viewer reads a *huipil* from its larger to its smaller graphic features. That is, the overall "macro" form and shape of the *huipil* instantly mark the wearer as being "of Indian space." Geographically, that means the woman comes from the western highlands of Guatemala; but, more important in a society that is stratified by race and class, it implies that she acknowledges Indian/*ladino* boundaries and publicly places herself on the Indian side of the fence.

At a second level, the overall imagery of the total design (in this case, dense horizontal bands running across both fabric wefts) locates her as belonging to a community within the eastern Cakchiquel region. The color scheme coupled with distinctive elements of design (e.g., specific geometric patterns appearing on only one face of the fabric and pictorial motifs that are reversible) further signals the *municipio:* San Antonio Aguas Calientes. Virtually anyone from the highlands can make the identification without a second thought.

A third spatial order signaled by the *huipil* is the sub-*municipio* unit such as *cantón, aldea,* or *parraje.* Only a relative insider knows the design, color, and style well enough to make the finer distinction;[15] but only an insider would find the information relevant. For example, in *aldea* Santiago Zamora, women make their *pie de chuchu* design in one way; while two kilometers down the road, in the *cabecera municipal,* they do them another way. For most casual *huipil*-viewers (say *ladinos* interacting with Indians in the marketplace), this difference may be trivial. However, anyone for whom the Santiago Zamora–San Antonio distinction is important is also likely to know enough to instantly read, interpret, and mentally file the graphic code.

No two *huipiles* are ever precisely alike. The subtlest shades of variation in design and color mark "personal style" that distinguishes household from household, weaver from weaver, and generation from generation. In the finest nuances, a weaver says: this is me. She flies her colors, so to speak. With her bright floral *marcador* designs boldly across the chest (something her mother would never have used and her grandmother would never have seen) she tells the world: "Here I am, María, a somewhat free-thinking yet still traditional (probably Catholic) young Indian woman from the Sinay household in the *aldea* of Santiago Zamora, of the *municipio* of San Antonio Aguas Calientes, central Cakchiquel region, western Guatemala."[16]

Is there "religious significance" to this flying of colors? Absolutely. To the young Catholic woman, whose life and history are bound into community identity, the *huipil* is a badge of community and self. Protestantism is a process that separates community from self. That is why over two-thirds of Catholic women continue to wear the *huipil*, and just under two-thirds of the Protestant women *do not*, and more significantly, why only one in ten of the young Protestant women do. In brief, the self-locative function of the *huipil* continues to have significance to Catholic women; to Protestant women, it does not.

The Huipil *as Production Function Equation*

Toward the end of my fieldwork, several collaborators and I spent several months trying to decipher the "grammar" of the weaving language.[17] To lay a foundation for interpretive analysis, we studied in depth the physical construction of three sets of *huipiles:* a set of about one hundred worn day-to-day in the village; a set of about twenty made for sale to tourists; and a set of about one hundred high-quality *huipiles* collected in the early 1950s. In order to derive principles of design and color selection, we interviewed weavers and coded and recorded tens of thousands of bits of data on the *huipiles.*

Unfortunately, what emerged from the analysis was mostly a healthier respect for complexity, reams of print-outs, only the barest beginnings of a "grammar," and a methodology for comparing change over time and *huipiles*-for-use versus *huipiles*-for-sale.[18] Some general principles did become clearer, however. For example, we found that all *huipiles* are constructed around sets of accommodating frameworks—which I think of as empty shells—that can be correctly filled with only a narrow range of acceptable designs and colors. A woman works by "filling in" abstract patterns and empty forms. She is able to make substitutions of color, design, and thread type within these ranges. Through manipulation of design and color in relation to the collective norms, she publicly establishes her taste, skill, and personal style.

The basic unit of *huipil* design construction is the horizontal motif. That horizontal band—the "accommodating framework," the "shell"—contains within it innumerable micro-frameworks; and, in turn, it is nested within larger frameworks (i.e., sections of the *huipil* such as the shoulder piece or the design across the breast, or the whole *huipil*). As a woman works to fill in the forms, she makes thousands of barely conscious choices. At any moment, she may decide to devote relatively more or less attention to a particular design or procedure. She may pound down the weft harder or, alternatively, ease up and create a "looser" weave. She may choose to brocade a difficult, time-consuming design that requires much finger work, or a simpler, more mechanical design.

Take, for example, so straightforward a matter as choice of thread. By choosing a single- rather than a two- or three-ply cotton thread for her ground fabric, the weaver will pay eleven cents per *madeja* (a small hank of thread weighing one-twentieth of a pound) instead of thirteen cents per *madeja*. The single-ply is cheaper (a total savings of approximately sixty cents per *huipil*), but its use requires the weaver to expend more time in thread preparation, since it must be laboriously doubled (plied together) by hand. If this hand-plied thread is to be used, the weaver must decide whether the added value from selling the finished product on the specialized tourist/collector market (or, alternatively, the value that it has for her as "created wealth") offsets her sore fingers. Quite literally she might say, *"No vale la pena"* (It's not worth the pain).

If the weaver decides not to use single-ply, she then confronts a second choice. Two- and three-ply threads cost the same amount. The difference is that the two-ply thread must be sized (dipped in a starch bath) to give it the necessary strength for weaving. It also takes longer to warp two-ply threads (they are finer, so there are more warp ends per inch), but the result is a closer-textured cloth. The tradeoff now is between the weaver's time and her perception of quality, since in this case the capital investment stays constant.

Obviously, thread selection is dictated by several factors. Is the extra time available for plying or starching thread? How much ready cash is at hand to buy materials? What do potential customers want to buy? What is her sense of "quality"? But mostly it is a matter of what the *huipil* means to her, the significance of the process as expressed by the product.

The totality of the finished *huipil* is a tangible expression of how she decided to make those decisions. What is particularly interesting is that not only has she made the thing, but she has kept a minute *record* of the making by virtue of the graphic properties of design. In a sense, the *huipil* is a record of itself, a record of imbued significance.

In this respect, the *huipil* operates a bit like the economist's or engineer's production function equation.[19] If not precisely mathematical, it is at least a symbolic expression of a particular kind of input-output relationship. The inputs are capital, labor, skill, and knowledge of the collective consciousness; and the *relationship* of these elements to one another is symbolically expressed by the locally spoken language of design. The "weaving together"—in both

Figure 34. ". . . a minute record of the making by virtue of the graphic properties of design . . ."

the physical and the symbolic sense—expresses an optimized relationship of inputs. It is much the same as the mathematical production function, which is an equation that graphically expresses the largest amount of output that can be produced with all possible combinations of a given set of inputs (what an econometrics text would call the set of "efficient production possibilities"[20]).

The typical inputs of a more conventional textbook production function equation are units of land, labor, and capital. The output is often expressed in physical units and translated to dollars of product. An agricultural economist might ask what is the best possible combination of hog feeds, fertilizers, transportation costs, and pig-sty material to produce a certain yield of pork in the most efficient manner. The equation expresses the solution. What is unusual about the *huipil*, unlike pounds of pork, is that the product is both the output and the expression: the thing and the representation are the same.

Intrigued by this idea, at the outset of our analysis I wished to assign numeric values to input elements and to treat individual *huipiles* as literal equations to be "solved." That didn't work very well for several reasons. One reason—which I think even more important than the formidable technical obstacles—was that there were really two kinds of equations rather than one: Protestants and Catholics each had a different optimization logic expressed through design.

This difference strikes to the heart of respective conceptions of wealth. Both Protestants and Catholics weave in order to produce wealth. But the wealth they produce is not the same. To Catholics, the *huipil* expresses and celebrates the fusion of self and community, just as the religious fiesta does. The weaver *adds* as much input as possible. The more generous the gift, the better. By creating a product that expresses what she put into it, the weaver creates a kind of social currency expendable only in the local economy.

Protestantism, on the other hand, is a process in which women redefine self as *me*, not community. Each has adopted a one-to-one relationship with a personal savior instead of religious practice based on communal ritual. The *municipio* is no longer her controlling frame of action and identity. So the wealth she wishes to create is the more familiar kind, negotiable in dollars *outside* the community. To her, time and capital that are nonremunerable in this external currency are merely another form of cultural tax. Given her likely "*suelo al cielo*" aspirations, it is a tax that probably has negative utility. From her point of view, an optimized and efficient relationship is, naturally, one that yields the maximum profit with the least investment.

To see this Catholic-Protestant distinction translated into *huipil* design, take, for example, the distinction between making a design by the *recogido* technique versus making the same design by *pepinado*. *Recogido* means inserting the brocading threads with a bone needle and by tedious finger-picking. Alternatively, the same design can be created by *pepinado*, simply holding apart sets of threads with a stick that is inserted horizontally through the warp. Only someone who is fairly expert in weaving—which of course would include virtually all San Antonio weavers and virtually no tourist buyers—can detect the difference between a design that is *pepinado* versus one that is *recogido*.[21] To a Catholic, the piece is better if it is *recogido* since it has more time and care invested in it. To a Protestant, the surplus investments impart no added cash value, unless she plans to sell it to a neighbor. The extra effort represents only a time loss. To weave a design *recogido* when one could do nearly the same thing *pepinado* is, flatly, a bit stupid.

The point here is that a *huipil*, as a kind of production function equation, is a graphic expression of wealth. As suggested in the previous section, it can also serve as a map. In both respects, the *huipil* is an organized collection of signs and symbols. These symbolic meanings emanate deeply from the character of indigenous culture. Any San Antonio weaver knows how to read a *huipil* as surely and precisely as a geographer knows how to read a map or an econometrician knows how to read a Cobb-Douglas equation. And as that culture changes, even splits under the pressure of religious conversion, the woven texts rewrite themselves to express the deeper underlying changes in communal values and self-identity.

Weaving for Commerce

The fact that the symbolism of weaving in San Antonio should be more economic than mythic/cosmological may be less surprising when one considers how long commercial handweaving has existed in Mesoamerica. Weaving for commercial purposes is sometimes assumed to be a relatively new phenomenon, the corrupted modification of an older and purer tradition, vaguely the fault of tourists. There is, however, nothing recent about the sale of handwoven textiles. Commerce in textiles is probably as old as the weaving technology itself and closely parallels its evolution.

Fibers, feathers, dyes, and textiles were among the first items exchanged on the earliest pre-urban trade routes. By the florescence of the great cities in the Valley of Mexico in the tenth and eleventh centuries, large rectangular pieces of cotton cloth were well established as a medium of commercial exchange and as payment of tribute.

Aztec *pochteca,* the hereditary long-distance traders who traversed the Aztec empire, carried with them richly brocaded, multicolored textiles to exchange for cacao beans, gold, and copper hand-axes. Even Columbus, the first European tourist to the New World, was offered (and bought) textiles from the Chontal Yucatec traders he encountered in Guananja in 1502.[22]

The tradition of using lengths of cotton cloth (*manta*) for tribute payment survived the Conquest and continued during the colonial period. Woodrow Borah and Sherbourne Cook say that, next to maize, cotton *manta* was the most important item of tribute in the immediate post-Conquest period.[23] The extensive tributary records that the Spaniards kept during the colonial period recount in detail payments extracted from Indian weaving centers.[24] In fact, one might argue that the survival and persistence of pre-Hispanic handweaving into the modern era owes more to its convenience as a means of wealth extraction and payment of rent than it does to any cultural attachment to the use of the loom. In this sense, backstrap weaving is purely post-Hispanic, not an atavism.

Numerous investigators during this century have described the intense importance of trade, particularly in textiles, among the contemporary Mayan population.[25] In a modern economy characterized by scarcity of income-generating employment for rural Indian women, textile sales represent an important, if not unique, opportunity. In 1976, an economist and I analyzed the Guatemalan tourist sector and calculated that the yearly tourist expenditure on textiles supported the equivalent of about eighteen thousand full-time weaving jobs, or employment for about forty-five thousand part-time, semiprofessional weavers.[26]

In San Antonio, commerce in textiles is of great importance as a source of revenue and as a means of mobility for women. Invariably, "to sell them"—not aesthetic pleasure or the creation of symbolic texts—is the answer that women give to queries about reasons for weaving. As might be expected from the analysis of agricultural production (Chapter 5), Protestant and Catholic women relate very differently to the opportunities created for textile entrepreneurship. That matter is taken up in greater detail in the following chapter.

7

Textile Entrepreneurship and the Economics of Culture

IF ASKED why they weave, most women are likely to give a short, simple answer: to earn money. Yet earning money, too, is a culturally constituted act. By exploring the differences between Catholic and Protestant textile entrepreneurship, this chapter shows how wealth creation—the object of weaving as an economic activity—adheres to a cultural as well as an economic logic. For Catholics, this means the "logic of the *milpa*"; for Protestants, the logic of "*suelo al cielo*."

To put this argument into context, the following section first reports on the town's total output of weavings and then looks at the rates of return to individuals. To understand the overall workings of the textile sector, it is important to understand the hierarchy in rates of return from the many kinds of subactivities involved in weaving.

After setting forth some basic operating principles, the chapter then looks at the character of entrepreneurship. It expands on an idea raised in the previous chapter—that handwoven textiles can be either an expression *of* or a means *to* wealth. For Catholics, entrepreneurship makes sense in order to possess textiles—because they are an expression of cultural well-being and because they manifest Indian identity. Protestants, on the other hand, trade in textiles insofar as it helps them acquire nontextile capital.

Background: The Town's "Gross Textile Product" and Rates of Return to Individuals

The importance of weaving for San Antonio is suggested by Table 17, which shows textile output for 116 women. All in all, these women generated a six-month textile product of almost $10,000—from which an annual "Gross Textile Product" of about $207,000 can be extrapolated for the whole town.[1]

Despite this impressively high aggregate production, rates of return to individual weavers remain remarkably low. Even a highly skilled backstrap weaver can generally produce no more than a few inches of brocaded cloth per day. In fact, despite buttressing from the

Table 17. Six-Month Weaving Output for 116 Women: Number of Pieces and Their Value

Textile Type	Number of Pieces[a]	% of Total	Value[b]	% of Total
Huipil—highest quality	56	6	3,416	35
Huipil—second quality	13	1	663	7
Huipil—plain	10	1	201	2
Huipil—"tourist junk"	8	<1	170	2
Tzut—best quality	28	3	1,575	16
Tzut—plain	8	1	47	<1
Servilleta	74	8	463	5
Faja—narrow, ornamental	15	2	264	3
Faja—wide, plain	38	4	274	3
Chalina—large "wall hanging"	82	9	1,164	12
Large decorative loom	109	12	676	7
Medium decorative loom	271	30	610	6
Small decorative loom	191	21	181	2
Child's cap	3	<1	23	<1
Placemat set	5	<1	38	<1
Total	911	100	9,765	100

[a] Data on the number of pieces produced during six months were derived from information that the women supplied from memory for the period between the two major fiestas of the year, the Dulce Nombre de Jesús fiesta in January and the Fiesta de San Antonio in June. For most women, the two fiestas are major highlights of the year—deadlines for having weavings finished so they can be sold or worn. Most women are unlikely to make more than two or three "large" items during a six-month period, and they are not likely to forget them, so error in reporting is more likely to occur with smaller items. One source of error is the tendency of many women to exaggerate the quality of their textiles (in case the interviewer is secretly contemplating purchase). Even though standard pieces were shown to the women as "definitions" for the various items, probably not quite so many "first-class" huipiles and tzutes were made during these six months as are shown in the table.

[b] The value of textile production was determined by a four-step process. First, the range of woven products in the town was classified in a way that corresponded to weavers' thinking; then actual samples of each type were collected in order to "define terms" during interviews. Second, each sample was shown to a "panel" of seven tienda owners, who estimated its wholesale value; these estimates were then averaged. Third, women were asked how many of each type they had made between the fiesta of Dulce Nombre de Jesús and the titular fiesta—a six-month period that had just ended when most of these interviews were conducted. Finally, the predetermined values established for each piece were multiplied times the number of pieces reported.

"Gross Textile Product" extrapolates to the town production by the women in the sample (multiplied by two, for two six-month periods).

tourist market, weaving as a full-time activity is almost as poorly remunerated as the town's least profitable full-time activity, *petate*-making (see Chapter 3).

To better understand the rates of return that an individual weaver can expect from her labor (more or less, the shadow wage rate of an elderly woman's time), I asked my "Protestant weaving teacher," Doña Paola (shown in Figure 35 and described in Chapter 6), a hypothetical question: "If I wanted you to work on a daily basis in my *tienda*—weaving full-time and selling to tourists who came by—would you do it for such-and-such amount of money?"

She responded as follows.

SA:	DOÑA PAOLA:
". . . 25 cents per day?"	"No way. That's a joke."
". . . 35 cents per day?"	"No. You shouldn't try to take advantage of a poor lady like me."
". . . 45 cents per day?"	"Well, maybe, but . . ."
". . . 55 cents per day?"	"Maybe . . . I suppose I might."
". . . 75 cents per day?"	"¡*Con mucho gusto!*"

Even by the cost-of-living standards of San Antonio during the late 1970s, fifty-five to seventy-five cents per day was a barely adequate income. With that amount, however, Doña Paola supported herself and helped provide for three dependent grandchildren. Her family was among the very poorest in my seventy-four-household sample.

To put matters into perspective, Doña Paola's income as a weaver represented less than half the daily minimal wage for an agricultural *mozo* (about $1.50 in the late 1970s). Like most women who are nearly full-time weavers, she has virtually no assets other than her clothing and her ability to weave, so she has a limited range of choices on how to make a living. To get by, she spends five or six hours a day at the loom, supplemented with innumerable bits of this and that—hand-knotting textile fringes (by candlelight) for other weavers, washing clothing, occasionally teaching foreign students such as myself, and hand-spinning crude cotton for the small connoisseur market.

With such a low rate of return from primary production, weaving can provide only the barest of livelihoods. Like the subsistence farmer, the weaver must constantly and imaginatively find new ways to upgrade the value of whatever meager resources lie at hand. To the farmer, that may mean harvesting weeds for some offbeat purpose or planting worn-out slope land with a hardy crop; to the woman who manages a household, it may mean weaving a belt during two pre-dawn hours before she starts making tortillas, teaching a small child to use a warp board and weave crude *telarcitos*, or assembling rustic

Figure 35. Doña Paola: "75 cents a day?" "¡Con mucho gusto!"

Table 18. *Textile Marketing Strategies*

	Number of Weavers	% of Total
(1) Don't sell	20	17
(2) Infrequent sales to vendors	18	16
(3) Frequent sales to vendors	46	40
(4) Family *tienda*	20	17
(5) Direct sales to tourists	7	6
(6) *Tienda* & high-volume sales outside San Antonio	2	2
(7) Coop sales	2	2
Total	115	100

dolls out of corn husks and scraps of cloth. In human terms, it also means long hours, exhaustion, the need to forego her grandchildren's schooling, and drastic vulnerability to the ebb and flow and the whims of foreign tourists.

None of these choices is very attractive. So the women keep their eyes open for new ways to upgrade the value of their time. How? The best alternative is *not* to weave more or faster, but to become an entrepreneur. As every weaver knows, selling textiles that someone else makes is far more profitable than selling your own.

How can sales be most remunerative? Table 18 categorizes seven distinct approaches to the problem of marketing textiles. Lopping off Rows 1 ("Don't sell") and 7 ("Coop sales"),[2] the five remaining alternatives can be viewed as a continuum of desirability in marketing alternatives. That is, the strongest marketing position for a weaver is to own her own *tienda* and also maintain a high volume of sales outside of San Antonio (Row 6). However, that is not easy to do; it requires capital and contacts in Antigua or Guatemala City. The middle position on the continuum, a family-owned *tienda* in San Antonio (Row 4), is a relatively strong position if the flow of tourists is steady and capital is available to acquire the *sitio* and build an inventory. The worst marketing alternative is to have to sell wholesale to the local vendors (Rows 2 and 3). As shown, wholesaling in this fashion is the major outlet for 56 percent of the women. Without the means to acquire an inventory or a place from which to sell, these primary producers have no choice but to sell their product to local vendors who can manipulate their personal resources in order to become higher-level intermediaries.

Who Are the Entrepreneurs?

From the foregoing analysis, I had initially expected that wealth would be the principal predictor of textile entrepreneurship. A woman with capital can build an inventory, offering buyers a more attractive selection of goods; she can afford to turn down low offers for her goods; she can weather periods of slack tourism; she can afford transportation and accommodations for longer selling trips; she can afford to set up a *tienda* locale; and, most important, she can commission work from nonprivileged weavers who lack the options that capital makes possible.

One would expect textile entrepreneurs to come mainly from the ranks of the local well-to-do: those best able to capitalize an enterprise would exploit the obvious opportunity. My assumption was that a certain brand of entrepreneurialism ("penny capitalism") is so engrained in the Indian economy and culture that virtually any weaver would "move up" to small-scale commerce given the opportunities made possible by the fact of capital accumulation.

In fact, the situation is not so simple, as suggested in Table 19. "Resellers" in the table refers to people who sell textiles that they buy, as opposed to selling textiles that they make. These are the true textile entrepreneurs.

As previously discussed, land is the traditional basis for wealth in San Antonio and the nearby towns; and, as shown in Table 13, there is a strong and statistically significant association between land, wealth, and income, at least among Catholics. Surprisingly, Table 19 shows that the "low resellers" (the non-entrepreneurs) have an initial advantage in land. They own more land (Row 1), and their prop-

Table 19. *Characteristics of Textile Resellers*

	High Resellers	Low Resellers
(1) Number of *cuerdas* owned	11.2	14.2
(2) Land value ($)	1,999	2,590
(3) % of land planted	132	99
(4) Agricultural income ($)	479	272
(5) Livestock income ($)	27	6
(6) Family business income ($)	421	168
(7) Total income ($)	1,488	973
(8) Total wealth ($)	5,657	3,989

Data for 38 high resellers and 39 low resellers.

erty has a higher dollar value (Row 2). Yet despite this advantage, the "high resellers" are evidently more productive farmers, at least judged by the intensity of cultivation (Row 3) and by overall agricultural income (Row 4), which greatly exceeds that of the land-richer "low resellers."

Why? Entrepreneurship, it seems, is not simply a function of initial competitive position. The "high resellers" are persons whose minds, values, and activities are "geared" toward entrepreneurship, whatever the sector. As shown in the table, entrepreneurship is an across-the-board pattern of maximization: so even if members of this group start with less, they end up with more. For example, they earn more from animal husbandry (Row 5), probably by raising hogs for the market rather than chickens for domestic consumption. Their average business income (excluding textiles) is about two and one-half times that of the group of "low resellers" (Row 6). As measured both by total income and total wealth (Rows 7 and 8), they are substantially better off economically than the group of "low resellers."

Religion and Textile Entrepreneurship

Religious conversion, I believe, is the driving force behind this "re-gearing" that causes those in the less-favored position to financially overcome their initial competitive disadvantage. That, however, was not immediately evident. At the outset of my research, I had hypothesized that the incentives for textile entrepreneurship were ordered in such a way that increased access to capital would gradually lead weavers to replace their traditional production with commercial production (i.e., make easily salable tourist items rather than *huipiles* and *tzutes* for their own use), and then move from commercial production to reselling. Further, I assumed that assets accumulated in the form of traditional textiles were viewed as a kind of potential savings account and a natural starting point for a commercial inventory.

This hypothesis seemed to be confirmed by my first pass at the data. Running regression analyses on reselling, the variable that best represented entrepreneurial behavior,[3] generally confirmed that variables associated with wealth advantage (such as total wealth, land wealth, value of land per capita) were good indicators of propensity toward entrepreneurial behavior in the textile sector.

On the other hand, knowing and talking to weavers day-to-day gradually convinced me that entrepreneurial behavior was rooted in cultural behavior and was not simply a function of capital availability. This prompted me to rerun the regressions, using religion as an explanatory variable. By dichotomizing religion (0=Catholic; 1=

Table 20. *Sales Outlets for Catholic and Protestant Women* [a]

	(A) Does Not Sell	(B) Sells to Local Vendors	(C) Owns Tienda; Sells Direct to Tourists; High-Volume Wholesaler	(D) Sells to Coop
Catholic women Number in this category	13	59	18	2
(% of Total)	(14)	(64)	(20)	(2)
Protestant women Number in this category	6	4	11	—
(% of Total)	(29)	(19)	(52)	—

[a] Data for 92 Catholic and 21 Protestant women.

Protestant) and adding "years of school," which also appeared to be an important factor, an impressive amount of the total variance in textile entrepreneurship was "explained." As expected, wealth was highly correlated with entrepreneurial behavior—but religion turned out to be even more important, and years of school bore little relation.[4]

The conclusion to be drawn is that wealth is indeed an important factor in explaining entrepreneurial mobility; but a more important factor is a cultural understanding (captured by the Catholic/Protestant religious distinction) of what capital means and why one wants to be an entrepreneur in the first place.

How do Catholic and Protestant women differ in their thinking about and their responses to the micro-opportunities offered in the weaving sector?

In the first place, if Protestant women weave at all, they are almost certain to weave commercially. Unlike Catholics, for whom textiles *are* wealth, textiles for Protestants are a *means* to wealth. If they weave, they do so in clear relation to their access to a particular kind of sales opportunity. By inference, this is suggested in Table 20, which compares where Protestant and Catholic weavers sell what they produce.

The table indicates that Protestant women are relatively more likely not to sell at all (Column A); but if they do, more than half manage to sell within one of the favored environments: their own *tiendas*, direct to tourists, or as high-volume wholesalers (Column C). Although relatively more Catholics weave and sell, nearly two-thirds market from the less-favored environment (Column B): they wholesale their product to the *tienderas* (a disproportionate number of whom are Protestant of course), who then resell to tourists.

The implication here is not necessarily that Catholics are not "good businesswomen," but perhaps that they are less focused on textile sales as an exclusive business activity. For the typical Catholic family, following the cultural and economic logic of the *milpa*, weaving is likely to be carried out for two basic reasons: first, to create symbolic objects which in themselves represent wealth, even if that kind of wealth cannot easily be converted to wealth and power outside of the village frame of reference; and, second, to provide supplemental income that fits into the optimizing pattern that characterizes the Catholic economy. Rather than reorient their lives around the fact of the family business, they tend to weave steadily to fill in their least-productive hours with a reasonably lucrative activity. By contrast, the Protestants are generally maximizers, not optimizers. They weave as if they were cash-crop farmers.

The fundamental differences in approach to textile activity are illustrated in Table 21, comparing the statistical means for nine variables according to religion. The variables are listed in ascending order according to the Catholic/Protestant ratio. That is, the "most Protestant" variables are listed first; the "most Catholic" variables are listed last. In the first three rows—at the "Protestant end" of the scale—are the variables that most reflect entrepreneurial activity: value of the family's commercial textile inventory, the family's income from textiles that were bought to be resold, and total income from textile sales. The mean values for the first two variables are more than four times greater for the Protestants than for the Catholics.

In contrast, in the last two rows—at the "Catholic end" of the scale—are value from production of traditional textiles and the most "Catholic" of activities, production of *petates*, which virtually no Protestants make.

Toward the middle of the scale, more or less in one-to-one ratio, are variables for which Protestants and Catholics produce similar dollar amounts—though not necessarily for the same reasons. For example, both kinds of families produce a similar amount of commercial textiles (Row 5); but, as Table 20 shows, Protestant women tend to produce commercial textiles in order to maximize returns in family *tiendas* or other commercially oriented, touristic textile enterprises. Catholics who produce commercial textiles, on the other

Table 21. *Catholics and Protestants in the Textile Sector: Variables Ranked by Catholic/Protestant Ratio*[a]

	(A) Catholic Average ($)	(B) Protestant Average ($)	(C) Catholic/ Protestant Ratio
(1) Value of family's inventory of commercial textiles	66	315	.21
(2) Family's income from textiles that it bought and resold	15	68	.22
(3) Total income from textile sales	64	111	.58
(4) Value of *huipil* inventory	194	200	.97
(5) Value of commercial textiles that family made	75	76	.99
(6) Value of family's inventory of traditional textiles	362	358	1.01
(7) Family's income from textiles that it made and sold	48	43	1.12
(8) Value of traditional textiles that family made	65	17	3.82
(9) Income from *petates*	17	1	17.00

[a] Data from survey of 74 households.

hand, tend to be poorer women who sell their products to intermediaries, which makes sense if the family is directing itself toward stabilizing and then building upon a *milpa*-based family economy. Row 6 of Table 21 shows that Protestants and Catholics possess a similar average value of "traditional textiles." While many Protestant women continue to own and wear high-quality *huipiles, tzutes,* and old-style *fajas* (see, for example, Margarita López, shown in Figure 36), many others own none at all, or else own only those that they intend to sell (for example, Margarita López' daughters). Ownership of traditional textiles among Catholic women is far more even: women tend to own a few highest-quality textiles, which they normally have made themselves and have no intention of selling short of a financial emergency.[5]

The contrasting patterns of entrepreneurialism are illustrated in Table 22, which shows the correlations between total family income from textiles and the portion derived from textiles made by the family versus the portion derived from textiles that the family bought to

Figure 36. Margarita López, flawlessly presented to the outside world.

Table 22. *Correlations between Total Family Income from Textiles and Related Variables*

	(A) Income from Textiles Made	(B) Income from Textiles Bought for Resale
Catholic family textile income	.90***	.35**
Protestant family textile income	.12	.95***

*p ≤ .05
**p ≤ .01
***p ≤ .001

resell. What this table says, in brief, is that Catholics earn money from textiles as producers, and Protestants as sellers. Among Protestants, "income from textiles" is virtually synonymous with profit from textiles bought for resale. There is virtually no correlation between family income from textiles and family income from *making* textiles. Although there is a positive and significant correlation among Catholics between family textile income and income from reselling, the correlation with income from primary production is much stronger. It is true that many poor Protestant women, like Doña Paola (Figure 35), earn their living almost entirely from their own textiles and almost never have the cash to purchase products for resale. But their incomes are so small compared to that of the wealthy Protestant *tienderas*, like Florentina Carmona (Figure 23), that they barely affect the direction and strength of these correlations.

Table 23 illustrates how, among Protestants, textile entrepreneurship is a pattern carried over to other sectors. The table shows the correlations between bought-for-resale textiles and various related measures of wealth and income. What is significant is that among Catholics textile reselling seems to bear virtually no relation to the degree of wealth (in the sense of hard capital). For Catholics, textile entrepreneurship is additive; it stabilizes rather than changes the basic productive system. Among Protestants, however, capital is far more fungible. Capital is transferred laterally from sector to sector; a surplus here is used to create and expand an opportunity there.

This kind of cross-tacking from sector to sector can be described in quantitative terms and captured with statistical techniques such as correlation matrices and regression analysis. But complicated

Table 23. *Correlations between Income from Textiles Bought for Resale and Related Variables*

	(A)	(B)	(C)	(D)
			Machinery, Vehicles,	
	Cuerdas Owned	Land Value	Business Inventory	Total Wealth
Catholic income from textiles bought for resale	−.15	−.11	−.10	−.09
Protestant income from textiles bought for resale	.73**	.68**	.92***	.92***

*p ≤ .05
**p ≤ .01
***p ≤ .001

analysis should not obscure the human content of what is happening. Looked at in local terms, the Protestant tendency to transfer capital from sector to sector (illustrated in Table 23) is simply the working out of the *"suelo al cielo"* story (see Chapter 5). Starting the journey with his or her feet on the earth (or in the dirt, to lend the proper pejorative connotation), the spiritual-cum-economic traveler aspires upward. Then, on either the spiritual or the economic ladder, it's two steps forward and one back on the unsteady ascent toward salvation.

Not all persons, of course, are quite so normative as the generalized Protestant and Catholic "types" described here. Most probably are not. In reality, most human (as opposed to statistical) Protestants and Catholics are complicated blends of both "types."

Yet the point behind this microscopic analysis is that empirically observable Catholic/Protestant differences such as these in the textile sector tend to take hold and repeat themselves in other economic sectors and other domains of behavior. Not every Protestant businessperson is necessarily a spiritual traveler in the *"suelo al cielo"* sense; an irreligious son may just have learned a set of business assumptions from his father, never himself having seriously struggled with the temptations of alcohol or the passionately seductive drama of an Easter procession. But as these economic differences are reinforced through generations by religious doctrine, family values, and external pressures such as growing landlessness, they take on a self-reinforcing coherence as a pattern of cultural behavior. Slowly, the social, economic, and psychological anchorings of the village are knocked askew. So that when an Edgardo Robertson, an Efraín Ríos Montt, or a Vinicio Cerezo arrives on the scene, he meets a world that has ever less in common with the stolid Indianness of past generations.

8

Conclusion

WITH CONQUISTADOR Pedro de Alvarado himself as the founder of the town, San Antonio is in every sense a product of "colonial relations." Its initial "Indianness" was more the Spaniards' creation than the Indians'. Yet over the years, the descendants of those slaves and captives who were settled in San Antonio recreated Indianness in order to meet *their* needs. They built a society that gave to the Hispanic mainstream what it had to but provided the villagers with a stable and dignified culture.

Today, the equilibrium of the town is fractured by a complex bombardment of twentieth-century forces. As a result, Indianness is under siege and changing. This change is probably different from and more profound than any that has previously occurred in the town's 450 years because it affects the community's very idea of itself—who people think they are, what they think their community is and means. It is this change that has opened the new receptivity to Protestantism, not only in San Antonio but throughout the Guatemalan highlands.

Such receptivity, I believe, begins with the stresses and strains that are pulling apart the *milpa*-based economy. As analyzed here, the *milpa* is both the processor of resources and the producer of subsistence, but more broadly it is a metaphor for the "logic" of traditional Indian culture. As a set of ideas, the logic of the *milpa* and indigenous Catholic religious ideology are inseparable.

Most *milpa* farmers now find themselves under pressure. Individually, they have less land and more dependents than ever, so making a living is harder and harder. On the other hand, for a significant minority, things are getting better.

Taken together, these two trends mean that wealth and class differentiation are rising. This undercuts the traditional cultural equilibrium, which was based on social egalitarianism (or at least the assumption of shared poverty).

Most San Antonio families today find themselves in one of two positions. First, they can continue to operate within a traditional *milpa* economy, even without much land. As a way to manage micro-quantities of resources or as a model for developing off-farm activity, the *milpa* adapts remarkably well. As things worsen, farmers can compensate by crop intensification, renting land from their neighbors, wage labor, and supplemental business enterprise; with luck, they can hold on. But the *milpa* has limits: a minimum threshold of resources is always necessary. It also has a major disadvantage. The *milpa* is better suited to adjustment to perpetual poverty than to commercial production.

So the traditional economy itself has bred a second set of people who no longer fully fit and now increasingly stand outside its boundaries. These include both the landless who have no reasonable hope of surviving as farmers and, at the other extreme, those better-off individuals who sense and want greater economic opportunity. These people find new mobility within the newly class-differentiated local economy, or are drawn toward the world beyond the village. They begin to shift from lower-output to higher-output agriculture—that is, they become "maximizers" (cash croppers) rather than "optimizers" (*milpa* farmers).

Protestantism (or Protestant-like brands of Catholicism) finds fertile ground for converts among those who are alienated from the traditional economy. To those who are economically marginalized by an abject poverty or socially marginalized by increased entrepreneurial activity, Protestantism says: Come to me.

The mechanics and ideology of wealth accumulation—the "*suelo al cielo*" trek—are discussed and illustrated in several sections of this work. The practical outcome—better economic performance by Protestants—is shown first for agriculture and then developed in more detail for textile entrepreneurship. The case study of textiles illustrates how the Catholic and Protestant cultural paths diverge. For Catholics, handweaving is a kind of celebration of the integrative power of the identity of Indianness. But for Protestants, handweaving and textile entrepreneurship are a path leading away from Indianness and on to a different kind of salvation.

Much of this book has centered upon economic analysis. Yet one need only attend prayer in any village church—watch the faces and listen to the singing—to know that Protestantism means far more than just rationalizing economic gain.

But what then?

For nearly ten years I have been thinking about Edgardo Robertson's advice on how to get an Indian's attention—how to talk to Indians about God. Considering that nearly a quarter of Guatemala's

Indian population is now Protestant, certainly *something* has gotten their attention. But was it God? Was it theatrics like Edgardo's? Was it the earthquake? Was it a zealot evangelical president, army repression, a guerrilla war?

Perhaps all these, and also something more subtle: each individual translating the growing chaos of a disordered world into his or her consciousness. Was it fear of chaos that so riveted attention?

In an earlier chapter, I described some Protestants as "anorexic" savers. "Anorexia" may be apt psychologically as well as economically, for it suggests the obsessive, overcompensating desire to tame what is feared to be out of control.

It is not hard to understand why contemporary Guatemala, especially for poor Indians, should be threatening and in desperate need of taming. It is a place where the earth itself goes mad and can shake villages apart; where gunmen tear into homes in the middle of the night (or day); where sick children die of infections instead of going to hospitals; where livelihood becomes ever more precarious with each passing year; where the old rules and beliefs seem ever less authoritative, ever less comforting.

In such a world, how does anyone feel in control? For poor Indians, certainly not by taming the earth, the army, poverty, or the loss of a culture.

For some Indians, Protestantism may provide one kind of answer. Each person can make his or her body the battlefield and, perhaps, triumph over chaos. On this battlefield, all the cruelty and disorder of the outside world is embodied in the living Satan; and although Satan wins round after round, he can be vanquished by humanly possible assertions of will.

On the soul's battlefield, whoever is powerless becomes powerful. Whatever the personal demons—lust, drink, profligacy with wealth—they can be rejected; and the greater the struggle, the greater the victory. Salvation through self-denial represents a kind of human triumph—in the long run because it can lead to wealth and a new stability, and in the short run as proof that any control is possible.

Amid the pain of struggle, the tambourines go on banging. A new Christian warrior's spirit is moved, and he shouts for joy.

Anorexia. A cruel and ironic metaphor. But is that perhaps the meaning of the tear-stained faces of the Protestant Indians of Guatemala?

Notes

1. How to Get an Indian's Attention

1. I have changed his name and blurred the details of this story slightly in order to spare "Edgardo" recognition and possible embarrassment.

2. The effects of political violence in San Antonio are described in Sheldon Annis, "A Story from a Peaceful Town," in *Harvest of Violence: Guatemala's Indians and the Counterinsurgency War*, ed. Robert M. Carmack.

3. The fraudulence of the 1974 election was well documented at the time by the foreign press, i.e., *New York Times, Miami Herald*; and it has been well documented since.

4. Ríos Montt's conversion and personal life are well described in his biography, *He Gives—He Takes Away*, by Joseph Anfuso and David Sczeponski.

5. A discussion of the rise of the guerrilla movement and the army's counterinsurgency effort is contained in Jim Handy, *Gift of the Devil: A History of Guatemala*; see especially pp. 244–281. For an analysis of Guatemala's successive periods of peace and terror, see Gabriel Aguilera Peralta, Jorge Romero Imery, et al., *Dialécticas del terror en Guatemala*.

6. Phillip Berryman, *The Religious Roots of Rebellion: Christians in Central American Revolutions*, p. 7. See especially pp. 173–180 for the church's pastoral and political work among the poor. For other insider/outsider views, see Luisa Frank and Philip Wheaton, *Indian Guatemala: Path to Liberation*, and Thomas R. Melville, "The Catholic Church in Guatemala, 1944–1982," *Cultural Survival Quarterly* 7 (Spring 1983): 23–27. On the political implications of liberation theology, see Penny Lernoux's moving account, *Cry of the People*.

7. This is my own conclusion, based on visits to the area—especially on interviews conducted around Nebáj in October 1984.

8. See Shelton H. Davis and Julie Hodson, *Witness to Political Violence in Guatemala: The Suppression of a Rural Development Movement* (1982); Inter-American Commission on Human Rights, *Report on the Situation of Human Rights in the Republic of Guatemala* (1983); Americas Watch Committee, *Guatemala: A Nation of Prisoners* (1984); United Nations Commission on Human Rights, *Situation of Human Rights in Guatemala: Report Prepared by the Special Rapporteur, Viscount Colville of Colcross* (1983 and 1984); Christine Krueger and Kjell Enge, *Security and Development Conditions in the Guatemalan Highlands* (1985); and British Parliamentary Hu-

man Rights Group, *Bitter and Cruel: Report of a Mission to Guatemala* (1985).

9. This includes Mayor Carmelo Santos and Alcides López Hernández, to whom this book is dedicated. The circumstances of their deaths is described in Annis, "A Story from a Peaceful Town."

In the late 1970s, on a consultancy for AID, I wrote a humorous memo called "Yo soy líder," which chided AID and private voluntary organizations for creating a popular new occupational category in the countryside. Virtually any village male when asked what he did in his particular village would opportunistically respond, "Yo soy líder." Traveling for the Inter-American Foundation in late 1984, I found that the joke had turned sour indeed. No one other than army-appointed heads of civil defense committees (generally army veterans) would claim organizational membership, much less leadership. In response to queries, people immediately brought me into the presence of proper authorities, lest they be accused of establishing independent relations with outsiders. I quickly stopped asking questions, realizing that people feared I was adding names to a hit list.

10. On the dismantling of the organized rural development movement, see especially Davis and Hodson, *Witness to Political Violence*, Ch. 3.

11. In Guatemala, the term "reconstruction" initially referred to reconstruction after the 1976 earthquake. A centralized institutional mechanism was created to handle the huge inflow of disaster relief funds. The National Reconstruction Committee waned in the early 1980s, but was revived for reconstruction from the effects of war. Through means of the *coordinadora* system, the activities of government social service ministries, foreign private voluntary organizations, and village self-help committees were all brought under army scrutiny and centralized government control. In a sense, the village civil defense patrols were the bottom rung of the ladder.

12. As will be discussed in succeeding chapters (especially Chapter 4), Protestantism also attracted many of the poorest and least economically successful village Indians.

13. Of course, many Catholics belonged to and positively identified with civil defense patrols; and many Protestants belonged to and identified with coops. What I wish to suggest here is that there is only a kind of rough congruence between Protestantism and the government, and Catholicism and the guerrillas. In Guatemala, the idea of an "evangelical guerrilla" would be absurd; a "Catholic guerrilla" is not. Since *everyone* had to participate in the rural civil defense patrols in the early 1980s (an estimated 700,000 men), one cannot easily distinguish Protestant from Catholic participation. Yet common sense suggests that had 700,000 men psychologically identified with the guerrillas—with no ideological counterforce, such as that provided by the evangelicals—the government would certainly have had second thoughts about arming them.

14. On traditional Guatemalan antipathy for involvement of the Church in state affairs and the unusual repression of the Church that began with the liberal regime in 1871, see Richard N. Adams, *Crucifixion by Power*, Ch. 5, "The Renaissance of the Guatemalan Church," pp. 278–317.

15. To Guatemalans, the implication here is that, unlike his predecessors, he had neither the inclination to leave nor the brains and venality to have stolen enough to lead a stylish life in Miami. To many Guatemalans, there is a childish innocence about that.

16. Robert Carmack, ed., *Harvest of Violence: Guatemala's Indians and the Counterinsurgency*, presents a set of village case studies that illustrate the cultural toll of the violence of the early 1980s.

17. A census map and sampling frame were drawn up with ten tracts of approximately equal size. A proportionate number of households were drawn from each tract. A perplexing decision was whether to select a purely random sample or allow for limited "choices" among several households within a narrow range of those suggested by the sampling procedure. The difficulty was that our survey instrument was highly detailed. Although painstakingly designed to minimize awkward questions, it called for information that was personal, sometimes sensitive, and required that the interviewer establish a certain amount of *confianza* with his or her informant. All the interviewers concurred that information from people we knew or were "referred to" was more likely to be complete and truthful. To take advantage of established *confianza*, we devised a somewhat complicated formula for classifying people as "friends," "referrals," and "unknowns." Within narrow ranges of acceptable alternatives we gave preference to "friends" and "referrals," though the three categories tended to balance out naturally. Among us, we knew a great many families in the town and we made friends and contacts in many diverse ways. With the apparent exception of knowing a disproportionate number of *tienda* owners (at whose stores we shopped) and persons who wished to sell textiles to foreigners, we could see no clear-cut bias inherent in our selection technique. Subsequent analysis of the three kinds of informants showed that "friends" (followed by "referrals") did have noticeably higher incomes and greater assets, but I do not know whether that is because the set of informants who were friends or referrals were "richer" or whether they simply gave us more reliable information. I suspect the latter and strongly believe that the probable gain in accuracy was well worth the slight loss in statistical purity.

2. Colony of a Colony

1. My thanks to archaeologists Ed Torres and Edwin Shook for consultations in this matter.

2. Archaeologist William Swezey, of the Centro para Investigaciones Regionales de Mesoamérica, disagrees that the valley was unoccupied. He notes the difficulty of distinguishing Late Classic from Postclassic peasant utilitarian ware. He believes that the valley was too rich agriculturally to have been uninhabited prior to the Conquest and that the resident Indians probably died or fled from Spanish control. These and other matters relating to the initial settlement of this area are touched upon in a forthcoming volume by George Lovell, Christopher Lutz, and William Swezey on the colonial demography of southern Guatemala. The best and most up-to-date

source on the archaeology of this region is Fredrick Lange and Doris Stone, eds., *The Archaeology of Lower Central America.*

3. The place name "Quinizilapa," used throughout this text, is today largely forgotten, a relic (with several orthographic variants) from colonial and nineteenth-century documents. The most common alternative spelling is "Quilizinapa," though Quinizilapa is probably closer to the original term, which in Nahuatl means "place of the intermittent waters" (Alfonso de Molina, *Vocabulario en lengua castellana y mexicana,* p. 90).

4. The term *milpa,* in this historical sense, does *not* mean a garden-like plot of corn and beans, the contemporary meaning of the word used in the previous chapter and the rest of this text.

5. For a more complete account of the founding of the Quinizilapa towns and the settlement of the region, see Christopher Lutz, *Historia sociodemográfica de Santiago de Guatemala, 1541–1773.* More complete surveys of colonial history are provided in Murdo MacLeod, *Spanish Central America: A Socioeconomic History, 1520–1720,* and Miles L. Wortman, *Government and Society in Central America, 1680–1840.* Both have excellent bibliographies on colonial history. For a broader, well-annotated overview of Central American history, see Ralph Lee Woodward, Jr., *Central America: A Nation Divided.*

6. Archivo General de Indias, Seville (cited hereafter as AGI), "Los indios que eran esclavos . . ." (1576), leg. 54, fol. 29. For contextual background on the Conquest and colonization periods, see also William Sherman, *Forced Native Labor in Sixteenth-Century Central America,* and Peter Gerhard, *The Southeast Frontier of New Spain.*

7. AGI, "Los indios," fol. 29.

8. Lutz, *Historia sociodemográfica.*

9. Curiously, in available sixteenth-century documents, there is no specific reference to these people as "Guatimaltecas," the term then used to describe Cakchiquel speakers who were descended from the inhabitants of the destroyed Cakchiquel capital at nearby Iximché (near modern Tecpán), and who were among the principal inhabitants of Spanish Guatemala. Nor is there reference to previous native inhabitants (Cakchiquel-speaking or otherwise) in the valley itself.

In fact, Cakchiquel was apparently the second non-native language introduced to the newly settled Indians. The first was Nahuatl. As early as the mid-sixteenth century, Indians writing to the King of Spain required a translator who spoke the "Mexican language" as well as the emerging local language, "Achí" (see AGI, "Los indios," fol. 9.) Although Achí is a distinct Mayan language spoken today in the Rabinal area of Baja Verapaz (and formerly in the northwestern zone of El Salvador), in the sixteenth century it had a generic meaning of "the people" and probably referred to the language that eventually evolved into the Cakchiquel dialect now spoken in the region.

10. Rodolfo Stavenhagen, "Classes, Colonialism, and Acculturation," in *Masses in Latin America,* ed. Irving L. Horowitz, p. 269.

11. This term was popularized in the anthropological literature in Eric Wolf, "Closed Corporate Communities in Mesoamerica and Central Java," *Southwestern Journal of Anthropology* 13 (1957): 1–18; and idem, *Sons of the Shaking Earth.* Virginia Lathbury analyzes San Antonio as a "closed corporate community" in "Textiles as the Expression of an Expanding World View: San Antonio Aguas Calientes" (M.A. thesis, University of Pennsylvania, 1974).

12. Two now-classic and much-discussed works that have shaped this particular interpretation of Guatemalan social history are Severo Martínez Peláez, *La patria del criollo: Ensayo de interpretación de la realidad colonial guatemalteca,* and Carlos Guzmán Böckler and Jean-Loup Herbert, *Guatemala: Una interpretación histórico-social.*

13. Christopher Lutz, "Historia de la población de la Parroquia de San Miguel Dueñas, 1530–1770," *Mesoamérica,* 2, no. 2 (June 1981): 64–82; MacLeod, *Spanish Central America,* especially pp. 98–100; Robert M. Carmack, John Early, and Christopher Lutz, eds., *The Historical Demography of Highland Guatemala;* Lutz, *Historia sociodemográfica,* Appendix VI, pp. 743–752.

14. The view that the present-day Indian society, which is often called "traditional," acquired many of its features during the nineteenth century after being relatively stable for the preceding two hundred years has been discussed by many anthropologists. For classic statements, see Oliver LaFarge, "Maya Ethnology: The Sequence of Cultures," in *The Maya and Their Neighbors,* ed. C. L. Hay et al., pp. 281–291; Manning Nash, "The Impact of Mid-Nineteenth Century Economic Change upon the Indians of Middle America," in *Conference on Race and Class in Latin America,* ed. Magnus Morner, pp. 173–180; and Richard N. Adams, "Cultural Components of Central America," *American Anthropologist* 58 (1956): 881–907.

15. On this subject, see Lutz, *Historia sociodemográfica,* and idem, "Population History of San Miguel Dueñas, ca. 1530–1770," in *The Historical Demography of Highland Guatemala,* ed. Robert M. Carmack, John Early, and Christopher Lutz.

16. Manuel Rubio Sánchez has written extensively on the histories of several important export commodities. On indigo, see *Historia de añil o xiquilite en Centro América;* on cacao, "El cacao," *Anales de la Sociedad de Geografía e Historia de Guatemala* 31 (1958): 81–129; on cochineal, "La grana o cochinilla," *Antropología e Historia de Guatemala* 13 (1961): 15–46. On coffee, see J. C. Cambranes, *Coffee and Peasants: The Origins of the Modern Plantation Economy in Guatemala, 1853–1897,* and more generally, idem, *Introducción a la historia agrícola de Guatemala.* The standard and most comprehensive overview of Guatemalan economic history is Valentín Solórzano Fernández, *Evolución económica de Guatemala.*

17. Unlike those Indian settlements that sprawl in dispersed clusters over large areas (generally farther north and west in the highlands), San Antonio is unambiguously nucleated. Virtually the entire population of two *municipios* lives in the dense node formed by San Antonio, Santa Catarina Bara-

hona, and San Andrés Ceballos. For more information about the characteristics and classification of Guatemalan cities by size, see Bernard Hackel, *Urban Poverty in Guatemala;* and Robert Fox and Jerrold Huguet, *Population and Urbanization to the Year 2000 in Central America and Panama.*

18. This statement was true in 1979, when fieldwork for this study was carried out. When I visited San Antonio in 1982, however, a small refugee settlement had formed on the eastern edge of the town. The residents were mostly rural women whose husbands had been killed or had fled during sweeps by the army above the town.

19. The original Catholic church, an imposing eighteenth-century edifice, was almost completely destroyed by the earthquake that devastated central Guatemala in February 1976. The massive ruins of the old church have been torn down and are gradually being replaced. The town's tiny municipal buildings were also leveled by the earthquake. Since 1980, three small structures have been erected in the plaza to replace them.

20. In 1977–1979, the number of tourist *tiendas* was at an all-time high. Between the 1976 earthquake and the escalation of political violence around 1980, many families set up *tiendas* with loans from the Corporación Financiera Nacional (CORFINA), a national development bank that loaned money to artisans as part of an earthquake recovery program financed through the Inter-American Development Bank. The number of tourist stalls greatly declined when tourism fell. As tourism has recovered, the number of tourist stalls has not necessarily increased, since a few entrepreneurial families have been able to achieve a relatively monopolistic grip on the local tourist industry (see Chapters 6 and 7).

21. For an analysis of the Almolonga and Zuñil cases, see, for example, Carol Smith, "Production in Western Guatemala: A Test of Von Thünen and Boserup," in *Formal Methods in Economic Anthropology,* ed. Stuart Plattner.

22. San Miguel Dueñas, until the draining of the lake in 1928, was the principal town within the region. In recent years, however, San Miguel has become functionally and administratively integrated into the higher-altitude coffee-growing zone, which stretches upward along the slopes of the Acatenango volcano and towards Yepocapa.

23. Population projection based on tables in Rodolfo Poitevin, *República de Guatemala: Departamento de Sacatepéquez, población calculada, año 1972–1980.*

24. Marina Flores and Emma Reh, "Estudios de hábitos dietéticos en poblaciones de Guatemala, III, San Antonio Aguas Calientes y su aldea San Andrés Ceballos," *Boletín de la Oficina Sanitaria Panamericana,* Publicaciones de INCAP, Suplemento No. 2 (1955); pp. 149–162.

25. The *cuerda* is a local, and highly variable, measure, equivalent to 40 × 40 *varas,* about 1,600 square meters.

In 1874, José María Navarro reported 16 *caballerías,* about 6,400 *cuerdas.* There were 398 persons in Santiago Zamora according to the 1880 census. In other words, 100 years ago there were theoretically 80 *cuerdas* of land available per family—probably ten times the amount of land now available per family. See José María Navarro, *Memorias de San Miguel Dueñas.*

26. The term *mestizo*, which is not commonly used in Guatemala, is sometimes employed to describe the people of San Lorenzo. Locally, the term implies "mixed blood," a mildly disdainful way of saying that a person has Indian blood but lacks the cultural integrity of being Indian. While the term *ladino* suggests class hierarchy based on race, in this area *mestizo* simply suggests alienation from cultural roots.

27. See Cambranes, *Coffee and Peasants.*

28. Navarro, *Memorias,* p. 153.

29. The demographic history of these towns is discussed by Lutz, *Historia sociodemográfica;* idem, "Historia de la poblacion"; idem, "Population History."

30. The residents of one tiny, all-*ladino* hamlet of nearby San Andrés Itzapa, Xeparquíy—which, like San Lorenzo el Cubo is virtually landless— have found their economic niche by specializing in transport as *arrieros* (mule drivers).

31. The depopulation of this area was accelerated during the political violence of 1980–1981 when government forces swept through the area, torturing men and carrying out exemplary executions to discourage rural support for the clandestine political action group CUC and the insurgent fraction ORPA.

32. In San Antonio, *mozo* generally conveys the sense of "day laborer"; the term carries less implication of servility than it does elsewhere in Latin America. The term *peón* carries with it some sense of indenture and personal obligation. A *peón* works someone else's land—and generally does that person's bidding—as a servant, principally in exchange for room and board. A *colono* is someone who has usufruct on a designated plot of land in exchange for a relatively fixed labor obligation. The term is more often applied on the large coffee, cotton, and cattle *fincas* of the Pacific coast than on the relatively small landholdings of San Antonio farmers. *Mozo* is the most generic of the three terms, which can at times be used interchangeably.

33. John Early, "Municipios Recommended as Sites of Experimental Programs," Appendix C, in "The Family Planning Program among the Indian Population of Guatemala" (study prepared by the American Public Health Association). Other *municipios* with similarly high levels of female Indian literacy are the nearby Sacatepéquez *municipios* of San Bartolomé Milpas Altas and the contiguous *municipio* of Santa Catarina Barahona.

34. República de Guatemala, Dirección General de Estadística, *VII Censo de Población, 1973,* ser. 3, vol. 1.

35. Ibid., p. xxxviii.

36. Sheldon Annis and Elena Hurtado, "Improving Family Planning Programs in the Highlands of Guatemala: A Case Study of the Department of El Quiché," for the American Public Health Association.

37. Despite this impressively high level of female literacy, there is still a substantial gap between males and females. In nearly every age category, the

male literacy rate is approximately double that of females. In part, this gap reflects the fact that boys in San Antonio are generally able to stay in school longer than girls. Both literacy and school attendance are slightly higher among girls in the early years. The female drop-out rate begins to rise after the second grade, while boys tend to remain in school.

38. Navarro, *Memorias*, p. 156.

39. Nima Yá was opened in the early 1920s under the direction of William Cameron Townsend, the first long-term Protestant missionary in the Cakchiquel area. Over the years the school has softened its explicit proselytizing, so many children of Catholic families now attend. Many Nima Yá graduates have left San Antonio to receive further education, including its best-known alumnus, Elena Trejo, an orphan who became the first woman, first Indian physician in Guatemala. (Under threats to her life, she had to flee the country in the early 1960s when she attempted to practice medicine as an Indian among Indians.)

40. Navarro, *Memorias*, p. 149; Instituto Indigenista Nacional, *San Antonio Aguas Calientes: Síntesis socio-económico de una comunidad indígena*, p. 32; Flores and Reh, "Estudios de hábitos dietéticos," p. 151.

41. According to my field survey, which included 409 persons, about 70 percent of the population are fully bilingual. Another 20 percent claim to understand Cakchiquel but not to speak it very well. About 8 percent are monolingual in Spanish (mostly children of ladinoized Indian families or children of Indian parents who are not native to San Antonio). Fewer than 1 percent claim to understand Spanish but not to speak it very well, and only 0.3 percent (one very elderly woman) is monolingual in Cakchiquel.

3. The Economy of a "Rich" Indian Town

1. Other "rich" towns are Patzún and Comalapa in the Department of Chimaltenango, San Pedro Sacatepéquez in San Marcos, and Almolonga and Zuñil in Quezaltenango.

2. Total family income was computed as the sum of U.S. dollar values of: the net value of all agricultural crops (commercial and domestic); adult male and adult female wage income from sources outside the household; income from any household-based business enterprise; wage contributions from children's nonhousehold work; income from small-scale vegetable marketing by women; income from *petate* (mat) production; income from sale or maturation of animals; and profit from sale of textiles to tourists. My estimate of total income is about twice that of a previous researcher, Julia Marina Arreola Hernández ("Diagnóstico de la situación del grupo materno-infantil, año 1975, San Antonio Aguas Calientes, Sacatepéquez" [Thesis, University of San Carlos, 1976]). For the year 1975, she estimates total family income at $519 and per capita income at $104. She does not elaborate her methods, but I infer from similar medical thesis research conducted in Guatemala that she used a closed-ended questionnaire that simply asked, "What is your total family income?" I assume that my income estimate is higher because I quantified a wider range of "micro-incomes," not because

the economic situation in the town improved substantially in the three-year interval between her research and mine.

3. Total family wealth was computed as the sum of dollar values of: all plots of agricultural land (value adjusted according to location); the household *sitio* (adjusted for the number of rooms and type of building material, location, fruit trees, water, or electricity); machines and tools; vehicles; business inventory; animals; and inventory of textiles for personal and commercial use. The reason that the mean (average) is so much higher than the median (midpoint) is, of course, that a relatively few better-off families have a disproportionately large amount of land (see Chapter 4), the principal source of wealth in San Antonio. Because most distributions are skewed, medians rather than means are generally used in the following text.

4. See, for example, U.S. Agency for International Development, *Country Development Strategy Statement, 1979–1980*, for Guatemala; and Consejo Nacional de Planificación Económica, *Plan nacional de desarrollo, 1975–1979: Educación, ciencias y cultura*. However, such income estimates generally do not consider the secondary and "minor" sources of income that characterize peasant households. In studies I have carried out elsewhere in rural Guatemala, I have crudely estimated regional or village income using the shadow wage rate of local labor, i.e., the current opportunity cost of unskilled rural labor multiplied by an estimate of available family work days. In this case, however, I used the more comprehensive method because I wished to be able to explore income variations within the sample.

5. One might argue that some of the illustrations used here are not indicators of well-being but of cultural preference, or of the tendency of Guatemalan Indians to invest disposable income in increased production rather than in consumption. In my view, the "cultural preference argument" is overused and not at all certain under conditions of choice. Granted, a propensity to invest in production rather than consumption is an Indian trait; however, my previous work in adoption of health, family planning, water, and environmental sanitation practices persuades me that Indians view such services (as well as nutrition and primary education) as long-term productive investments—essentially a "basic human needs" approach to local development. In short, when they have money to invest in such services, they will; and noninvestment in such services implies primarily poverty.

6. About three-fourths of the individual rooms belonging to families in my survey sample were made of *caña*; only 19 percent of the rooms were built of rough, unfinished, pine boards; 6 percent used cinder block; and 3 percent employed a board-and-block combination.

7. Eighty-four percent of the homes that Arreola Hernández surveyed had plain dirt floors ("Diagnóstico," p. 24).

8. In Guatemala, the term *potable* simply means that the water comes from a protected source, usually a spring at an elevation above the village. But *agua potable* does not necessarily mean water that is "uncontaminated," much less "pure." In a field study of 105 "potable water systems" in the departments of Totonicapán, Sololá, and San Marcos, I found that 16 per-

cent of supposedly potable water systems were "dangerously contaminated" and 25 percent were "borderline contaminated" with coliforms (Sheldon Annis, "Estudio de los servicios de salud en los departmentos de Sololá, Totonicapán y San Marcos").

9. Although distance to the standpipe and public laundry area (*pila*) is usually short, lines waiting there can be quite long, especially when water slows to a trickle toward the end of the dry season. During the driest months, lines at the *pilas* begin to form in the predawn hours.

10. Arreola Hernández classified more than half of these as "unsanitary" ("Diagnóstico," p. 13).

11. Annis, *"Estudio de los servicios"*; Leonel Cabrera and Sheldon Annis, "Estudio comunitario: Evaluación del sistema de salud rural, Informe No. III."

12. Childhood diarrhea was studied in depth during a major, longitudinal study on nutrition and infection undertaken during the early 1960s by the Instituto para Nutrición para Centroamérica y Panamá (INCAP). San Antonio's contiguous, neighboring town of Santa Catarina Barahona served as a control "feeding village." The study documents and analyzes rates of diarrheal infection, approaching epidemic proportions during some periods, and relates such infections to nutritional disorders, respiratory disease, and child mortality. The findings were reported in a series of articles: see Werner Ascoli et al., "Nutrition and Infection Field Study, 1959–1964: Part IV, Deaths of Infants and Preschool Children," *Archives of Environmental Health* 15, no. 4 (October 1967): 439–449; Nevin Scrimshaw et al., "Nutrition and Infection Field Study, 1959–1964: Part V, Disease Incidence among Preschool Children under Natural Village Conditions, with Improved Diet and with Medical and Public Health Services," *Archives of Environmental Health* 16 (February 1968): 223–234; John E. Gordon et al., "Nutrition and Infection Field Study: Part VI, Acute Diarrheal Disease and Nutritional Disorders in General Disease Incidence," *Archives of Environmental Health* 16 (March 1968).

13. Arreola Hernández in her "Diagnóstico" evidently calculated these rates from vital statistics in the municipal registry. If so, the estimates are probably low. Under-reporting of deaths in rural Guatemala is near universal, though San Antonio, with its high literacy and close proximity to Antigua, probably has more reliable records than most towns.

14. See, for example, Nevin Scrimshaw, Lance Taylor, and John E. Gordon, *Interaction of Nutrition and Infection*; and Nevin Scrimshaw, "Synergism of Malnutrition and Infection: Evidence from Field Studies in Guatemala," *Journal of the American Medical Association* 212 (June 1970): 1685–1692.

15. For an analysis of the income-nutrition relationship for the Quinizilapa region, see Gary Smith, "Income and Nutrition in the Guatemalan Highlands" (Ph.D. dissertation, University of Oregon, 1972).

16. These data from Arreola Hernández' "Diagnóstica" are presumably based on clinical observation made during the year that she was assigned to the government health center in San Antonio as a final-year medical student. The classifications are based on pre-established, age-specific norms for

height, weight, muscle mass, and head and arm circumferences. She also alludes (without citation) to a 1973 INCAP study in San Antonio that reports an overall malnutrition rate in San Antonio of 81.4 percent.

17. In terms of cash, the main contributor to total income was male wage labor, which accounted for nearly 38 prcent of total family income—an average of $475 per family. Nearly 70 percent of families received some income from male labor outside the household. The dollar amount reported here is probably proportionately too high because of a survey bias that tends to overestimate cash income (and male income) in relation to noncash (and female) income. The second largest source in dollar terms is agriculture (*milpa* and cash-cropping combined), which accounts for about a quarter of family income. Eighty-two percent of families have *some* income from agriculture. The third source is family-based small business. Nearly half of all families earned some business income, generating about $522 per year for those affected. Fourth, over three-fourths of families have some income from textile sales. Women's earnings from wage labor produce about 4 percent of the total, and children's labor about 1 percent, while vegetable marketing (by women) is responsible for about 4 percent. Even though the dollar amounts from these activities are small relative to total income, they are vital to those families that depend on them nearly exclusively. The relatively low amount of small-scale vegetable marketing, a traditionally female activity during these years, does not reflect a decline of female participation in the workforce but the displacement of vegetable marketing by textile commerce as the locus of female entrepreneurial activity.

18. In Chapter 2 the term *milpa* was used in a historical sense to mean the *encomiendas* that were given to the lieutenants of Pedro de Alvarado as rewards for service during the Conquest. The term is used here in the contemporary sense: a plot of corn intercropped with beans and small quantities of secondary crops.

19. In this text, I have chosen to use the more colloquial word "corn" (American usage) rather than the slightly more precise word "maize." For a historical synopsis of the cultivation of corn/maize in Guatemala, see Angel Palerm, "Agricultural Systems and Food Patterns," in *Handbook of Middle American Indians*, vol. 6, *Social Anthropology*, ed. Robert Wauchope and Manning Nash; pp. 26–52; Richard S. MacNeish, "The Food-gathering and Incipient Agriculture Stage of Prehistoric Middle America," in ibid., vol. 1, *Natural Environment and Early Cultures*, ed. Robert Wauchope and Robert West, pp. 413–426; and Paul Mangelsdorf, Richard S. MacNeish, and Gordon R. Willey, "Origins of Agriculture in Middle America," in ibid., pp. 427–445.

20. U.S. Agency for International Development, "Results of Small Farmer Survey: Rural Cooperatives, 1974–75," in "Guatemala Small Farm Improvement—Progress and Projections," an evaluation of the Small Farmer Improvement Program in USAID agricultural loan 520-T-026, Attachment I, p. 3. This estimate is buttressed further by unpublished BANDESA (the national agricultural development bank) data from Region V, Subregion 4 (kindly provided by an agricultural technician, René Asturias, of the Antigua regional office) and by my own field data from San Antonio.

21. Data represent an average of input and yield estimates from a "panel" of eight farmers. Their responses varied considerably due largely to the hypothetical nature of the question (more concretely: "Was the land for which the estimate is made planted the year before or left fallow? Does it have to be cleared? Is it flat or on a slope? How much fertilizer was used? What kind of fertilizer was used? Do you include transport cost if your own horse was used?") Moreover, farmers tend to think about quantities in terms of their own *milpa*, not a hypothetical one-*cuerda* plot. Because of these methodological difficulties and because of the counter-intuitive conclusion that the most common form of economic activity produced a rate of return evidently lower than the prevailing wage rate for day labor, I carefully reviewed the data with my informants and compared these estimates with production data from other sources. I also consulted with agronomists for the INCAP Patalul nutrition project who were analyzing corn production, and with Dr. Donald Cass, an agricultural researcher at the Instituto Centroamericano de Técnica Agrícola. In general, my initial findings were supported by these consultations and the review. If anything, my calculation of rate of return for corn was slightly higher than those of the other researchers.

22. According to the substudy on corn, bean, and vegetable production that was used to establish standard values for the larger survey, San Antonio farmers consider a "low" yield to be about 450 pounds (4.5 *quintales*) per *cuerda*; a "high" yield is around 700 pounds. Low yields are far from uncommon. In 1977–1978, which was not a particularly bad agricultural year, farmers reported just under a third of their principal crops as "low" yields.

23. The resilience of corn, and the contrasting fragility of most other crops, was underscored for me by the astonishing rapidity with which my neighbors' chickens destroyed my home vegetable garden, or rather, what had survived the predations of usual garden pests and my inexpert, irregular maintenance. But only a rampaging pig, loose to root unrestrained for an entire afternoon, could completely destroy my green and thriving corn crop.

24. Marina Flores and Emma Reh, "Estudios de hábitos dietéticos en poblaciones de Guatemala: III, San Antonio Aguas Calientes y su aldea San Andrés Ceballos," *Boletín de la Oficina Sanitaria Panamericana*, Publicaciones de INCAP, Suplemento No. 2. (1955), pp. 149–162; Marina Flores, Zoila Flores, and Marta Lara, "Food Intake of Guatemalan Children, Ages 1–5," *Journal of the American Dietetic Association*, June 1966, pp. 400–487.

25. In my efforts to calculate *total* economic output of households, I arrived at an intermediate solution to the "large number of small quantities problem." Through field observation and interviews, we developed a comprehensive inventory of intercrops and, then, a conversational method of prompting informants. Interviewers first ascertained the location and size of each plot of land that the seventy-four families owned or farmed (309 plots in all). The interviewers then inquired, plot by plot, which crops were planted on each piece. An informant's first response was usually corn or beans. The interviewers then prompted for secondary crops—first by asking a general question ("What else do you plant besides corn on that piece of land in Chicarona?"), and with those answers exhausted, by suggesting com-

mon intercrops ("Do you plant any carrots there, *guicoy,* cabbages?"). The questionnaire format was constructed to allow fractions of *cuerdas* and numbers of trees (*matas,* or large stalks), but quantities smaller than that (a few handfuls of carrots or three blackberry bushes) were judged to be substatistical, even for these purposes. Seldom more than four crops were recorded for a single plot, but if more were offered, the information could be accommodated as a second plot on the questionnaire format. In a separate step, dollar values per units of crops were established, so that total dollar output could be computed for individual plots of land and then tallied for families. A formula programmed for the computer-adjusted output, according to land location, number of harvests, and the informant's subjective appraisal of "good harvest"/"bad harvest." This technique is still obviously biased toward underreporting; nevertheless, I believe that the data far more accurately reflect actual production than does the standard agricultural survey research with which I am familiar.

26. U. Gutiérrez, M. Infante, and P. Pinchinat estimate that fully 73 percent of bean production is grown in association with other crops, particularly maize ("Situación del cultivo de frijol en América Latina," *Boletín Informe,* E.S. 19 (1975).

27. On how the *milpa* system fits together with other inputs of Indian family-centered production, see Oscar Horst, "El rancho y la milpa: Una simbiosis significativa en la economía agrícola del occidente de Guatemala, *Cuadernos de Antropología,* No. 7 (1966): 13–18; and idem, "Assessing Peasant Agriculture: Western Perception and Traditional Realities" (paper presented to the International Geographic Union Symposium on Rural Development, Fresno, Calif., April 1981). Because of the particular kind of "efficiency" that the *milpa* represents, many development technicians have recommended programmatic incentives to increase output by making marginal improvements in the *milpa.* See Richard Bernstein and Robert Herdt, "Towards an Understanding of Milpa Agriculture: The Belize Case," *Journal of Developing Areas* 11 (April 1977): 373–392; and S. G. Manger Cats, "Socio-economic Development in Guatemala through Incentives to the Subsistence Sector," *Netherlands Journal of Agricultural Science* 18 (1970): 116–124.

28. José María Navarro, *Memorias de San Miguel Dueñas.*

29. The figure of 350 pounds per *cuerda* is based on the Instituto Indigenista's yield without commercial fertilizer during the 1940s of 350 *quintales* (hundredweights) per *cuerda* (adjusted to the San Antonio *cuerda* of 40 × 40 *varas*), as well as local verification in the Quinizilapa towns from elderly informants. Similar prefertilizer yields from the Lake Atitlán area are reported by John Early, "Education via Radio among Guatemalan Highland Maya," *Human Organization* 32 (Fall 1973): 228; Sol Tax, "The Towns of Lake Atitlán" (University of Chicago Microfilm Collection of Manuscripts on Middle American Cultural Anthropology, No. 13 [1946]); and Felix Webster McBryde, *Cultural and Historical Geography of Southwest Guatemala.* I presume that higher modern yields due to improved hybrids would be offset by the better state of the land in the past due to longer fallowing.

30. One problem with making a very precise calculation in this regard is not knowing the ratio of privately held to communal land in 1874 (i.e., the extent of the *astillero*). My supposition is that most individuals would have "owned" approximately the amount of land for which they could actually provide labor, and the surplus was held communally in the *astillero*. Elderly informants confirm that the *astillero* was much larger in the past than it is today.

31. Although general and growing inequity of land distribution is doubtless the case, I suspect that these data somewhat overstate the actual maldistribution. Asking a San Antonio family for exact information on landholding is a delicate matter, no matter how subtle the questionnaire. Interviewers used several techniques to enhance the accuracy of responses: directing inquiries to more than one family member, visiting repeatedly to double-check information, occasionally asking neighbors about someone else's land (which is how San Antoneros normally find the answers to questions that are none of their business). Yet none of these approaches was foolproof, and there is certainly substantial error in the data. Fortunately, the nature of the bias is fairly evident. The more frequent inaccurate response was to under-report family land: a cautious but common reluctance on the part of Indians to admit wealth, especially to foreigners, in case such knowledge by an outsider might put the family at a competitive disadvantage in some future negotiation. At the other extreme was a tendency, probably less common, to exaggerate landholding, either through pride, through boastfulness, or in a collegial spirit of helpfulness. Thus, the aggregate data probably incorporate considerable under-reporting and some over-reporting, causing a shift in skew to the right.

32. AGI, "Los indios que eran esclavos . . ." (1576), leg. 54, fol. 28. It is noteworthy that more than three hundred years later—fifty years *after* Guatemalan independence—the situation had probably worsened rather than improved. On May 10, 1886, the Indians of San Antonio sent a bitter petition to the Legislative Assembly asking that laws be written to abolish the "slavery" through which they were legally compelled to work in the neighboring *finca*, Panteleón, "from five in the morning to six at night for a miserable compensation that often worked out to less than one *real* per day" (from Archivos Generales de Centroamérica [AGCA], Correspondencia al Congresso, Caja Numero 4131).

33. For the sake of simplicity, I have not attempted to distinguish among the numerous varieties of several of these crops. There are, for example, at least six common types of beans grown for market. I also recognize that a *camote* in San Antonio is not exactly a "sweet potato," the English term used above; and a *guicoy* or *ayote* is not exactly a "squash." Furthermore, I have lumped into "others" all the many products for which I know no English equivalents (e.g., *jocotes, guynános, nisperos, chiltomates, chilequaque, güisquiles*). In addition to the crops reported in my survey, others (e.g., marijuana, garbanzos, and celery) are grown locally but for one reason or another were not reported. Among several families whose lands extend down

into the Pacific piedmont, tropical crops such as bananas, mangos, papaya, and sugarcane were not included.

34. Potatoes, of course, can be and are commonly intercropped; however, the data used here refer to potatoes grown in a strictly commercial fashion, i.e., as a BANDESA agricultural technician might advise a San Antonio farmer to grow them.

35. Beginning in the late 1970s, a lawyer from Guatemala City, who had been hired by a local family to regularize a land title for purposes of inheritance, began acquiring tracts of land in the *laguna*. He used outright fraud (*he* became the beneficiary of his first client's will) and legal intimidation ("You might as well sell me this land because if you don't, I'll just take it from you—and you know lawyers know how to do that"). During the time that I lived in San Antonio, farmers who owned land in the *laguna* exhausted one remedy after another in futile attempts to stop this incursion. When the lawyer dammed a spring to create an artificial carp pond, the pattern of drainage was disrupted, drying out some fields, inundating others, and ruining much of the vegetable crop. Anger and frustration erupted into violence when farmers finally stormed the *finca*, wounded the lawyer's son with machetes, and tore down the retaining wall of the pond. Mass arrests and occupation of the town by the army followed; and then gunmen murdered six townsmen (including the mayor, Carmelo Santos) who had been involved in opposing the lawyer's actions. Soon thereafter, guerrillas machine-gunned the lawyer in his office in Guatemala City. That led to further crackdowns in San Antonio by the army and by paramilitary groups from Antigua. These events are described more fully in Sheldon Annis, "A Story from a Peaceful Town," in *Harvest of Violence: Guatemala's Indians and the Counterinsurgency War*, ed. Robert M. Carmack.

36. According to local informants, San Antonio farmers were the only regional beneficiaries of the land reforms. None of the nearby towns received land.

37. There is today an enormous literature on the U.S. intervention in Guatemala. See, for example, Richard H. Immerman, *The CIA in Guatemala*; and Stephen Schlesinger and Stephen Kinzer, *Bitter Fruit: The Untold Story*.

38. Guatemala's *caudillo*, Jorge Ubico, 1931–1944, expropriated nearly all lands belonging to Guatemalans of German descent at the outset of World War II. Unlike lands expropriated during the Arbenz reforms, these lands were not returned in 1954 but came under the jurisdiction of the Instituto Nacional de Transformación Agraria (INTA).

39. The wealthiest family in my sample of seventy-four households, for example, received a Calderas tract. In this case, the land is nominally owned by the male head-of-household but worked by his adult sons, each of whom will inherit a portion and farm it separately after his father's death.

40. Townsend's point of view emerges clearly in his voluminous writings from the field during the 1920s, mostly articles and reports to mission constituencies in publications such as the *Central American Bulletin* and the

Christian Herald. Townsend's values are also reflected in his novel, *Tolo, the Volcano's Son,* published serially in a missionary publication, *Revelation,* from April through October of 1936. For an adoring biography, with Townsend cast as a missionary hero, see James and Marti Hefley, *Uncle Cam.*

41. Charles Katy and Geraldine Katy, "Private Voluntary Organizations in Health," in *Guatemala Health Care Sector Assessment.*

42. Typically, a San Antonio farmer will borrow about $300 for inputs and labor. For example, one elderly farmer has about ten *cuerdas* of prime coffee land but little cash. In January–February, he must find about ten workers (mostly women from San Antonio or the neighboring towns) to harvest his crop. He will pay them each $1.25 per day for about ten days of harvest work. The workers must be paid when the crop is picked; to get cash, he can either borrow from the middleman at the *beneficio* where he sells his coffee, or he can borrow more favorably from BANDESA. In 1977 and 1976, two years for which I was able to review BANDESA office records of the five Quinizilapa towns, twelve and twenty farmers, respectively, received BANDESA agricultural loans. In past years, the number of borrowers was higher, doubtless because of the generous availability of housing reconstruction and artisanal loans in 1976–1977 from BANDESA and CORFINA that could be, and were easily diverted into agricultural production.

43. Many studies have been carried out upon the effects of education upon productivity. Marilyn Lockheed, Dean T. Jamison, and Lawrence J. Lau surveyed thirty-seven studies from Asia, Africa, and Europe, as well as Latin America. The authors state: "Overall, we find confirmation for the hypothesis that education will have a positive effect on farmer efficiency . . . In six of these data sets education was found to have a negative (but statistically insignificant) effect, but in the remaining 31, the effect was positive and usually significant." In Latin America, however, results were more mixed; only four of thirteen education coefficients were found to be positive and significant (Marilyn Lockheed, Dean T. Jamison, and Lawrence J. Lau, "Farmer Education and Farm Efficiency: A Survey," *Economic Development and Cultural Change* 29, no. 1 [October 1980]: 37–76).

44. See, for example, U.S. Agency for International Development and Guatemalan Ministry of Education, Tables VIII-1 and VIII-2 in *Education Sector Assessment* and U.S. Agency for International Development, "Small Farmer Survey," Attachment I.

45. For a discussion of the Almolonga/Zuñil situation see Carol Smith, "Production in Western Guatemala: A Test of Von Thünen and Boserup," in *Formal Methods in Economic Anthropology,* ed. Stuart Plattner.

46. The purchase of vehicles accelerated noticeably between 1976 and 1978, when nearly two hundred "loans" for "artisanal recovery" from the earthquake of February 1976 were made by CORFINA, the national development finance corporation. Since the tourist textile market was saturated and administrative controls on use and recovery of the loans was weak, many families quietly (but wisely) used the money for, among other things, partial down-payments on pickup trucks. For a description of this entrepreneurial use of "free money," see Sheldon Annis, "Artisanal Entrepreneurship in a

Guatemalan Village" (Paper presented to the International Geographic Union Symposium on Rural Development, Fresno, Calif., April 1981).

47. See Stephan F. de Borhegyi's archaeological review, "Archaeological Synthesis of the Guatemalan Highlands," in *Handbook of Middle American Indians*, vol. 2, *Archaeology of Southern Mesoamerica, Part One*, ed. Robert Wauchope and Gordon R. Willey, pp. 3–58; and in particular, with reference to mat, basket, and rope impressions found in the Early Preclassic (Village Formative) period, 1500–600 B.C., see p. 10.

48. The term *petate* refers to the finished product (i.e., the mat) and sometimes to a particularly fine, thin variety of the reed. *Tul* is used generically to describe the reeds but also refers specifically to the thicker, heavier reed that is used for a cruder, more rustic mat.

49. Two oft-cited statements on this subject are Alexander V. Chayanov, *The Theory of Peasant Economy*, p. 109; and V. I. Lenin, *The Development of Capitalism in Russia*, pp. 177–178. Among Mexican artisans, the case of *metate* (grinding-stone) makers in Oaxaca is described by Scott Cook: ". . . the typical *metatero* situation can be described as one characterized by relative landlessness, low income (in cash and kind), and chronic indebtedness that places him invariably in the lower half of the socio-economic structure of his community" ("Price and Output Variability in a Peasant-Artisan Stoneworking Industry in Oaxaca, Mexico," *American Anthropologist* 72 [1970]: 780). For a description of much the same situation for pottery makers in Jalisco see May N. Diaz, *Tonalá: Conservatism, Responsibility, and Authority in a Mexican Town*. For a description of Yucatec hammock artisans see Alice Littlefield, "The Hammock Industry of Yucatan: A Study in Economic Anthropology" (Ph.D. dissertation, Michigan State University, 1976).

50. *Petate* income also correlates positively and significantly with the number of women in the family over fifteen years of age ($r = .35$, $p = .002$), with income from textile production ($r = .53$, $p = .000$), and with the sale of self-made (as opposed to bought) textiles ($r = .32$, $p = .006$). It shows no correlation with activities that require capitalization, e.g., cash-cropping or resale of purchased textiles.

51. I suspect that reported production would have been higher had interviews been carried out at the end of the rainy season rather than during the dry season.

52. The dollar value of their production was determined as follows. Each woman over fifteen was queried as to whether she made *petates*. Through a series of structured probes and adjustments by the interviewers (for seasonality and size of mat produced), a theoretical "monthly" production equivalent representing the number of "standard-size" *petates* was derived for each woman. The average sales price of a standard-size *petate* (less the approximate value of raw materials) was determined in a separate step, so that each woman's yearly *petate* income could be calculated by multiplying times twelve (months per year). Male *petate* income was calculated in a separate step but added to the family total.

53. The oldest person in my sample, a wizened wraith of a woman said by

her family to be ninety-two years old, weaves *petates* for five or six hours each day. With a teenage great-great-great-grandson to guide her, carry the mats, and help bargain, she travels regularly to rural *aldeas* on two- and three-day selling trips—bargaining with her fingers, since she is nearly deaf and speaks almost no Spanish.

54. Since wage income is easier to remember, report, and compute than nonwage sources of income, these findings may over-represent wage income and under-represent traditional agricultural production, the value of exchanged services, and interhousehold sales of miscellaneous goods and services. Nevertheless, considerable attention was paid to quantifying such incomes. Even though the relative contribution of wage income to total income may have been inadvertently magnified, I feel fairly confident that the general sense of the findings reported here is correct.

55. The relationship between these two groups of farmers and the role of *mozo* labor and land rental in regulating the distribution of labor and land is taken up in Chapter 4.

56. Small business in San Antonio was given an unusual boost in 1977 and 1978. Following the earthquake, "artisan recovery" funds from the Inter-American Development Bank were made available through CORFINA, the national development finance corporation. By cosigning for each other, about 190 families received "loans" of from a few hundred to two thousand dollars, nominally to buy primary materials (information provided by CORFINA). The weak tourism textile market was soon inundated, so most families, realizing that the government would not foreclose, treated the loans as "free money" for house reconstruction or business purposes. As discussed elsewhere (see note 46 above), families used the money creatively: they made down-payments on vehicles, bought sewing machines, musical instruments, typewriters, land, a refrigerator for a family store, coffee seedlings for a nursery, and so forth.

4. *Milpa* Logic and Wealth Differentiation

1. As mentioned in Chapter 2, Juan de Chávez, the original *señor de la tierra* of San Antonio, legally bequeathed the town to his Indians when he returned to Spain about 1550. In that the San Antonio Indians then owned their own land, they were quite exceptional.

2. Kay B. Warren, *The Symbolism of Subordination: Indian Identity in a Guatemalan Town.*

3. Manning Nash, "The Social Context of Economic Choice in a Small Society," *Man* 61 (1961): 186–191.

4. See Richard N. Adams, ed., *Political Changes in Guatemalan Indian Communities;* Robert Wasserstrom, "Revolution in Guatemala: Peasants and Politics under the Arbenz Government," *Comparative Studies in Society and History* 17, no. 4 (October 1975): 443–478.

5. A recent study estimates that in the year 2000 nearly all departments of Guatemala will have population densities equal to that of present-day Totonicapán, the nation's most densely inhabited department (about 134

people per square kilometer). There will be several hundred thousand new, landless, rural families. See Robert Fox and Jerrold Huguet, *Population and Urbanization in the Year 2000 in Central America and Panama.* Innumerable studies have documented the loss of self-sufficiency for highland farmers. In Santiago Atitlán, for example, over 90 percent of farmers were found to be no longer self-sufficient in corn production by the late 1960s (John Early, "Education via Radio among Guatemalan Highland Maya," *Human Organization* 32 [Fall 1973]: 221–229). Overall, nine out of ten highland farmers are estimated to own too little land for self-sufficiency (U.S. Agency for International Development, *Country Development Strategy Statement, 1979–1980*).

6. See several case studies in Robert Carmack, ed., *Harvest of Violence: Guatemala's Indians and the Counterinsurgency.*

7. For a typology of cargo systems along a traditional-modern continuum based on broadened economic opportunity and a discussion of comparative evidence in communities whose cargo systems have changed, see Billie de Walt, "Changes in the Cargo System of Mesoamerica," *Anthropological Quarterly* 48 (April 1975): 87–105. For an example of how economic opportunities created by tourism have drawn many entrepreneurial Indians away from the traditional cargo system, see Robert Hinshaw, *Panajachel: A Guatemalan Town in Thirty Year Perspective.* For an investigation of how factory workers in Cantel use their earnings, see Paul McDowell, "Guatemalan Stratification and Peasant Marketing Arrangements: A Different View," *Man* 11 (1975): 273–278. Waldemar R. Smith in *The Fiesta System and Economic Change* argues that "barriers of social class . . . entrap and isolate peasants, [so] that ceremonial giving is a result rather than a cause of their constrained position." He concludes that social incentives serve to inspire generosity in a closed society, but when the community is no longer closed, then the fiesta system breaks down. Even Frank Cancian, whose frequently cited description of the fiesta system in Zinacantán, Chiapas, in the early 1960s stands as perhaps the most dramatic description of the classic impoverishing-but-equalizing Mesoamerican cargo system, speculates that changing economic circumstances may alter the operation and structure of the cargo system (*Economics and Prestige in a Maya Community*, pp. 188–192).

8. William Roseberry, "Rent, Differentiation, and the Development of Capitalism among Peasants," *American Anthropologist* 78 (1976): 52. A similar point of view is developed more fully by Alain De Janvry and Carmen Deere. They argue that mechanisms for surplus extraction are a dominant factor shaping peasant behavior. As I have here, they show how increasing differentiation is taking place among peasants: certain groups of campesinos become capitalist farmers; others remain dominated by forms of surplus extraction ("A Conceptual Framework for the Empirical Analysis of Peasants," *American Journal of Agricultural Economics* 61 [November 1979]: 601–611).

Roseberry, in "Rent, Differentiation . . ." (p. 51), uses the concept "rent" in the broad, Marxian sense of "any extraction of surplus value not based on the sale of labor power." He includes "actual rent, taxes, interest on loans,

forced presale of produce at less than market price, etc." As he himself acknowledges, he loses the economic/empirical sense of the term, substitut-
ing a meaning in which rent comes to be, more simply, "a broad category
which refers to the principal form exploitation takes among peasants." De
Janvry and Deere, in "A Conceptual Framework," are more specific. As a
basis for empirical analysis, they cite six points at which surplus is extracted: the home production process, the circulation process on the supply
side, the circulation process on the demand side, the reproduction process,
and finally the differentiation process.

9. "Constant" and "variable" capital correspond to the familiar account-
ing dichotomy between fixed and variable costs. The split presupposes a distinction between those productive resources that are in fixed supply in the
short run (principally land) and factors of production that can be purchased
on the market (principally labor but also fertilizer, seed, etc.).

10. Like Sol Tax's famous "penny capitalist" (*Penny Capitalism: A Guatemalan Indian Economy*).

11. For an example of this kind of bank borrowing, see Chapter 3, note 42.

12. The range in the total wealth variable was from $117 to $31,417; the
mean was $4,006 (standard deviation, 5,636); the 25th percentile was $1,008;
the median was $1,980; the 75th percentile was $5,341; kurtosis was 10.5;
skew was 3.1. "Surplus" was assumed to be highly correlated with total family wealth (and per capita wealth). The top 20 percent of families on the total
wealth variable were classified as "petty capitalists." The lower 30 percent
were classified as "dispossessed"; and the half of the families between the
30th and 80th percentiles were classified as "*milpa* technologists."

13. Two cautionary notes: First, I have used simple arithmetic means here
and in several subsequent tables, despite their drawbacks with nonnormal
distributions. It is relatively easy to normalize distributions with log transformations or by dropping outliers (which I did in earlier iterations of the
data); however, for purposes of presentation, the straightforward, intuitively
understandable mean seemed preferable. Second, the reader should keep in
mind that the three peasant types are not statistically independent categories but were defined operationally in terms of their position on a ranking of
families by wealth. Thus, one would logically expect the "petty capitalist"
to have greater wealth than the "dispossessed peasant." What the table illustrates, however, is difference in magnitude.

14. The overall correlation between land and wealth in the sample is .93,
significant at the .001 level.

15. The poorer families tend to be young and include many heads-of-
household who work land that they do not own but may one day inherit.
Since young families usually have many more at-home children, they appear
to be even poorer when per capita rather than total family wealth is used as a
measure (Column D). This tends to exaggerate the difference between richest
and poorest families shown in the table.

16. During the course of the fieldwork, I established a "panel" of farmers
to whom I frequently turned for answers to questions such as this one: "Approximately how much land can one man comfortably farm alone without

help from additional laborers?" I would obtain five or six responses to such questions. If answers were roughly consistent, as in this case, I would accept the responses and calculate an average value. If there was an erratic pattern or wide variation, I would investigate further until a pattern was clear.

17. Altogether, information was obtained for 140 agricultural plots in the seventy-four-family survey. As shown in Table 8, 50 of these plots were rented. The average size of "owned" plots was 13.5 *cuerdas* (median, 4.7 *cuerdas*); the average size of rented plots was 4.7 *cuerdas* (median, 2 *cuerdas*).

18. In addition to his own labor and that of the other ".5 male," a farmer can also call upon women and younger children for some labor. Although most San Antonio women and children do not regularly perform heavy field work, they are available to help out during times of peak labor demand. Of 117 women over fifteen who were surveyed, only 12 percent claimed to work in the fields "often." Twenty-one percent responded that they work in the fields "occasionally" (meaning in times of peak labor demand, e.g., coffee picking or carrot cleaning). Fully 68 percent claimed to "never" or "almost never" work in the fields (though many of these same women invest considerable time and effort cultivating home gardens). Similarly, among eight- to fourteen-year-old children, 14 percent "always" or "almost always" work in the fields; 14 percent work "frequently"; about 40 percent help out a little when not in school; and the rest do no agricultural work at all. (Relative terms like "often" and "occasionally" were not used in the actual field query; these ideas were expressed by concrete examples.)

19. This estimate is based on data drawn from several sources. First, an unpublished study for which I was an investigator, "Feasibility Study on the Production of Low-Cost Protein-Enriched Wheat Products in the Guatemalan Highlands" (Ecotecnia Associates and the Instituto para Nutrición para Centroamérica y Panamá [INCAP] (carried out for the United Nations Development Programme in 1977) collected data on corn and wheat consumption in one *ladino* and four highland Indian towns. Second, when queried directly, San Antonio women generally responded that they consume "about a pound" of *masa* (ground corn for tortillas) per person per day. Third, similar findings were reported by Marina Flores, Zuila Flores, and Berta Meneses, "Estudio de hábitos dietéticos en poblaciones de Guatemala, IX, Santa Catarina Barahona," *Archivos Venezolanos de Nutrición* 8, no. 1–2 (1957): 67.

5. The Production of Christians

1. A 1978 field survey of Protestant church membership in Guatemala found 40 large denominations and 160 smaller sects. See Instituto Internacional de Evangelización a Fondo (IINDEF) and Servicio Evangelizador para America Latina (SEPAL), *Directorio de iglesias, organizaciones y ministerios del movimiento protestante*, p. 15.

2. The missionary view of the often-recounted story of Barrios inviting in the Presbyterian Mission is told in Paul Burgess, *Justo Rufino Barrios: A Biography*.

3. Julian Lloret, "The Mayan Evangelical Church in Guatemala" (Doctor

of Theology dissertation, Dallas Theological Seminary, 1976), pp. 65–84; Paul Burgess, ed., *Historia de la obra evangélica presbiteriana en Guatemala.*

4. William Read, Victor Monterroso, and Harmon Johnson, *Latin American Church Growth,* p. 157. They do not provide sources or explain their methodology. Lloret, who studied church growth in the late 1970s, doubts this 1.6 percent estimate and believes their estimated 9 percent rate of annual growth is unrealistically high (Lloret, "Mayan Evangelical Church," p. 246).

5. William Cameron Townsend, like a whole generation of evangelists before him, astutely worked the market routes as a traveling Bible salesman fully twenty years before anthropologists such as Robert Redfield "discovered" the organizational importance of Indian markets. See Robert Redfield, "Primitive Merchants of Guatemala," *Quarterly Journal of Inter-American Relations* 1, no. 4 (1939): 42–46.

6. In reviewing church growth over the last decades, a church researcher recently wrote, "When the Gospel first reaches someone in a previously unchurched family, village or small community it can frequently spread rapidly. Each new church is a seed planted with the potential to grow 30 fold, 60 fold or 100 fold" (James Montgomery, "The Case for Research: Part 4, Factors of Growth, *Global Church Growth* 20 [July–August, 1983]: 265).

7. See Ethel Wallis and Mary Bennett, *Two Thousand Tongues to Go;* and Wycliffe Bible Translators and Summer Institute of Linguistics, *Who Brought the Word.* Less friendly views of Wycliffe-SIL activity in Latin America are David Stoll, *Fishers of Men or Founders of Empire? The Wycliffe Bible Translators in Latin America;* Peter Aaby and Soren Hvalkof, *Is God an American? An Anthropological Perspective on the Missionary Work of the Summer Institute of Linguistics;* and Pedro Alisedo et al., *El Instituto Lingüístico de Verano.*

Despite ample SIL/Wycliffe publicity that Townsend's was the first Bible in an Indian language, a British and Foreign Bible Society had translated one Gospel into Cakchiquel at least fifteen years earlier. Townsend must have known about it since the Central American Mission distributed it (David Stoll, personal communication). By the early 1930s, Townsend had shifted away from his missionary work in San Antonio and Patzún and refocused his energies on linguistics. He dropped out of the Central American Mission and largely relegated San Antonio to his less effective brother, Paul.

8. Ricardo Falla, "Evolución político-religiosa del indígena rural en Guatemala 1945–65," *Estudios Sociales Centroamericanos* 1 (January–April, 1972): 27–41; Robert Wasserstrom, "Revolution in Guatemala: Peasants and Politics under the Arbenz Government," *Comparative Studies in Society and History* 17, no. 4 (October 1975): 443–478.

9. For a report on the conversion of nearly a third of San Pedro la Laguna's population to five competing Protestant sects, see Benjamin Paul and Lois Paul, "Changing Marriage Patterns in a Highland Guatemala Community," *Southwest Journal of Anthropology* 19 (1963): 131–148. See also June Nash, "Protestantism in an Indian Village in the Western Highlands of Guatemala," *Alpha Kappa Deltan* 30 (Special Issue, 1960): 49–58; and Benson

Saler, "Religious Conversion and Self-Aggrandizement: A Guatemalan Case," *Practical Anthropology* 12 (1965): 107–149.

10. J. Nash, "Protestantism"; Saler, "Religious Conversion"; E. A. Nida, "The Relationship of Social Structure to the Problem of Evangelism in Latin America," *Practical Anthropology* 5 (1958): 101–123.

11. W. E. Carter, "Innovation and Marginality: Two South American Case Studies," *América Indígena* 30 (1965): 383–392, 436; Bryan Roberts, "Protestant Groups and Coping with Urban Life in Guatemala City," *American Journal of Sociology* 73 (1967): 753–767.

12. James D. Sexton and Clyde Woods, "Development and Modernization among Highland Maya: A Comparative Analysis of Ten Guatemalan Towns," *Human Organization* 36 (1977): 156–172.

13. H. Siverts, "Political Organization in a Tzeltal Community in Chiapas, Mexico," *Alpha Kappa Deltan* 30 (Special Issue, 1960): 14–28.

14. Saler, "Religious Conversion"; Sol Tax and Robert Hinshaw, "The Maya of the Midwestern Highlands," in *Handbook of Middle American Indians*, vol. 7, *Ethnology, Part One*, ed. Robert Wauchope and Evon Z. Vogt, pp. 69–100; and Ricardo Falla, *Quiché rebelde: Estudio de un movimiento de conversión religiosa rebelde a las creencias tradicionales, en San Antonio Ilotenango, Quiché, 1948–70*, pp. 185–187.

15. Robert Harmon and William Kurtz, "Missionary Influence on Maya Medical Behavior: Results of a Factor Analysis" (Paper presented to the 33rd Annual Meeting of the Society for Applied Anthropology, Tucson, 1973).

16. Ruben Reina and Norman Schwartz, "The Structural Context of Religious Conversion in Petén, Guatemala: Status, Community, and Multicommunity," *American Ethnologist* 1 (1974): 157–192.

17. Lloret, "Mayan Evangelical Church," p. 246. For an analysis and critical interpretation of Protestant church growth in Guatemala, see also Jesús García-Ruiz, *Las sectas fundamentalistas en Guatemala*.

18. By 1981, the total active, baptized twelve-years-or-older membership of *all* Protestant groups, not just evangelicals, was enumerated as 334, 453. Accepting the four-to-one ratio of nonactive members/children to active members used in this study, the "Protestant community" stood at about 1.3 million, or just over 18 percent of the total population (IINDEF and SEPAL, *Directorio*, p. 61). A more conservative estimate put the Protestant portion of the population at 15 percent (Julian Lloret, "Forces Shaping the Church in Central America," *CAM Bulletin*, Summer 1982, p. 3). In 1982, unidentified Protestant groups were reported as claiming 22 percent of the population, with some sects boasting of annual growth rates of 15 percent (Marlise Simons, "Latin America's New Gospel," *New York Times Magazine*, November 7, 1982, p. 45). A claim of "20 percent or more" for 1983 is made by James Montgomery, "The Case for Research: Part 3, The Factors of Growth," *Global Church Growth* 20 (March–April 1983): 250. On the basis of recent growth patterns, he further projects that Guatemala will be fully 50 percent Protestant by 1990 ("The Case for Research: Part 6, Projections for Growth," *Global Church Growth* 20 [September–October 1983]: 303).

19. Following a pattern similar to that in other parts of Latin America,

Pentecostal churches in Guatemala have grown much faster than the original "pioneer" missions, such as the Presbyterians. According to Montgomery, "By 1950, Pentecostals comprised 13 percent of the evangelical community. This increased to 20 percent in 1960, to 31 percent in 1967 and all the way up to 54 percent in 1980." At present, Pentecostal and non-Pentecostal churches are of roughly equal size. See "The Case for Research: Part 3."

20. Robert Redfield, *The Village That Chose Progress: Chan Kom Revisited.*

21. Julian Lloret, for many years field director of the Central American Mission (CAM), pointedly used this phrase, "functional substitute," in his dissertation while describing "strategies for future expansion." Of Bible conferences, for example, he says: "In a real sense these conferences are a functional substitute for the traditional religious festivals and provide opportunity for everyone to contribute to corporate religious activity just as they did before" ("Mayan Evangelical Church," p. 269). Ironically, but perhaps with a certain poetic justice, this is the same pattern that occurred during the Catholic evangelization of the Indians in sixteenth-century Mexico and Guatemala. Robert Ricard, in *The Spiritual Conquest of Mexico*, discusses the friars' attempts to relate particular cults to particular prehistoric gods. To do that, they placed churches or shrines on the sites of pre-Hispanic temples to gods with attributes similar to those of the Christian saints to whom the post-Conquest shrines were dedicated.

22. G. Alexander Moore, in *Life Cycles in Atchalán: The Diverse Careers of Certain Guatemalans*, provides a particularly effective description and interpretation of Semana Santa ritual in the town of Alotenango, a few kilometers southwest of San Antonio.

23. James and Marti Hefley, *Uncle Cam;* Stoll, *Fishers of Men*, pp. 28–29.

24. Despite his liberationist attitude at the grassroots, Townsend appeared to make no political judgments against the larger system of debt peonage. He did not attack *finca* owners or *contratistas*. In fact, in his novel, *Tolo, the Volcano's Son*, he portrays God as a kindly *finquero*.

25. In an analysis of eight San Antonio–Santa Catarina conversion stories published by Townsend between 1919 and 1929, Stoll found that seven contained explicit economic motivation. The stories describe people who were severely taxed, indebted, and even bankrupted by costly ritual obligation. Their present or future prosperity was tied to freedom from this obligation (David Stoll, "The Founder in Guatemala," unpublished draft of *Fishers of Men*).

26. William Cameron Townsend, "A Rich Chief's Family Getting 'Saved,'" *Central American Bulletin*, vol. 15 (September 1926).

27. From alcoholic profligacy, the family has risen to be the wealthiest household among my seventy-four-household survey sample. Florentina and her daughters operate one of the largest tourist *tiendas*. Her husband and son-in-law farm considerable land and operate a bus between San Antonio and Antigua.

28. William Cameron Townsend, *One of Guatemala's Indians: His Witch Doctor and a Torn Tract* (missionary brochure). Silverio López, like Don Apolinario, then began his climb. With the revelatory scrap of paper in hand,

he sought out the evangelical pastor in Antigua, who saved Silverio on the spot and cured the daughter with simple medication for parasites. By 1926, Silverio was working with Townsend as the pastor of five small congregations. This follow-up account of the Silverio story is reported in W. F. Jordan, *Central American Indians and the Bible*, pp. 15–16. However, according to Stoll, who followed up the story in the field, "Fifty years later the man's son could not recall Townsend's story of swindle and woe. He did describe his father's drinking problem, which together with his weakness for women forced him to leave the Protestant church" (Stoll, *Fishers of Men*, p. 33).

29. By way of contrast, as late as the early 1960s in Zinacatán (whose ceremonial organization was intensively studied during the years of the Harvard Chiapas Project), an adult male was described as having to spend from $4 to $1,100 in order to discharge one of fifty-five yearly ceremonial posts (Frank Cancian, *Economics and Prestige in a Maya Community*). Eric Wolf says, "Evidence from Middle America indicates that a man may have to expend at least the equivalent of one year's local wages to act as sponsor in a community ceremonial. Expenditures of from two to twenty times this amount are noted for particular communities" (*Peasants*, p. 7). Paul Diener reports ritual expenditures of about 25 percent of income ("The Tears of St. Anthony: Ritual and Revolution in Eastern Guatemala," *Latin American Perspectives* 5 [1978]: 92–116).

30. Among the many discussions on this subject, see several pertinent chapters in Daniel H. Levine, *Churches and Politics in Latin America;* also, Margaret E. Crahan, "International Aspects of the Role of the Catholic Church in Central America," in *Central America: International Dimensions of the Crisis,* ed. Richard E. Feinberg, pp. 213–235; and more generally, Penny Lernoux, *Cry of the People.* In reference to Guatemala, see Luisa Frank and Philip Wheaton, *Indian Guatemala: Path to Liberation;* Thomas R. Melville, "The Catholic Church in Guatemala, 1944–1982," *Cultural Survival Quarterly* 7 (Spring 1983): 23–27; and Phillip Berryman, *The Religious Roots of Rebellion: Christians in Central American Revolutions.* For a historical view of the Church's prerevolutionary period, see B. J. Calder, *Crecimiento y cambio de la iglesia católica guatemalteca, 1944–1966.*

31. For a detailed description of contemporary Mayan religion in Momostenango, Quiché, see Barbara Tedlock, *Time and the Highland Maya.*

32. Kay B. Warren's analysis of the subject is particularly helpful. See *The Symbolism of Subordination: Indian Identity in a Guatemalan Town.*

33. The struggle between Catholic Action and traditionalist sects in San Antonio Ilotenango, Quiché, is described in Falla, *Quiché rebelde.*

34. San Antonio *cofradías* are of the "faded" type, to use the classificatory system in Billie de Walt, "Changes in the Cargo Systems of Mesoamerica," *Anthropological Quarterly* 48 (April 1975): 87–105.

35. This is slim fare for a family of seven. All but the oldest children appear to be mildly malnourished. The two- and three-year-old children have been treated in a clinical malnutrition project at the Instituto para Nutrición para Centroamérica y Panamá (INCAP) in Guatemala City.

36. Several hundred thousand pilgrims visit the Black Christ at Esquipulas throughout the year. It is one of Central America's most important pilgrimage centers. The major celebration and peak migration is during January. To the best of my knowledge, no one from San Antonio still makes the trip by foot—much less on their knees, as many did in the past. Each year, at least one or two buses are chartered in the town (ironically, from a Protestant family in 1978, the year that I joined a local group for the pilgrimage). To reduce expenses, most food for the two-to three-day trip is packed picnic-basket style. About ten people jammed into our tiny, two-twin-bed hotel room. All in all, a family's total cost for the trip is roughly $30. Keep in mind, however, that a $30 "vacation expense" on an annual income of $650 is equivalent to $1,100 out of a $24,000-a-year income, without taking into account the greater elasticity of the latter.

37. The difficult question arises as to whether or not *all* alcoholic consumption should be viewed as a Catholic ceremonial expense. Certainly, the Catholic Church does not openly condone drinking; in fact, priests inveigh against drunkenness, and most parishes sponsor vigorous abstinence programs, including active support for Alcoholics Anonymous chapters in towns such as San Antonio. Nevertheless, while Catholics condemn *drunkenness*, Protestants condemn *alcohol*—and in this regard all Protestant sects are unbending. The critical difference, then, is that Protestants believe it is sinful to drink (whether or not they do), and Catholics do not. Indeed, Catholic ritual is associated with drinking; the Church advocates moderation but sends ambiguous signals by looking the other way during fiestas. Among Protestants, on the other hand, abstinence has been elevated to a tenet of faith.

38. See Diener, "Tears of St. Anthony," p. 92, for comparable figures in eastern Guatemala. He reports: "While it is impossible to estimate exactly the amount of 'ritual waste' resulting from ritual practices, on the basis of nearly 200 very detailed household economic surveys gathered over two years, I would suggest that traditional Indians may spend as much as 25 percent of their income in this fashion."

39. Parenthetically, if the heads of this family were inclined to pursue such logic—which they are not—they would be quite capable of carrying it out. Both husband and wife are frequent newspaper readers, and they are adept with numbers. The husband frequently borrowed books that happened to be around my house: *A Hundred Years of Solitude* by Gabriel García Marquez, *The Wonderful Clouds* by Françoise Sagan, a Spanish translation of the *SPSS Manual*. When and if he returned them, he was prepared to discuss them.

40. Since Weber, there have been a plethora of Catholic-Protestant comparative economic studies. As N. D. Glen and R. Hyland noted in 1967, "the relationship of religion to economic and occupational success is the most viable topic of debate in the sociology of religion in the United States" ("Religious Preference and Worldly Success: Some Evidence from National Surveys," *American Sociological Review* 32, no. 1 [1967]: 73). For a fairly good review of the literature on Catholic-Protestant economic performance in

Latin America and a case study of the central Mexican town of Nealticán, see David Clawson, "Religious Allegiance and Economic Development in Rural Latin America," *Journal of Interamerican Studies and World Affairs* 26, no. 4 (November 1984): 499–524.

41. Waldemar R. Smith, in *The Fiesta System and Economic Change*, develops the argument that "it is barriers of social class which entrap and isolate peasants, and that ceremonial giving is a result rather than a cause of their constrained position."

42. Boys begin accompanying their fathers to the fields at the age of six or seven. When they are even smaller, both boys and girls begin running errands and taking care of their even-younger siblings. In a separate survey of household chores by twenty-one children, I found that parents generally view an eight-year-old as capable of providing about two hours of productive work per day, rising to nearly a full day's work by an out-of-school fifteen-year-old.

43. A second reason is specific to this particular sample. The largest landholder in the seventy-four-family sample is a Catholic who received land during the 1950s land reform. He claimed to have planted 150 *cuerdas* of corn during the year in which this survey was carried out. This exceptionally large amount was sufficient to significantly raise the overall Catholic average.

44. See notes 18 and 19 above for estimates and projections of the number of Guatemalan Protestants.

6. Religion and Why Women Weave

1. Numerous technical studies are available on the technology of backstrap weaving. See, for example, H. Ling Roth, *Studies in Primitive Looms;* Lila M. O'Neale, *Textiles of Highland Guatemala;* idem, "Weaving," in *Handbook of South American Indians,* ed. Julian H. Steward, 5: 97–138; Raoul d'Harcourt, *Textiles of Ancient Peru and Their Techniques;* Marilyn Anderson, *Guatemalan Textiles Today;* and Eric Broudy, *The Book of Looms.*

2. For more complete descriptions of Guatemalan weaving techniques, see Lilly de Jongh Osborne, *Indian Crafts of Guatemala and El Salvador;* O'Neale, *Textiles;* O'Neale, "Weaving"; Hilda Schmidt Delgado Pang, "Aboriginal Guatemalan Handweaving and Costume" (Ph.D. dissertation, Indiana University, 1963); idem et al., "Central American Ethnographic Textiles," in *Ethnographic Textiles of the Western Hemisphere,* ed. Irene Emery and Patricia Fiske, pp. 89–156; Suzanne Baizerman and Karen Searle, *Latin American Brocades: Explorations in Supplementary Weft Techniques;* Lena Bjerregaard, *Techniques of Guatemalan Weaving;* Anderson, *Guatemalan Textiles Today;* Norbert Sperlich and Elizabeth Katz Sperlich, *Guatemalan Backstrap Weaving.*

3. In regard to the sexual division of labor, the general rule in the highlands is that women are backstrap weavers and men (and *ladinos*) operate the larger, foot-operated treadle looms. In San Antonio, men are associated with field labor and women are associated with weaving, but there is nothing un-

usual or unacceptable about a man doing backstrap weaving. When I first began to weave, I was reassured on this score by being told the names of several local and foreign backstrap weavers. Nevertheless, I *was* the cause of considerable behind-the-hand chuckling. It took some time to realize that weaving, per se, was acceptable for a male, but "sitting like a woman" (see Figure 29) was not. I had gamely declined the initial offer of a chair. When I reconsidered and sat in the chair, I restored my manly image.

4. Forty-six percent of Catholic women and 48 percent of Protestant women weave every day for three or more hours. Although a higher proportion of Protestant women don't weave at all (29 percent, versus 14 percent for Catholics), this is somewhat offset by the fact that a correspondingly higher proportion of Catholic women who weave do so infrequently (17 percent, versus 5 percent for Protestants).

5. In some towns, the terms are interchangeable, but in San Antonio *servilleta* usually refers to a plain or striped everyday cloth, while a *tzut* is a more formal, stylized cloth that is dense with designs unique to San Antonio. A *tzut* is primarily a decorative complement to a woman's formal attire—something carried in a religious procession, worn to Guatemala City, or exchanged between mother- and daughter-in-law at a marriage. A *servilleta* is more mundane. It seldom sells for more than $12; the cost of a high-quality *tzut* (though only rarely sold among neighbors) ranges from $40 to $60.

6. There is an extensive literature on humoral hot/cold associations in Latin America generally and Mesoamerica specifically. Anthropologists have found that this hot/cold logic applies to many domains. For example, with regard to food, see Robert Redfield and Alfonso Villa Rojas, *Chan Kom: A Maya Village*, p. 162; John McCullough, "Human Ecology, Heat Adaptation, and Belief Systems: the Hot-Cold Syndrome of Yucatán," *Journal of Anthropological Research* 29, no. 1 (1973): 32–36; C. H. Molony, "Systematic Valence Coding in 'Hot'-'Cold' Food," *Ecology of Food and Nutrition* 4 (1975): 67–74. For illness, see J. M. Ingham, "On Mexican Folk Medicine," *American Anthropologist* 72 (1970): 78–79; George M. Foster, "Disease Etiologies in Non-Western Medical Systems," *American Anthropologist* 78 (1976): 773–782; Juan José Hurtado and Julie Glavis, "Calor-frío, una categoría cognitiva: Un estudio de creéncias y prácticas médicas populares en el municipio de San Juan Sacatepéquez, Guatemala," in *Seminario nacional sobre tecnología apropriada*. For herbal remedies, see Michael Logan, "Digestive Disorders and Plant Medicinals in Highland Guatemala," *Anthropos* 68 (1973): 537–547. For astrological and worldly elements, see W. Madsen, "Hot and Cold in the Universe of San Francisco Tecospa, Valley of Mexico," *Journal of American Folklore* 68 (1955): 123–140. For breastfeeding, see Richard Currier, "The Hot-Cold Syndrome and Symbolic Balance in Mexican and Spanish American Folk Medicine," *Ethnology* 5 (1966): 257.

7. The "saddest" colors are black, the color of death, and purple, the mourning color of Easter. "Happy" colors are generally those that we would call "bright." But the terms are also often used in a relational sense, i.e.,

"happy" in that they "go together." There is no widespread agreement about which colors (or sets) are "happy" or "sad."

8. To say that "textiles are like texts" is a misdirected simile since, etymologically, "texts" are like "textiles" (*text:* from the Latin *texere,* to weave), not the other way around. "Lat. *textum,* that which is woven, a fabric, also the style of an author; hence, a text. Orig. neut. of *textus,* pp. of *texere* to weave" (Walter Skeat, *An Etymological Dictionary of the English Language,* p. 633).

9. See, for example, Bjerregaard, *Techniques of Guatemalan Weaving.*

10. Walter F. Morris, *Flowers, Saints, and Toads: Chiapas Maya Textile Design Symbolism.*

11. Walter F. Morris, "A Textured Script: Classic and Modern Maya Textile Designs" (research proposal to the National Geographic Society, 1980).

12. Flavio N. Rodas, *Simbolismo (Maya Quiché) de Guatemala.* Writing in the late 1930s, Rodas analyzed Quichean weaving from Chichicastenango and found color and design symbolism related to pre-Columbian roots. Although he presents scant evidence that suggests systematic investigation and bases much of his case on obvious conjecture, his analysis and linguistic material are so rich that I at least am persuaded that "something is there."

13. Barbara and Dennis Tedlock, "Text and Textile: Language and Technology in the Arts of the Quiché Maya," *Journal of Anthropological Research* 41 (1985): 121–146. The Tedlocks present a far more sophisticated semantic analysis based on their extensive studies of Quichean ethnopoetics. Through the notion of "intertextuality" they explore how textual "dialogue" transcends itself and crosses boundaries from one cultural medium to another.

14. Pang, "Aboriginal Guatemalan Handweaving and Costume."

15. Margaret Wilhite argues that *huipiles* in San Antonio and the nearby Cakchiquel-speaking town of Santa María de Jesús explicitly reveal the "status" and identify the family of the intended user. She found that the exact manner of weaving these designs is known only to specific families, but that they are nonetheless recognizable to most people in the town. See R. Margaret Wilhite, "First Language Acquisition: Textile Design Terminology in Cakchiquel (Mayan)" (Ph.D. dissertation, Washington University, 1977), esp. pp. 71–74.

16. Not all *huipiles* function so neatly or ideally as this fictitious example. With the emergence and growing popularity of regional styles, "mass-produced" *huipiles* made by machine, footloom, or professional handweavers replace the *municipio* and lower locative orders with a pan-regional design such as "the Totonicapán style," the "Chimaltenango style," or the "Alta Verapaz style." For discussion of textile design as spatial representation, see Wilson Popenoe, "Regional Differences in the Guatemalan Huipil," *Anales de XX Congreso Internacional de Americanistas* 1 (1950): 217–220; Felix Webster McBryde, *Cultural and Historical Geography of Southwest Guatemala;* Hilda Delgado Pang, "Guatemalan Indian Handweaving: Conservatism and Change in a Village Handicraft," in *Verhandlungen des*

XXXVIII Internationalen Amerikanisten Kongresses 2: 449–457; Cherri Pancake, "Textile Traditions of the Highland Maya: Some Aspects of Development and Change" (paper presented to the International Symposium on Maya Art, Architecture, Archaeology, and Hieroglyphic Writing, Guatemala City, 1978); Osborne, *Indian Crafts;* Cherri Pancake and Suzanne Baizerman, "Guatemalan Gauze Weaves: A Description and Key to Identification," *Textile Museum Journal* 19–20 (1980–1981): 1–26; R. C. Morrissey, "Continuity and Change in Backstrap Loom Textiles of Highland Guatemala" (Ph.D. dissertation, University of Wisconsin–Madison, 1983), pp. 144, 173–174; Anne P. Rowe, *A Century of Change in Guatemalan Textiles,* pp. 22–24.

17. I wish to acknowledge again the close collaboration of Cherri Pancake, formerly director of the Museo Ixchel (textile museum) in Guatemala City, who worked to develop the coding system and computer analysis for this study; to Wendy Kramer and Lydia Parks, who collected design and price data in the field and ran a series of "time trials" that were used to establish the difficulty and the average times for particular designs; and to Gordon Smith, formerly of Antigua, who generously allowed us to study and photograph his collection of San Antonio *huipiles.*

18. Preliminary findings are reported in Cherri Pancake and Sheldon Annis, "El arte de la producción: Aspectos socio-económicos del tejido a mano en San Antonio Aguas Calientes, Guatemala," *Mesoamérica* 3, no. 4 (1982): 387–413.

19. The general form of a production function equation is:

$$Y = f(X_1 \ldots X_i \ldots X_n)$$

where Y is the observed output, having different sets of inputs $X_1 \ldots X_n$. Production function equations have many specific algebraic forms. The best known and most conventional form is called the Cobb-Douglas function. The Cobb-Douglas form is:

$$Y = AX_1^{b_1} \ldots X_i^{b_i} \ldots X_n^{b_n}$$

where Y is the output, X_i are the inputs, A is a constant term, and b_i defines a transformational parameter for the particular level of input, X_i. All variables in this function are measured in physical units. The computational characteristic of this form that has made it so popular is that it becomes linear in the logarithms of the variables. See Charles W. Cobb and Paul H. Douglas, "A Theory of Production," *American Economic Review Supplement* 18, no. 1 (1928): 139–165.

20. A. A. Walters, *An Introduction to Econometrics,* p. 272.

21. If the two completed designs are held side by side, one is likely to say, "Yes, I see the difference." But the quality judgment must be learned.

22. Many accounts of the pre-Conquest period discuss use of textiles as a medium of exchange. Bartolomé de Las Casas, among the first on-site historians, in *Apologética historia de las Indias,* p. 621, describes the exchange "of cloaks of cotton for gold and hand-axes of copper, and gold for emeralds and turquoises and plumes, which are the merchandise most valued." The *Popul Vuh* describes painted or embroidered *mantas* that Quichean maidens were given by the storm gods and refers to cotton *manta* as a tribute item (Munro S. Edmonson, trans., *The Book of Counsel: The Popul Vuh of*

the Quiché Maya of Guatemala, pp. 197, 230. Patricia Anawalt has published extensively on pre-Conquest and immediate post-Conquest use of textiles in Middle America: see, for example, her "Costume and Control: Aztec Sumptuary Laws," *Archaeology* 53 (January/February 1980): 33–43.

23. Woodrow Borah and Sherbourne F. Cook, "Price Trends of Some Basic Commodities in Central Mexico, 1531–1570," *Ibero-Americana,* vol. 40 (1958).

24. Alonso de Cerrato et al., "Tributos, 1553–1555" (AGCA, legajo A3.16/2797, expediente 40466) list in some detail tribute paid from various weaving centers in the mid-sixteenth century. The document describes a standard tribute textile that was made from several smaller pieces and measured 8 × 1.5 meters.

25. See, for example, Sol Tax, *Penny Capitalism: A Guatemalan Indian Economy;* McBryde, *Cultural and Historical Geography;* Manning Nash, "Indian Economies" in *Handbook of Middle American Indians,* vol. 6, *Social Anthropology,* ed. Robert Wauchope and Manning Nash, pp. 87–102; Alfred John Hagan, "An Analysis of the Hand-Weaving Sector of the Guatemalan Economy" (Ph.D. dissertation, University of Texas at Austin, 1970).

26. These calculations are based on extrapolation from reports of textile expenditures from a small sample of tourists and from calculations based on the shadow wage rates for unskilled Indian labor. If anything, they are conservative since we did not include sales of textiles to nontourists, i.e., to *ladino* Guatemalans or to other Indians. See Olivier Conrard and Sheldon Annis, "Handicraft Employment," in *Guatemalan Tourism Sector Analysis,* Technical Appendix, Annex II.

7. Textile Entrepreneurship and the Economics of Culture

1. The average textile product per family for the six-month period (January–June 1978) is about $280—or $560 for the year. Considering that median family wealth is only slightly over $2,000 and that median family income is only slightly over $1,000, an output of roughly $500 is significant in both absolute and relative terms. During the six-month period, the same women actually *sold* a reported 1,406 textiles, which yielded a net cash return of $5,221. Of the textiles sold, just over half (762) were woven and marketed by the seller herself; the rest were either commissioned, purchased from local weavers, or purchased from textile vendors from outside the town. The sales value of textiles (excluding the cost of materials) that were made and then sold was $3,515 (i.e., the value added by labor). In other words, the average annual net gain from sales of all made-and-bought textiles was $141 ($5,221 × 2 ÷ 74) and for personally made-and-sold textiles was $95 ($3,515 × 2 ÷ 74).

2. The artisan coop is moribund. It is a carry-over from external pressures to form cooperatives. Even in its heyday, it was never vigorous. As it happened, two coop members (both from the same household) fell into this sample, but only about a dozen or so women in the town actively participate in coop activities. Although local nonmembers occasionally sell through or

to the affiliated coop store in Antigua, the coop is only another kind of *tienda*.

3. For purpose of this analysis, I computed values for eight textile variables: the dollar value of a family's six-month production of traditional textiles, the dollar value of a family's six-month production of commercial textiles, the dollar value of a family's inventory of traditional textiles, the dollar value of a family's inventory of commercial textiles, the dollar value of a family's *huipil* inventory, the dollar value of a family's six-month textile sales, the dollar value of that portion of textile sales that were made by family members, and the dollar value of textiles that were purchased for the purpose of resale. In a variety of tests, this last variable proved to be the best and most reliable indicator of purely entrepreneurial behavior.

4. The Beta coefficient showing the relationship between the independent variable (i.e., wealth obtained from the resale of purchased textiles, the proxy indicator of "entrepreneurial behavior") and total wealth was .3471 (significant at the .999 level); the relationship between the independent variable and religion was .3815 (significant at the .999 level); and between the independent variable and years of school was −.1262 (significant at the .90 level).

One quirk that complicates these data is the presence of two "outliers" among the small set of Protestant families, that is, two women from a single family that is both "rich" and the highest textile reseller in the sample. Their income from textile resales is very much larger than that of the family that has the next highest income from textile resales. If this distortion is adjusted either by dropping the two outliers or by using logs of bought-textile income to smooth out the distribution, the effect of the wealth variable becomes even less dramatic. In re-running the regression, the explanatory power of total wealth all but disappears; religion, and then years of school, emerge as far more important independent variables.

5. For both Catholic and Protestant women, high-quality textiles serve as rainy-day savings accounts; though a woman under pressure to sell may not be able to command a good or even fair price, a high-quality *huipil* can nevertheless almost always be converted to some ready cash.

Glossary

AID: The U.S. Agency for International Development.

alcaldía: The mayor's office.

aldea: A rural hamlet, usually linked administratively and culturally to a larger urban center, like San Antonio.

alfombra: Outdoor "rug" made of pine needles, colored sawdust, and flowers, as part of the Catholic celebration of Holy Week. See Figure 20.

anda: A religious "float," carried in the Holy Week processions. See Figure 22.

astillero: Communal land belonging to the *municipio*, used for firewood and *milpa* farming by the town's poorest inhabitants.

BANDESA: El Banco Nacional para Desarollo Agrícola, a state-operated bank for rural development.

básico: A post-primary school, in Antigua.

caballería: Land measure equal to 400 *cuerdas* (about 33.5 acres).

cabecera municipal: The "municipal seat," i.e., San Antonio.

cantón: A neighborhood, quarter of town, or rural zone.

cédula: The identification card that Guatemalan Indians are required to carry.

chirimía: A primitive flute-like instrument often played on fiesta days.

cofrade: A member of a *cofradía*, a civil-religious "cargo association" that venerates a particular saint or holy image.

comité: A civil village committee, usually for self-help projects.

compadrazgo: Ritual godparenthood, common among Catholics.

contratista: A labor contractor.

corte: A long piece of rectangular, foot-loomed cloth, wrapped around a woman's waist to make the traditional Indian skirt.

costumbrista: A person practicing *costumbre*, traditional Mayan-Catholic ritual.

CUC: The Committee for Campesino Unity, a political party that was driven underground in the late 1970s.

cuerda: Land measure equal to about 1,600 square meters (but can vary).

encomienda: A concession or land grant given to conquistadores which gave them the right to the land and to the labor of the Indians living on it.

evangélico: "Evangelical," the term commonly used in Guatemala for Protestant churches, including Pentecostal groups, but usually excluding Jehovah's Witnesses, Mormons, and Adventists.

faja: Hand-loomed belt, part of the traditional woman's costume.

finca: Farm; in Guatemala, usually implies a large, export-oriented farm.

finquero: The owner of a *finca*.

gabán: A man's traditional heavy woolen overgarment. See Figure 30.

huipil: A woman's traditional handwoven blouse. See Figure 32.

INCAP: Instituto para Nutrición para Centroamérica y Panamá, an OAS-affiliated research and training institution that specializes in health and nutrition.

Indianness: A term used here to refer to a post-Conquest social identity—created in large measure in response to the needs of the Hispanic overclass—for Maya-descended people.

ladino: Non-Indian, in language and culture.

marcador: A "modern" floral design usually woven at the breast region of a *huipil*.

milpa: Historically, one of the *encomiendas* given to the lieutenants of Pedro de Alvarado as rewards for service during the Conquest; now, a plot of corn intercropped with beans and small quantities of secondary crops.

milpa logic: The cultural and economic "logic" of traditional Indian identity that is elegantly expressed by the *milpa* production process; particularly refers to resource transformations in which inputs are optimized, as opposed to outputs being maximized.

mozo: Day laborer, servant.

municipio: A political subdivision, similar to a county. Indians in a *municipio* usually share dress style, dialect, religious fiestas, and common civil authority.

ORPA: Organization of People in Arms, a guerrilla group.

petate: A woven reed mat; see Figure 24. Sometimes the term refers to the thin variety of reed used to make the mats.

pila: Laundry area; public *pilas* have communal standpipes for drinking water.

promotores: Village volunteers who help "promote" self-help activities.

quetzal: The basic monetary unit of Guatemala; on 1 : 1 par with the U.S. dollar until the mid-1980s.

Quinizilapa: The name of a dried-up lake bed around which five towns, including San Antonio, were founded ca. 1530. The lake no longer exists, and the term is not a recognized place name in contemporary Guatemala.

quintal: A hundredweight.

real: An old Spanish monetary unit.

servilleta: A square cloth for everyday use; in San Antonio, usually plain or striped.

sitio: Household compound containing several freestanding rooms surrounded by a cornstalk fence; may contain several families.

telarcitos: Small ornamental "loom weaving samplers" sold to tourists, often made by children.

tienda: A tiny "general store"; or a stall where textiles are sold to tourists.

tiendera: The owner of a *tienda*.

tul: The marsh reeds from which *petates* are woven; sometimes refers to the thick reed used for cruder mats.

tzut: A formal, stylized type of *servilleta*, used as a decorative complement to a woman's formal attire.

vara: A unit of length, equivalent to about a meter.

Bibliography

Aaby, Peter, and Soren Hvalkof. *Is God an American? An Anthropological Perspective on the Missionary Work of the Summer Institute of Linguistics.* Copenhagen: International Work Group for Indigenous Affairs, and London: Survival International, 1981.

Adams, Richard N. *Crucifixion by Power.* Austin: University of Texas Press, 1970.

———. "Cultural Components of Central America." *American Anthropologist* 58 (1956): 881–907.

———, ed. *Political Changes in Guatemalan Indian Communities.* New Orleans: Middle American Research Institute, Publication 21, 1957.

AGCA. *See* Archivo General de Centroamérica.

AGI. *See* Archivo General de Indias.

Aguilera Peralta, Jorge Romero Imery, et al., *Dialécticas del terror en Guatemala.* San José, Costa Rica, 1982.

Alisedo, Pedro, et al. *El Instituto Lingüístico de Verano.* Mexico City: Proceso, 1981.

Americas Watch Committee. *Guatemala: A Nation of Prisoners.* New York, 1984.

Anawalt, Patricia. "Costume and Control: Aztec Sumptuary Laws." *Archaeology* 53 (January/February 1980): 33–43.

Anderson, Marilyn. *Guatemalan Textiles Today.* New York: Watson-Guptill, 1978.

Anfuso, Joseph, and David Sczeponski. *He Gives—He Takes Away: The True Story of Guatemala's Controversial Former President Efraín Ríos Montt.* Eureka, Calif.: Radiance Publications, 1983.

Annis, Sheldon. "Artisanal Entrepreneurship in a Guatemalan Village." Paper presented to the International Geographic Union Symposium on Rural Development, Fresno, Calif., April 1981.

———. "Estudio de los servicios de salud en los departamentos de Sololá, Totonicapán y San Marcos." Guatemala: U.S. Agency for International Development and Ministry of Health, 1980.

———. "A Story from a Peaceful Town." In *Harvest of Violence: Guatemala's Indians and the Counterinsurgency War,* edited by Robert M. Carmack. Norman: University of Oklahoma Press, 1987.

Annis, Sheldon, and Elena Hurtado. "Improving Family Planning in the

Highlands of Guatemala: A Case Study of the Department of El Quiché."
Washington, D.C.: American Public Health Association, 1978.

Archivo General de Centroamérica (AGCA). Guatemala City. Correspondencia al Congresso. Cajo no. 4131.

Archivo General de Indias (AGI). Seville. "Los indios que eran esclavos . . ."
(1576). Guatemala, legajo 54, folios 9, 28, 29.

Arreola Hernández, Julia Marina. "Diagnóstico de la situación del grupo
materno-infantil, año 1975, San Antonio Aguas Calientes, Sacatepéquez."
Thesis, School of Medicine, University of San Carlos, Guatemala, 1976.

Ascoli, Werner, Miguel Guzmán, Nevin Scrimshaw, and John E. Gordon.
"Nutrition and Infection Field Study, 1959–1964, Part IV: Deaths of In-
fants and Preschool Children." *Archives of Environmental Health* 15, no. 4
(October 1967): 439–449.

Baizerman, Suzanne, and Karen Searle. *Latin American Brocades: Explorations in Supplementary Weft Techniques.* St. Paul, Minn.: Dos Tejedo-
ras, 1976.

Bernstein, Richard, and Robert Herdt. "Towards an Understanding of Milpa
Agriculture: The Belize Case." *Journal of Developing Areas* 11 (April
1977): 373–392.

Berryman, Phillip. *The Religious Roots of Rebellion: Christians in Central
American Revolutions.* Maryknoll, N.Y.: Orbis Books, 1984.

Bjerregaard, Lena. *Techniques of Guatemalan Weaving.* New York: Van
Nostrand Reinhold, 1977.

Borah, Woodrow, and Sherbourne F. Cook. "Price Trends of Some Basic Commodities in Central Mexico, 1531–1570." *Ibero-Americana*, vol. 40
(1958). Berkeley and Los Angeles: University of California Press.

Borhegyi, Stephan F. de. "Archaeological Synthesis of the Guatemalan High-
lands." In *Handbook of Middle American Indians*, vol. 2, *Archaeology of
Southern Mesoamerica, Part One*, edited by Robert Wauchope and Gordon
R. Willey, pp. 3–58. Austin: University of Texas Press, 1965.

Bowen, Gordon. "Guatemala: The Origins and Development of State Ter-
rorism." In *Revolution and Counterrevolution in Central America and
the Caribbean*, edited by Donald E. Shulz and Douglas Graham. Boulder,
Colo.: Westview Press, 1984.

Brintnall, Douglas. *Revolt against the Dead: The Modernization of a Mayan
Community in the Highlands of Guatemala.* New York: Gordon and
Breach, 1979.

British Parliamentary Human Rights Group. *Bitter and Cruel: Report of a
Mission to Guatemala.* London: 1985.

Broudy, Eric. *The Book of Looms.* New York: Van Nostrand Reinhold, 1979.

Burgess, Paul. *Justo Rufino Barrios: A Biography.* 2d ed. Quezaltenango:
Tipografíca El Noticiero, 1946.

———, ed. *Historia de la obra evangélica presbiteriana en Guatemala.*
Quezaltenango: El Noticiero Evangélico, 1957.

Cabrera, Leonel, and Sheldon Annis. "Estudio comunitario: Evaluación del
sistema de salud rural, Informe No. III." Guatemala City: Académia de
Ciencias de Guatemala, 1979.

Calder, Bruce. *Crecimiento y cambio de la iglesia católica guatemalteca, 1944–1966.* Guatemala City: Seminario de Integración Social Guatemalteca, 1970.

Cambranes, J. C. *Coffee and Peasants: The Origins of the Modern Plantation Economy in Guatemala, 1853–1897.* Stockholm: Institute of Latin American Studies, 1985. Distributed in U.S.A. and Canada by CIRMA/Plumsock Mesoamerican Studies, South Woodstock, Vt.

———. *Introducción a la historia agrícola de Guatemala.* Guatemala City: Facultad de Agronomía, Universidad de San Carlos de Guatemala, 1978.

Cancian, Frank. *Economics and Prestige in a Maya Community.* Stanford: Stanford University Press, 1965.

Carmack, Robert M., ed. *Harvest of Violence: Guatemala's Indians and the Counterinsurgency War.* Norman: University of Oklahoma Press.

Carmack, Robert M., John Early, and Christopher Lutz, eds. *The Historical Demography of Highland Guatemala.* Albany, N.Y.: Institute for Mesoamerican Studies, SUNY-Albany, 1982.

Carter, W. E. "Innovation and Marginality: Two South American Case Studies." *América Indígena* 30 (1965): 383–392, 436.

Chayanov, Alexander V. *The Theory of Peasant Economy.* Edited by Daniel Thorner, Basile Kerblay, and R. E. F. Smith. Homewood, Ill.: Published for the American Economic Association by R. D. Irwin, 1966. (The original Russian edition was published in Moscow in 1925.)

Clawson, David. "Religious Allegiance and Economic Development in Rural Latin America." *Journal of Interamerican Studies and World Affairs* 26, no. 4 (November 1984): 499–524.

Cobb, Charles W., and Paul H. Douglas. "A Theory of Production." *American Economic Review Supplement* 18, no. 1 (1928): 139–165.

Conrard, Olivier, and Sheldon Annis. "Handicraft Employment." In *Guatemalan Tourism Sector Analysis,* Technical Appendix, Annex II. Washington, D.C.: World Bank, 1977.

Consejo Nacional de Planificación Económica. *Plan nacional de desarrollo, 1975–1979: Educación, ciencias y cultura.* Guatemala City, 1975.

Cook, Scott. "Price and Output Variability in a Peasant-Artisan Stoneworking Industry in Oaxaca, Mexico." *American Anthropologist* 72 (1970): 780.

Crahan, Margaret E. "International Aspects of the Role of the Catholic Church in Central America." In *Central America: International Dimensions of the Crisis,* edited by Richard E. Feinberg, pp. 213–235. New York and London: Holmes & Meier Publishers, 1982.

Currier, Richard. "The Hot-Cold Syndrome and Symbolic Balance in Mexican and Spanish American Folk Medicine." *Ethnology* 5 (1966): 257.

Davis, Shelton H., and Julie Hodson. *Witness to Political Violence in Guatemala: The Suppression of a Rural Development Movement.* Boston: Oxfam America, 1982.

De Janvry, Alain, and Carmen Deere. "A Conceptual Framework for the Empirical Analysis of Peasants." *American Journal of Agricultural Economics* 61 (November 1979): 601–611.

Delgado Pang, Hilda Schmidt. *See* Pang, Hilda Schmidt Delgado.

De Walt, Billie. "Changes in the Cargo Systems of Mesoamerica." *Anthropological Quarterly* 48 (April 1975): 87–105.

d'Harcourt, Raoul. *Textiles of Ancient Peru and Their Techniques.* Seattle: University of Washington Press, 1962.

Diaz, May N. *Tonalá: Conservatism, Responsibility, and Authority in a Mexican Town.* Berkeley: University of California Press, 1966.

Diener, Paul. "The Tears of St. Anthony: Ritual and Revolution in Eastern Guatemala." *Latin American Perspectives* 5 (1978): 92–116.

Early, John. "Education via Radio among Guatemalan Highland Maya." *Human Organization* 32 (Fall 1973): 221–229.

————. "Municipios Recommended as Sites of Experimental Programs, Appendix C." In "The Family Planning Program among the Indian Population of Guatemala." Study prepared by American Public Health Association, Washington, D.C., under U.S. Agency for International Development contract no. 582-006, 1979.

Edmonson, Munro S., trans. *The Book of Counsel: The Popul Vuh of the Quiché Maya of Guatemala.* New Orleans: Middle American Research Institute, Publication 35, 1971.

Falla, Ricardo. "Evolución político-religiosa del indígena rural en Guatemala, 1945–65." *Estudios Sociales Centroamericanos* 1 (January–April 1972): 27–41. San José, Costa Rica.

————. *Quiché rebelde: Estudio de un movimiento de conversión religiosa rebelde a las creencias tradicionales, en San Antonio Ilotenango, Quiché, 1948–70.* Guatemala City: Editorial Universitaria de Guatemala, 1978.

Flores, Marina, Zoila Flores, and Marta Lara. "Food Intake of Guatemalan Children, Ages 1–5." *Journal of the American Dietetic Association,* June 1966, pp. 400–487.

Flores, Marina, Zoila Flores, and Berta Meneses. "Estudio de hábitos dietéticos en poblaciones de Guatemala, IX, Santa Catarina Barahona." *Archivos Venezolanos de Nutrición* 8, no. 1–2 (1957): 67.

Flores, Marina, and Emma Reh. "Estudios de hábitos dietéticos en poblaciones de Guatemala, III, San Antonio Aguas Calientes y su aldea San Andrés Ceballos." *Boletín de la Oficina Sanitaria Panamericana.* Publicaciones de INCAP, Suplemento No. 2 (1955), pp. 149–162.

Foster, George M. "Disease Etiologies in Non-Western Medical Systems." *American Anthropologist* 78 (1976): 773–782.

Fox, Robert, and Jerrold Huguet. *Population and Urbanization to the Year 2000 in Central America and Panama.* Washington, D.C.: Inter-American Development Bank, 1977.

Frank, Luisa, and Philip Wheaton. *Indian Guatemala: Path to Liberation.* Washington, D.C.: EPICA Task Force, 1984.

García-Ruíz, Jesús. *Las sectas fundamentalistas en Guatemala.* Cuaderno 4. Guatemala City: Ciencia y Tecnología para Guatemala, April 1985.

Gerhard, Peter. *The Southwest Frontier of New Spain.* Princeton, N.J.: University of Princeton Press, 1979.

Glen, N. D., and R. Hyland. "Religious Preference and Worldly Success:

Some Evidence from National Surveys." *American Sociological Review* 32, no. 1 (1967): 73–85.

Gordon, John E., Werner Ascoli, Leonardo Mata, Miguel Guzmán, and Nevin Scrimshaw. "Nutrition and Infection Field Study, 1959–1964: Part VI, Acute Diarrheal Disease and Nutritional Disorders in General Disease Incidence." *Archives of Environmental Health* 16 (March 1968).

Gutiérrez, U., M. Infante, and P. Pinchinat. "Situación del cultivo de frijol en América Latina." *Boletín Informe.* E.S. 19 (1975). Cali, Colombia: CIAT.

Guzmán Böckler, Carlos, and Jean-Loup Herbert. *Guatemala: Una interpretación histórico-social.* Mexico City: Siglo Veintiuno, 1970.

Hackel, Bernard. *Urban Poverty in Guatemala.* Guatemala City: Abeles and Schwartz, under contract to U.S. Agency for International Development, 1980.

Hagan, Alfred John. "An Analysis of the Hand-Weaving Sector of the Guatemalan Economy." Ph.D. dissertation, School of Business, University of Texas at Austin, 1970.

Handy, Jim. *Gift of the Devil: A History of Guatemala.* Boston: South End Press, 1984.

Harmon, Robert, and William Kurtz. "Missionary Influence on Maya Medical Behavior: Results of a Factor Analysis." Paper presented to the 33rd Annual Meeting of the Society for Applied Anthropology, Tucson, 1973.

Hefley, James and Marti. *Uncle Cam.* Waco, Tex.: Word Books, 1974.

Hinshaw, Robert. *Panajachel: A Guatemalan Town in Thirty Year Perspective.* Pittsburgh: University of Pittsburgh Press, 1975.

Horst, Oscar. "Assessing Peasant Agriculture: Western Perceptions and Traditional Realities." Paper presented to the International Geographic Union Symposium on Rural Development, Fresno, Calif., April 1981.

———. "El rancho y la milpa: Una simbiosis significativa en la economía agrícola del occidente de Guatemala." Cuadernos de Antropología (Instituto de Investigaciones Históricas, Universidad de San Carlos, Guatemala) 7 (1966): 13–18.

Hurtado, Juan José, and Julie Glavis. "Calor-frío, una categoría cognitiva: Un estudio de creéncias y prácticas médicas populares en el municipio de San Juan Sacatepéquez, Guatemala." In *Seminario nacional sobre tecnología apropriada.* Guatemala City: CEMAT, 1977.

IINDEF. *See* Instituto Internacional de Evangelización a Fondo.

Immerman, Richard H. *The CIA in Guatemala.* Austin: University of Texas Press, 1982.

Ingham, J. M. "On Mexican Folk Medicine." *American Anthropologist* 72 (1970): 78–79.

Instituto Indigenista Nacional. *San Antonio Aguas Calientes: Síntesis socioeconómico de una comunidad indígena.* Guatemala City: Instituto Indigenista Nacional, 1948.

Instituto Internacional de Evangelización a Fondo (IINDEF) and Servicio Evangelizador para America Latina (SEPAL). *Directorio de iglesias, organizaciones y ministerios del movimiento protestante.* Guatemala City, 1981.

Inter-American Commission on Human Rights. *Report on the Situation of Human Rights in the Republic of Guatemala.* Washington, D.C.: Organization of American States, 1983.

Jordan, W. F. *Central American Indians and the Bible.* New York: Fleming H. Revell, 1926.

Katy, Charles, and Geraldine Katy. "Private Voluntary Organizations in Health." In *Guatemala Health Care Sector Assessment.* Guatemala: U.S. Agency for International Development and Guatemalan Ministry of Health, 1977.

Krueger, Christine, and Kjell Enge. *Security and Development Conditions in the Guatemalan Highlands.* Washington, D.C.: Washington Office on Latin America, 1985.

La Farge, Oliver. "Maya Ethnology: The Sequence of Cultures." In *The Maya and Their Neighbors,* edited by C. L. Hay et al., pp. 281–291. New York: Appleton-Century, 1940.

Lange, Frederick, and Doris Stone, eds. *The Archaeology of Lower Central America.* Albuquerque: University of New Mexico Press, 1984.

Las Casas, Bartolomé de. *Apologética historia de las Indias.* Madrid: M. Serrano y Sanz, 1909. Cited in *National Union Catalog: Pre-1956 Imprints* 97: 533.

Lathbury, Virginia. "Textiles as the Expression of an Expanding World View: San Antonio Aguas Calientes." M.A. thesis, Department of Anthropology, University of Pennsylvania, 1974.

Lenin, V. I. *The Development of Capitalism in Russia.* Moscow: Progress Publishers, 1966.

Lernoux, Penny. *Cry of the People.* London: Penguin, 1982.

Levine, Daniel H. *Churches and Politics in Latin America.* Beverly Hills and London: Sage Publications, 1980.

Littlefield, Alice. "The Hammock Industry of Yucatan: A Study in Economic Anthropology." Ph.D. dissertation, Michigan State University, 1976.

Lloret, Julian. "Forces Shaping the Church in Central America." *CAM Bulletin,* Summer 1982, p. 3.

———. "The Mayan Evangelical Church in Guatemala." Doctor of Theology dissertation, Dallas Theological Seminary, 1976.

Lockheed, Marilyn, Dean T. Jamison, and Lawrence J. Lau. "Farmer Education and Farm Efficiency: A Survey." *Economic Development and Cultural Change* 29, no. 1 (October 1980): 37–76.

Logan, Michael. "Digestive Disorders and Plant Medicinals in Highland Guatemala." *Anthropos* 68 (1973): 537–547.

López de Cerrato, Alonso, Alonso de Zorita, Pedro Ramírez, Alonso Ortiz Quezada, and Tomás López. "Tributos, 1553–1555." Archivo General de Centroamérica (AGCA), Guatemala City. Legajo A3.16/2797, expediente 40466.

Lutz, Christopher. "Historia de la población de la Parroquia de San Miguel Dueñas, 1530–1770." *Mesoamérica* 2, no. 2 (June 1981): 64–82.

———. *Historia sociodemográfica de Santiago de Guatemala, 1541–1773.*

Serie Monográfica, no. 2. Antigua, Guatemala: Centro de Investigaciones Regionales de Mesoamérica, 1983.

——. Population History of San Miguel Dueñas, ca. 1530–1770." In *The Historical Demography of Highland Guatemala*, edited by Robert M. Carmack, John Early, and Christopher Lutz. Albany, N.Y.: Institute for Mesoamerican Studies, SUNY-Albany, 1982.

McBryde, Felix Webster. *Cultural and Historical Geography of Southwest Guatemala*. Washington, D.C.: Smithsonian Institution, Institute of Social Anthropology, 1947.

McCullough, John. "Human Ecology, Heat Adaptation, and Belief Systems: The Hot-Cold Syndrome of Yucatán." *Journal of Anthropological Research* 29, no. 1 (1973): 32–36.

McDowell, Paul. "Guatemalan Stratification and Peasant Marketing Arrangements: A Different View." *Man* 11 (1975): 273–278.

MacLeod, Murdo. *Spanish Central America: A Socioeconomic History, 1520–1720*. Berkeley: University of California Press, 1973.

MacNeish, Richard S. "The Food-gathering and Incipient Agriculture Stage of Prehistoric Middle America." In *Handbook of Middle American Indians*, vol. 1, *Natural Environment and Early Cultures*, edited by Robert Wauchope and Robert West, pp. 413–426. Austin: University of Texas Press, 1964.

Madsen, W. "Hot and Cold in the Universe of San Francisco Tecospa, Valley of Mexico." *Journal of American Folklore* 68 (1955): 123–140.

Mangelsdorf, Paul C., Richard S. MacNeish, and Gordon R. Willey. "Origins of Agriculture in Middle America." In *Handbook of Middle American Indians*, vol. 1, *Natural Environment and Early Cultures*, edited by Robert Wauchope and Robert West, pp. 427–445. Austin: University of Texas Press, 1964.

Manger Cats, S. G. "Socio-economic Development in Guatemala through Incentives to the Subsistence Sector." *Netherlands Journal of Agricultural Science* 18 (1970): 116–124.

Martínez Peláez, Severo. *La patria del criollo: Ensayo de interpretación de la realidad colonial guatemalteca*. 5th ed. San José, Costa Rica: Editorial Universitaria Centroamérica (EDUCA), 1983.

Melville, Thomas R. "The Catholic Church in Guatemala, 1944–1982." *Cultural Survival Quarterly* 7 (Spring 1983): 23–27.

Molina, Alfonso de. *Vocabulario en lengua castellana y mexicana*. Facsimile ed. Mexico City: Editorial Porrúa, 1970.

Molony, C. H. "Systematic Valence Cooling in 'Hot'-'Cold' Food." *Ecology of Food and Nutrition* 4 (1975): 67–74.

Montgomery, James. "The Case for Research: Part 3, The Factors of Growth." *Global Church Growth* 20 (March–April 1983): 250. Santa Clara, Calif.: Overseas Crusaders Ministries.

——. "The Case for Research: Part 4, Factors of Growth." *Global Church Growth* 20 (July–August 1983): 265. Santa Clara, Calif.: Overseas Crusades Ministries.

———. "The Case for Research: Part 6, Projections for Growth." *Global Church Growth* 20 (September–October 1983): 303. Santa Clara, Calif.: Overseas Crusades Ministries.

Moore, G. Alexander. *Life Cycles in Atchalán: The Diverse Careers of Certain Guatemalans.* New York: Teachers College Press, 1973.

Morris, Walter F. *Flowers, Saints, and Toads: Chiapas Maya Textile Design Symbolism.* St. Paul: Science Museum of Minnesota, 1979.

———. "A Textured Script: Classic and Modern Maya Textile Designs." Research proposal to the National Geographic Society Committee for Research and Exploration, 1980.

Morrissey, R. C. "Continuity and Change in Backstrap Loom Textiles of Highland Guatemala." Ph.D. dissertation, University of Wisconsin–Madison, 1983.

Nash, June. "Protestantism in an Indian Village in the Western Highlands of Guatemala." *Alpha Kappa Deltan* 30 (Special Issue, 1960): 49–58.

Nash, Manning. "The Impact of Mid-Nineteenth Century Economic Change upon the Indians of Middle America." In *Conference on Race and Class in Latin America,* edited by Magnus Morner, pp. 173–180. New York: Columbia University, 1970.

———. "Indian Economics." In *Handbook of Middle American Indians,* vol. 6, *Social Anthropology,* edited by Robert Wauchope and Manning Nash, pp. 87–102. Austin: University of Texas Press, 1967.

———. "The Social Context of Economic Choice in a Small Society." *Man* 61 (1961): 186–191.

Navarro, José María. *Memorias de San Miguel Dueñas.* Guatemala City: Imprenta de Luna, 1874.

Nida, E. A. "The Relationship of Social Structure to the Problem of Evangelism in Latin America." *Practical Anthropology* 5 (1958): 101–123.

O'Neale, Lila M. *Textiles of Highland Guatemala.* Washington, D.C.: Carnegie Institution of Washington, 1945; reprint, 1976.

———. "Weaving." In *Handbook of South American Indians,* edited by Julian H. Steward, 5: 97–138. Washington, D.C.: Smithsonian Institution, Bureau of American Ethnology, 1949.

Osborne, Lilly de Jongh. *Indian Crafts of Guatemala and El Salvador.* Norman: University of Oklahoma Press, 1965.

Palerm, Angel. "Agricultural Systems and Food Patterns." In *Handbook of Middle American Indians,* vol. 6, *Social Anthropology,* edited by Robert Wauchope and Manning Nash, pp. 26–52. Austin: University of Texas Press, 1967.

Pancake, Cherri. "Textile Traditions of the Highland Maya: Some Aspects of Development and Change." Paper presented to the International Symposium on Maya Art, Architecture, Archaeology, and Hieroglyphic Writing, Guatemala City, 1978.

Pancake, Cherri, and Sheldon Annis. "El arte de la producción: Aspectos socio-económicos del tejido a mano en San Antonio Aguas Calientes, Guatemala." *Mesoamérica* 3, no. 4 (1982): 387–413. Antigua, Guatemala: Centro de Investigaciones Regionales de Mesoamérica.

Pancake, Cherri, and Suzanne Baizerman. "Guatemalan Gauze Weaves: A Description and Key to Identification." *Textile Museum Journal* 19–20 (1980–1981): 1–26.

Pang, Hilda Schmidt Delgado. "Aboriginal Guatemalan Handweaving and Costume." Ph.D. dissertation, Indiana University, 1963.

———. "Guatemalan Indian Handweaving: Conservatism and Change in a Village Handicraft." In *Verhandlungen des XXXVIII Internationalen Amerikanisten Kongresses* 2: 449–457. Stuttgart-Munich, 1968.

Pang, Hilda Schmidt Delgado, et al. "Central American Ethnographic Textiles." In *Ethnographic Textiles of the Western Hemisphere*, edited by Irene Emery and Patricia Fiske, pp. 89–156. Washington, D.C.: Textile Museum, 1977.

Paul, Benjamin, and Lois Paul. "Changing Marriage Patterns in a Highland Guatemalan Community." *Southwest Journal of Anthropology* 19 (1963): 131–148.

Poitevin, Rodolfo. *República de Guatemala: Departamento de Sacatepéquez, población calculada, año 1972–1980.* Guatemala: Ministerio de Salud Pública, n.d.

Popenoe, Wilson. "Regional Differences in the Guatemalan Huipil." *Anales de XX Congreso Internacional de Americanistas* 1 (1950): 217–220.

Read, William, Victor Monterroso, and Harmon Johnson. *Latin American Church Growth.* Grand Rapids, Mich.: William B. Eerdmans Publishing Company, 1969.

Redfield, Robert. "Primitive Merchants of Guatemala." *Quarterly Journal of Inter-American Relations* 1, no. 4 (1939): 42–46.

———. *The Village That Chose Progress: Chan Kom Revisited.* Chicago: University of Chicago Press, 1962.

Redfield, Robert, and Alfonso Villa Rojas. *Chan Kom: A Maya Village.* Chicago: University of Chicago Press, 1934.

Reina, Ruben, and Norman Schwartz. "The Structural Context of Religious Conversion in Petén, Guatemala: Status, Community, and Multicommunity." *American Ethnologist* 1 (1974): 157–192.

República de Guatemala. Dirección General de Estadística. *VII Censo de Población, 1973,* ser. 3, vol. 1. Guatemala City, 1975.

Ricard, Robert. *The Spiritual Conquest of Mexico: An Essay on the Apostolate and the Evangelizing Methods of the Mendicant Orders in New Spain, 1523–1572.* Translated by Lesley B. Simpson. Berkeley: University of California Press, 1974.

Roberts, Bryan. "Protestant Groups and Coping with Urban Life in Guatemala City." *American Journal of Sociology* 73 (1967): 753–767.

Rodas, Flavio N. *Simbolismo (Maya Quiché) de Guatemala.* Guatemala: Impreso de la Tipografía Nacional, 1938.

Roseberry, William. "Rent, Differentiation, and the Development of Capitalism among Peasants." *American Anthropologist* 78 (1976): 45–58.

Roth, H. Ling. *Studies in Primitive Looms.* 1918. Reprint, Halifax: Bankfield Museum, 1976.

Rowe, Anne P. *A Century of Change in Guatemalan Textiles.* New York: Center for Inter-American Relations, 1981.

Rubio Sánchez, Manuel. "El cacao." *Anales de la Sociedad de Geografía e Historia de Guatemala* 31 (1958): 81–129.

―――. "La grana o cochinilla." *Antropología e Historia de Guatemala* 13 (1961): 15–46.

―――. *Historia del añil o xiquilite en Centro América.* 2 vols. San Salvador: Ministerio de Educación, 1976 and 1978.

Saler, Benson. "Religious Conversion and Self-Aggrandizement: A Guatemalan Case." *Practical Anthropology* 12 (1965): 107–149.

Schlesinger, Stephen, and Stephen Kinzer. *Bitter Fruit: The Untold Story.* Garden City, N.Y.: Anchor Books, 1983.

Scrimshaw, Nevin. "Synergism of Malnutrition and Infection: Evidence from Field Studies in Guatemala." *Journal of the American Medical Association* 212 (June 1970): 1685–1692.

Scrimshaw, Nevin, Miguel Guzmán, Marina Flores, and John E. Gordon. "Nutrition and Infection Field Study, 1959–1964: Part V, Disease Incidence among Preschool Children under Natural Village Conditions, with Improved Diet and with Medical and Public Health Services." *Archives of Environmental Health* 16 (February 1968): 223–234.

Scrimshaw, Nevin, Lance Taylor, and John E. Gordon. *Interaction of Nutrition and Infection.* Monograph Series, no. 57. Geneva: World Health Organization, 1968.

Sexton, James D. "Protestantism and Modernization in Two Guatemalan Towns." *American Ethnologist* 5 (May 1978): 280–302.

Sexton, James D., and Clyde Woods. "Development and Modernization among Highland Maya: A Comparative Analysis of Ten Guatemalan Towns." *Human Organization* 36 (1977): 156–172.

Sherman, William. *Forced Native Labor in Sixteenth-Century Central America.* Lincoln: University of Nebraska Press, 1979.

Simons, Marlise. "Latin America's New Gospel." *New York Times Magazine,* November 7, 1982, p. 45.

Siverts, H. "Political Organization in a Tzeltal Community in Chiapas, Mexico." *Alpha Kappa Deltan* 30 (Special Issue, 1960): 14–28.

Skeat, Walter. *An Etymological Dictionary of the English Language.* Oxford: Clarendon Press, 1898.

Smith, Carol. "Production in Western Guatemala: A Test of Von Thünen and Boserup." In *Formal Methods in Economic Anthropology,* edited by Stuart Plattner. Washington, D.C.: American Anthropological Association, 1975.

Smith, Gary. "Income and Nutrition in the Guatemalan Highlands." Ph.D. dissertation, Department of Economics, University of Oregon, 1972.

Smith, Waldemar R. *The Fiesta System and Economic Change.* New York: Columbia University Press, 1978.

Solórzano Fernández, Valentín. *Evolución económica de Guatemala.* 4th ed. Guatemala City: Seminario de Integración Social Guatemalteca, 1977.

Sperlich, Norbert, and Elizabeth Katz Sperlich. *Guatemalan Backstrap Weaving.* Norman: University of Oklahoma Press, 1980.

Stavenhagen, Rodolfo. "Classes, Colonialism, and Acculturation." In *Masses in Latin America*, edited by Irving L. Horowitz, pp. 235–288. New York: Oxford University Press, 1970.

Stoll, David. *Fishers of Men or Founders of Empire? The Wycliffe Bible Translators in Latin America*. London: Zed Press, 1982.

Study Group on United States–Guatemalan Relations. *Report on Guatemala*. SAIS Papers in International Affairs, no. 7. Boulder and London: Westview Press, 1984.

Tax, Sol. *Penny Capitalism: A Guatemalan Indian Economy*. Smithsonian Institute of Social Anthropology Publication no. 16. Washington, D.C.: U.S. Government Printing Office, 1953.

———. "The Towns of Lake Atitlán." University of Chicago Microfilm Collection of Manuscripts on Middle American Cultural Anthropology, no. 13. 1946.

Tax, Sol, and Robert Hinshaw. "The Maya of the Midwestern Highlands." In *Handbook of Middle American Indians*, vol. 7, *Ethnology, Part One*, edited by Robert Wauchope and Evon Z. Vogt, pp. 69–100. Austin: University of Texas Press, 1969.

Tedlock, Barbara. *Time and the Highland Maya*. Albuquerque: University of New Mexico Press, 1982.

Tedlock, Barbara and Dennis. "Text and Textile: Language and Technology in the Arts of the Quiché Maya." *Journal of Anthropological Research* 41 (1985): 121–146.

Townsend, William Cameron. *One of Guatemala's Indians: His Witch Doctor and a Torn Tract*. Missionary brochure. Paris, Tex.: Central American Mission, ca. 1921.

———. "A Rich Chief's Family Getting 'Saved.'" *Central American Bulletin*, vol. 15 (September 1926).

———. *Tolo, the Volcano's Son*, edited by Hugh and Norma Steven. (First published serially in *Revelation*, April–October 1936.) Huntington Beach, Calif.: Wycliffe Bible Translators, 1981.

United Nations Commission on Human Rights. *Situation of Human Rights in Guatemala: Report Prepared by the Special Rapporteur, Viscount Colville of Colcross*. New York, 1983–1984.

U.S. Agency for International Development. *Country Development Strategy Statement, 1979–1980*. Guatemala City, 1979.

———. "Results of Small Farmer Survey: Rural Cooperatives, 1974–75." In "Guatemala Small Farm Improvement—Progress and Projections." Evaluation of Small Farmer Improvement Program in USAID agricultural loan 520-T-026, Attachment I, p. 3, 1978.

U.S. Agency for International Development and Guatemalan Ministry of Education. Tables VIII-1, VIII-2. In *Education Sector Assessment*. Guatemala City, 1978.

Wallis, Ethel, and Mary Bennett. *Two Thousand Tongues to Go*. 1st ed., 1959. London: Hodder and Stoughton, 1966.

Walters, A. A. *An Introduction to Econometrics*. New York: Norton, 1972.

Warren, Kay B. *The Symbolism of Subordination: Indian Identity in A Guatemalan Town.* Austin: University of Texas Press, 1978.

Wasserstrom, Robert. "Revolution in Guatemala: Peasants and Politics under the Arbenz Government." *Comparative Studies in Society and History* 17, no. 4 (October 1975): 443–478.

Weber, Max. *The Protestant Ethic and the Spirit of Capitalism.* New York: Charles Scribner's Sons, 1958.

Wilhite, R. Margaret. "First Language Acquisition: Textile Design Terminology in Cakchiquel (Mayan)." Ph.D. dissertation, Washington University, 1977.

Wolf, Eric. "Closed Corporate Communities in Mesoamerica and Central Java." *Southwestern Journal of Anthropology* 13 (1957): 1–18.

———. *Peasants.* Englewood Cliffs, N.J.: Prentice-Hall, 1966.

———. *Sons of the Shaking Earth.* Chicago: University of Chicago Press, 1959.

Woodward, Ralph Lee, Jr. *Central America: A Nation Divided.* 2d ed. New York and Oxford: Oxford University Press, 1985.

Wortman, Miles L. *Government and Society in Central America, 1680–1840.* New York: Columbia University Press, 1982.

Wycliffe Bible Translators and Summer Institute of Linguistics. *Who Brought the Word.* Santa Ana, Calif., 1963.

Index